NEW EVERY MORNING

FROM THE MESSAGES OF

ADRIAN ROGERS

innovo
PUBLISHING
innovopublishing.com

Published by Innovo Publishing, LLC
www.innovopublishing.com
1-888-546-2111

Publishing quality books, eBooks, audiobooks, music, screenplays & courses for the Christian & wholesome markets since 2008.

New Every Morning

ISBN: 978-1-61314-938-6

Cover Design & Interior Layout: Innovo Publishing, LLC

Printed in the United States of America
U.S. Printing History
First Edition: 2023

Has God called you to create a Christ-centered or wholesome book, eBook, audiobook, music album, screenplay, or online course? Visit Innovo's educational center (cpportal.com) to learn how to accomplish your calling with excellence.

IT'S MORNING!

Okay, get coffee first if you need, but quick, grab this
devotional, your Bible, and a pen, and get alone with God.

PRAY

You'll notice each daily entry in this volume begins with Scripture. Read it, dig
into the Bible to study the context, and pray over it, asking God to help you
hear His voice. Listen to what God has to say to you through His Word and pray
accordingly.

PONDER

Take time each day to ponder the devotional that follows the Scripture. Each
devotional thought comes straight from a message preached by Pastor Adrian
Rogers during his 50 years in the pulpit. Pastor Rogers was known for his
unique ability to simplify profound truth so that it can be applied to everyday
life. Because he was firmly committed to the Word of God, don't be surprised
when something written 20 or more years ago is exactly what you need to hear
on your brand new day.

PRACTICE

Following each daily devotional thought, you'll find a couple of questions and
an action idea. While your thinking is fresh, note in your journal what you plan
to do about what you've just learned. James said, "But be doers of the word, and
not hearers only, deceiving yourselves" (James 1:22). As you stand at the mirror
to brush your teeth and style your hair, style your day to conform to Christ. As
James continued, "For if anyone is a hearer of the word and not a doer, he is like
a man observing his natural face in a mirror; for he observes himself, goes away,
and immediately forgets what kind of man he was" (James 1:23-24).

Now, go out and win the new day, "strengthened in faith, giving glory to God"
(Romans 4:20).

God specializes in things
that seem to be impossible.

ADRIAN ROGERS

1

PRAY OVER THIS

Then the children of Joseph spoke to Joshua, saying, "Why have you given us only one lot and one share to inherit, since we are a great people, inasmuch as the LORD has blessed us until now?"

JOSHUA 17:14

PONDER THIS The people of Israel were living in self-confidence. They were boasting about their greatness. The same thing is true about so many of us. Pride is bad enough, but pride that lifts its head from the mire of failure is terrible. These people were failing to be, do, have, and say what God would have them be, do, say, and have, and they were saying, "Look how great we are."

"Pride goes before destruction, and a haughty spirit before a fall" (Proverbs 16:18). There's nothing that will put you more out of the reach of the devil than genuine humility. But if you're proud, you're going to find God as an enemy. The Bible says, "God resists the proud, but gives grace to the humble" (James 4:6). And what is grace? Grace is the desire and the ability to do the will of God.

- What are some ways you are tempted to live in confidence in yourself instead of in God?
- How have you experienced the reality that God resists the proud but gives grace to the humble?

PRACTICE THIS Today is the start of a new year. You are likely taking up new practices and setting new goals. Assess your goals for this year through the lens of dependence on self or dependence on the Lord. Take steps to rely further on the Lord this year.

2

PONDER THIS The reason that many people are not living in victory is that their lives are cluttered. Many believe they don't have enough time for prayer or Bible study. The reality is, if you don't have enough time for prayer and Bible study, you're doing something you ought not to do. I don't know what it is, but I will guarantee you that if you don't have time to read your Bible and pray, you're doing something God never assigned you to do. There's something cluttering your life.

Whatever is cluttering your life may not be overtly harmful, sinful, or wicked, but if it is cluttering your life, you need to get rid of it. There's enough time to do everything God wants us to do. But this often requires removing the clutter from our lives. Some people are so busy doing good they don't have time to be godly. We must remember that we never waste time that is spent at Jesus' feet.

- What is cluttering your life right now?
- What steps will you take to prioritize time with God and His Word?

PRACTICE THIS Plan for a specific time on your daily schedule to spend with God. Consider what needs to be removed from your life in order to prioritize this time.

PRAY OVER THIS

Commit your works to the LORD, and your
thoughts will be established.
PROVERBS 16:3

PONDER THIS You need a goal in your life, and it's got to be specific. If you don't have that, you're like a ship at sea on a dark night without a rudder, without a chart, and without a compass. Most people don't plan to fail; they just don't plan anything! You may say, "Sure, you're a pastor. You ought to have some goals." Mothers ought to have goals. Teachers ought to have goals. Students ought to have goals. Athletes ought to have goals. Medical doctors ought to have goals. And a church, in general, ought to have goals.

Is your goal specific enough you could put it on paper? What are you all about? What motivates you? I mean, what are you trying to do? If our goals are not from God and according to His will, even our success will be a failure.

- What are your goals for this year?
- How have you sought to put your goals in line with God's will?

PRACTICE THIS Take time today to write out not just your goal for this year, but for your life. How will you submit this before God that He might establish you?

PRAY OVER THIS

"This Book of the Law shall not depart from your mouth, but you shall meditate in it day and night, that you may observe to do according to all that is written in it. For then you will make your way prosperous, and then you will have good success."

JOSHUA 1:8

PONDER THIS You want to encourage your confidence? Get in the Word of God. Read the Scriptures. Saturate your soul with the Scriptures. You want a promise for a new year? Today's verse says: "This Book of the Law shall not depart from your mouth, but you shall meditate in it day and night, that you may observe to do according to all that is written in it. For then you will make your way prosperous, and then you will have good success." Wait before God until you get a promise and let that promise come out of the Word of God. We are not meant to take confidence in ourselves, but we can always take confidence in God and His promises. As you think toward this coming year, let your confidence rest in God and what He has promised.

- What are some of your favorite promises of God?
- How does your confidence in God's promises grow as you spend time in His Word?

PRACTICE THIS Write a list of at least five of your favorite promises of God found in Scripture. Spend time meditating on the truth of these verses.

5

PRAY OVER THIS

"But you shall receive power when the Holy Spirit has come
upon you; and you shall be witnesses to Me in Jerusalem, and
in all Judea and Samaria, and to the end of the earth."

ACTS 1:8

PONDER THIS The mission Jesus gave to the disciples must have seemed impossible. Look at them—a little group of ragtag apostles, some of them fishermen. Most of them didn't have any education. They had no seminaries. They had no finances. They had no prestige. They had no political pull. And yet they were commanded to go into all the world and tell the message of a Galilean peasant who died on a cross, crucified by the Roman government. This was mission impossible.

Not only did they not have the credentials, but they were also up against impossible foes. There was the imperial might of the iron legions of Rome. There was the intellectual sophistry of the Greeks. There was the religious bigotry of the Jewish religion. And here they were. This reads like a magnificent novel, but it is absolutely true. It is the story of the Church triumphant.

- What feels impossible in your life right now?
- How is the story of the Early Church an encouragement in this regard?

PRACTICE THIS Write down the things you are facing that seem impossible. Pray over these things, confessing that all things are possible with God.

PRAY OVER THIS

And suddenly there came a sound from heaven, as of a rushing
mighty wind, and it filled the whole house where they were sitting.

ACTS 2:2

PONDER THIS Have you ever heard a tornado? Everybody says it sounds like
a freight train and that's true. Twice I have been close enough to a tornado to
hear the noise, and it is an awesome sound! Now if you think a tornado sounds
awesome outside, what would you think about an indoor one? This one was
inside the house where the believers were sitting.

Just as the wind comes from Heaven, the Holy Spirit comes from Heaven.
As the wind moves at will, commanded by nobody, so the Holy Spirit of God
is sovereign and moves at will. As the wind is mysterious—we can't tell where
it comes from or where it's going—so is the Holy Spirit. And yet, as the wind
operates according to fixed laws, so does God's blessed precious Holy Spirit. The
wind is invisible but powerful! And there's an invisible powerful force living in
every believer in Jesus—the Holy Spirit of God.

- How easy or difficult do you find it to believe that the Holy Spirit is
  powerful in your life?
- Where do you currently feel that you need the power of the Holy
  Spirit?

PRACTICE THIS Consider the things that make it easy or difficult for you to
believe in the power of the Holy Spirit. What do you need to start or stop to lean
further into the power of the Spirit in your life?

PRAY OVER THIS

And being assembled together with them, He commanded
them not to depart from Jerusalem, but to wait for the
Promise of the Father, "which," He said, "you have heard
from Me; for John truly baptized with water, but you shall be
baptized with the Holy Spirit not many days from now."

ACTS 1:4-5

PONDER THIS Jesus told the disciples to tarry until they were endued with power from on high. But we don't need to tarry. The Holy Spirit has already come. We don't need to say, "Oh God, send Your Spirit." He's sent His Spirit. That would be like praying, "Oh God, send Jesus to die on the cross." No, He has died on the cross. Calvary's an accomplished fact. Pentecost is an accomplished fact. What we need now to do is to receive the promise.

If you are a Christian, if you are truly saved, you've already received that promise. You may say, "Well I don't feel it." I want to tell you something. You can be a part of a denomination and be lost. You can attend worship services and be lost. But you cannot be a Christian and not have the Holy Spirit in you. That's what makes you a Christian. If you repented of your sins, you have already received the Holy Spirit of God.

- How much would you say you rely on the power of the Holy Spirit in daily life?
- How might you learn to do this more?

PRACTICE THIS Take time today to pray frequently, asking the Holy Spirit to guide you in routine decisions; seek to honor and serve Him in all you do.

8

PRAY OVER THIS

The former account I made, O Theophilus, of all that Jesus began both to do and teach, until the day in which He was taken up, after He through the Holy Spirit had given commandments to the apostles whom He had chosen.

ACTS 1:1-2

PONDER THIS In the Gospels you find what Jesus did in His human body—the body of His flesh. In the book of Acts, you find out what Jesus is doing in His mystical body, the Church. You see, Jesus is still active and alive on Earth today and He still has a body. In the Gospels, it was His material, physical body. In the book of Acts, it is His new body, which is the Church. And Jesus is alive and well today in His mystical body. This is what the Bible calls in Colossians 1:27, "Christ in you." You see, we're not here just imitating the Lord Jesus. I love the idea behind the question, "What would Jesus do?" That implies, "What would He do if He were here?" But we need to realize He is here. So, it's not, "What would He do?" We need to recognize His presence in His body and let Him do what He will do.

- How easily do you recognize that Jesus is present with His people and working through His body, the Church, each day?
- How are you called to be part of that work?

PRACTICE THIS Make a list of ways you can see Jesus working through your church right now.

PRAY OVER THIS

Go therefore and make disciples of all the nations, baptizing them
in the name of the Father and of the Son and of the Holy Spirit.
MATTHEW 28:19

PONDER THIS Jesus commanded that we be baptized. Jesus began His public ministry with baptism. Jesus concluded His public ministry by commanding baptism. (See Matthew 28:19.) Once a person is a disciple of the Lord Jesus Christ, that person is to be baptized by immersion, saying, "I belong to Jesus Christ. I'm not ashamed of Jesus Christ."

You know why I wear a wedding ring? That ring shows that I belong to my wife. I'm a one-woman man. I belong to that girl, and I love her, and I'm not ashamed of her. When I go out of town, I don't take the ring off. I belong to one lady.

In a similar way, baptism means you belong to Jesus Christ. You're not ashamed of Jesus Christ. You want everybody to know. You are publicly buried in the likeness of His death and raised in the likeness of His resurrection.

- If you are a follower of Jesus, have you been baptized?
- If not, how is God calling you to respond today?

PRACTICE THIS Take time today to reflect on your baptism (or to respond to God if you have not yet been baptized). Consider how your baptism provides a picture of your death and resurrection in Jesus.

PRAY OVER THIS

"And I, if I am lifted up from the earth, will draw all peoples to Myself."

JOHN 12:32

PONDER THIS Peter preached a Christ-centered Gospel message. The Church grew because its people lifted up Jesus. Jesus said, "And I, if I am lifted up...will draw all people to Myself." No church is going to be a growing, vibrant church if it does not exalt the Lord Jesus Christ.

Some churches reserve Sunday morning for God the Father, Sunday night for God the Son, and Wednesday night for God the Spirit. This may not be literal but there's sort of an emphasis like that. Of course, we should magnify God the Father, but every service must exalt the Lord Jesus Christ. Do you believe that?

- Why is it important that Jesus be at the center of all the Church does?
- What is the danger if He is not?

PRACTICE THIS Consider the activities of your church. How is Jesus the center? If He is not, how could He be?

PRAY OVER THIS

Then Peter said to them, "Repent, and let every one of you
be baptized in the name of Jesus Christ for the remission
of sins; and you shall receive the gift of the Holy Spirit."

ACTS 2:38

PONDER THIS I read somewhere years ago about a little boy who got saved in the children's church service. The pastor of the children's church service said to the little fellow, "Now you need to go over and tell them at big church that you've been saved, and you need to get baptized." Well, the boy didn't quite understand what he was being told, so he went and told the pastor, "I've been saved, and I need to get advertised." This is a funny mix-up, but his words were true. Once you get saved, you get advertised. You're saying, "Here I am, and I belong to Jesus Christ. I want everybody who sees me to know that I have been buried with Him by baptism into death and raised to walk in newness of life. I am identifying myself with the death, burial, and resurrection of Jesus Christ."

- Why is it important to identify with Jesus—to advertise ourselves for Him?
- Read Matthew 10:32-33. What did Jesus say about our identification with Him?

PRACTICE THIS Do one thing today to "advertise" for Jesus.

PRAY OVER THIS

Now when they saw the boldness of Peter and John, and
perceived that they were uneducated and untrained men, they
marveled. And they realized that they had been with Jesus.

ACTS 4:13

PONDER THIS Are you a bold believer? Or are you a cowardly Christian? Do you want to be a bold believer? What is boldness in the first place? Boldness is not arrogance. It's not the ability to put your finger in somebody's face and tell them off. Boldness is not being rude or crude. Some people think they are bold but they're just arrogant, and they have bad manners. That's not boldness. Those people turn more people away from Jesus than they bring to the Lord Jesus. We're to be gentle, apt to teach, and not seek to give offense. Don't think that if you go around getting in people's faces that you're necessarily bold.

Rudeness is not boldness. Boldness is having the courage to stand for the Lord Jesus Christ in the face of opposition.

- How might you have had a wrong view of boldness in the past?
- What would it look like for you to display godly boldness?

PRACTICE THIS Make a list of people you know who are bold for Christ. Consider what makes them bold and how you might learn from and follow their example.

13

PRAY OVER THIS

So when they heard that, they raised their voice to God
with one accord and said: "Lord, You are God, who made
heaven and earth and the sea, and all that is in them,…"

ACTS 4:24

PONDER THIS What gives the believer boldness? It is the fact that God—who scooped out the oceans, who heaped up the mountains, and who dotted the universe with stars, billions and billions of stars, out over the velvety blackness of space—is on our side. In today's passage and the verses that follow, (See Acts 4:24-30.) the believers said, "God, You made it all. Why should we tremble when You are our Father? Why should we be intimidated when a God who can do such things is on our side?"

A college student once asked his pastor, "Pastor, do you believe there's life on other planets, other places out in space?" Pastor said, "No, son, I really don't believe there is." He said, "Now, Pastor, think about it. There are billions and billions of stars, and you don't believe there's life out there anywhere?" The pastor said, "I can't prove there's not, but I don't believe there is." And then the college student said, "Well, Pastor, then why did God go to the trouble to make all that stuff?" The pastor said, "What trouble? He only had to speak. Only God can do that. He spoke and universes dripped from His fingers." What a mighty God we serve.

- How often do you stop to consider the majesty of God's creation, even beyond our solar system and galaxy?
- What does this tell you about God and His power?

PRACTICE THIS Make time this week to behold God's majesty in His creation. As you do, submit your cares before Him, recognizing His power and might as displayed in His creation.

PRAY OVER THIS

Blessed be the God and Father of our Lord Jesus Christ,
the Father of mercies and God of all comfort.

2 CORINTHIANS 1:3

PONDER THIS Do you know why discouragement is so bad? Discouragement opens the door to all kinds of sins and failures. Someone once said, "Discouragement is a dark room where the negatives of failure are developed." Did you know the Bible calls God the God of all encouragement? Second Corinthians 1:3 says, "Blessed be the God and Father of our Lord Jesus Christ, the Father of mercies and God of all comfort." The word *comfort* actually means "encouragement." God is the God of all encouragement. That means God has cornered the market on encouragement. He's the God of all of it. Do you need encouragement? Do you feel trapped in discouragement? Take heart that the God of all comfort and encouragement is ready to hear your cry and give you encouragement today.

- Where do you currently feel most discouraged?
- What encouragement can you find in God?

PRACTICE THIS Make a list of ways you can be encouraged because of who God is and what He has done for you. Dwell on this list today.

PRAY OVER THIS

But Peter and John answered and said to them, "Whether it is right
in the sight of God to listen to you more than to God, you judge."

ACTS 4:19

PONDER THIS What is the biggest problem you are facing today? Think about it. Hold it in your mind. Now double it. Make it twice as bad. Now double what you've doubled. Now, I want to ask you a question: is that big to God? Of course not.

What is the basis of boldness? You must keep company with God the Son. You must have confidence in God the Father. When these people were terrified, they took their eyes off man and put their eyes on God. Take your eyes off your problems. Focus your eyes upon Almighty God, who is the Creator of all things, who is the Controller of all things, and the Conqueror of all things. That's the basis of our boldness.

- Where are you typically focused when you feel most fearful and anxious?
- How might your perspective change if you focused on God over the things of the world?

PRACTICE THIS Take time today to purposefully take your mind off the problems you face in the world and put them onto our God who is the Creator, Controller, and Conqueror of all things.

PRAY OVER THIS

Now, Lord, look on their threats, and grant to Your servants
that with all boldness they may speak Your word.

ACTS 4:29

PONDER THIS The word *servant* here is the Greek word that means "bondslave." Are you a slave of the Lord Jesus Christ? I try to make it a habit every day to lift my hands in surrender to the Lord. To say to the Lord, "I am Your servant." Boldness is not for rebels. You will never have boldness, true boldness, until you can say, "Now, Lord, grant to Your bondservant—to Your slave—boldness."

When you do that, the Holy Spirit of God will give you courage. You know, if there's any unconfessed sin in your life, any area that is not surrendered, you're not going to have boldness. But you can wake up and say, "There's nothing between my soul and the Savior. Lord, I am Your servant. I am Your slave. Jesus is with me. God the Father is above me. Holy Spirit of God, You're within me. Grant me boldness to declare Your Word."

- What remains in your life that you need to surrender to God today?
- How is that thing acting as an obstacle to boldness in your life?

PRACTICE THIS Write down the things you need to surrender to God. Pray over these things, asking Him to help you surrender to Him and to receive bold obedience to Him.

PRAY OVER THIS

Now Barnabas was determined to take with them John
called Mark. But Paul insisted that they should not take
with them the one who had departed from them in
Pamphylia, and had not gone with them to the work.

ACTS 15:37-38

PONDER THIS Barnabas knew John Mark had failed, but he also knew that failure is not final, and he wanted to mend a broken relationship. From today's passage, Barnabas took John Mark, and he continued to nurture him. Later, Paul was in a filthy, Roman prison. Time had passed. In 2 Timothy 4:11, Paul wrote: "Only Luke is with me. Get Mark and bring him with you, for he is useful to me for ministry."

How about that? This is the same guy that Paul wouldn't have anything to do with in today's passage. But later, he said, "Bring him. He is profitable to me for the ministry." How did that happen? Because there was a man named Barnabas, who refused to let go of a good man named Mark just because he failed. There are many around us who have failed, and they need you to help them be restored.

- Who do you know who might feel stuck in past failure?
- How might God be calling you to provide spiritual encouragement?

PRACTICE THIS Take time this week to connect with someone you know who has failed and could use godly encouragement.

PRAY OVER THIS

Then Peter said, "Silver and gold I do not have, but what I do have I give you: In the name of Jesus Christ of Nazareth, rise up and walk."

ACTS 3:6

PONDER THIS The apostles were not preaching facts about a dead Christ. That's the only way you can explain their boldness. How do you explain the Early Church? How do you explain the fact that Peter, the man who was talking, was eventually crucified? Tradition holds that when they were getting ready to crucify Peter, Peter said, "Look, don't crucify me right side up, crucify me upside down. I'm not worthy to even be crucified as my Lord was crucified." This was the same man who denied Jesus three times on the night He was arrested. Where did Peter get that boldness? Through the risen Christ, Peter had no fear of death. Of course, he didn't want to be crucified, but he had no fear of death because he knew his Savior was alive.

- How does it give you boldness to remember that Jesus has conquered death?
- What would look different in your life if you lived in this boldness each day?

PRACTICE THIS Take specific steps today to act in the name of Jesus with boldness because of the truth of His resurrection.

19

PRAY OVER THIS

So they departed from the presence of the council, rejoicing
that they were counted worthy to suffer shame for His name.

ACTS 5:41

PONDER THIS Don't get the idea that the will of God is something you have to do. God's not going to force His will on you. It is something you get to do. When you learn to obey, you learn the joy that's available in the Christian life. There's no such thing as a happy, disobedient Christian. It is a contradiction in terms. Obedience and rejoicing come together. It is a lie from Hell that doing the will of God is painful and makes you miserable. The Bible says, "His commandments are not burdensome" (1 John 5:3).

The reason some of us don't obey the Lord and fail to understand there's joy in obedience is that we don't trust the Lord; we have difficulty taking commands from a stranger we don't know. Once we get to know the Lord Jesus Christ, we learn that His commands are not grievous or burdensome.

- How have you experienced joy in being obedient to God?
- How have you been deceived into believing that following God is burdensome and grievous?

PRACTICE THIS Make a list of ways you feel God calling you to be obedient to Him this week. Pray over this list, asking God to remind you that joy is found in obedience to Him.

PRAY OVER THIS

But Peter and the other apostles answered and said:
"We ought to obey God rather than men."

ACTS 5:29

PONDER THIS You cannot obey God unless He enables you to do so: "We love Him because He first loved us" (1 John 4:19). And "it is God who works in [us] both to will and to do for His good pleasure" (Philippians 2:13). Obedience to God is like breathing. Is breathing a gift of God? Of course, it is. God gives you lungs and God gives you air. But you can suffocate if you want. Obedience is a gift of God in the sense that God gives you the will—God works in you—but there comes a decision, and God is not going to force you to obey Him. We can't shrug our shoulders and say, "Well, if God wants it to happen, it'll happen." No! There is a decision to be practiced. You must say, "I will obey Him."

- Where are you currently faced with a decision of obedience or disobedience?
- How will you respond today?

PRACTICE THIS Take steps toward obedience in a specific situation in your life today.

PRAY OVER THIS

Now an angel of the Lord spoke to Philip, saying, "Arise
and go toward the south along the road which goes
down from Jerusalem to Gaza." This is desert.

ACTS 8:26

PONDER THIS When you're sensitive to the direction of the Spirit, God will lead you to somebody who needs Jesus. Those of you who are students, tomorrow you're going to find some student, if you'll be sensitive. Perhaps God is preparing some student for you to witness to. Those of you who are business people, if you're sensitive, God's going to lead you to somebody. God is working on an individual. Perhaps there's somebody who went to church Sunday, seeking the wells of religion, but came away dry. Maybe that person knows the Bible, but doesn't know how to be saved. You may say, "Well God never brings anybody to me." Oh? Could it be that you're not listening?

- When was a time God enabled you to share with another person because you were sensitive to His prompting?
- When might have been a time you missed God's prompting because you were focused on other things?

PRACTICE THIS Take time in your normal routine today to stop and ask God where He is leading you, so that He might use you to point others to Him.

22

> ## PRAY OVER THIS
>
> Go, stand in the temple and speak to the
> people all the words of this life.
>
> **ACTS 5:20**

PONDER THIS The apostles had a command from God. The reason they took action is because they'd been told to do so. All true obedience is informed obedience. You must hear from God in order to obey God. Don't do things just because you want to do them and think you're living the Christian life. What God doesn't initiate, God doesn't appreciate. God is going to tell you what to do. And God has never promised to bless any endeavor that He has not commanded.

- How can we know what God wants us to do?
- How is regular time spent in God's Word and in prayer connected to knowing what He wants us to do?

PRACTICE THIS Take inventory. Consider the things you are doing because you feel God clearly called you to do them as well as those things you are doing according to your own desires. Seek to submit every area of your life to Him.

PRAY OVER THIS

And we are His witnesses to these things, and so also is the
Holy Spirit whom God has given to those who obey Him.

ACTS 5:32

PONDER THIS God is not going to give spiritual power to rebels. Why should
God release the anointing power of the Holy Spirit upon your life when you're
not living in obedience? The Holy Spirit is there to get His work done. Have
you ever taught a teen to drive an automobile? If so, one of the first things you
likely pointed out was the brake pedal. Now suppose that teen said, "I am not
interested in the brake. Show me how to make it go. I'm not interested in how
to make it stop. I want to go!" You'd take the keys back, put them in your pocket,
and say, "You're not ready yet." In the same way, you will never know the release
of the Spirit until you know the restraint of the Spirit. You will never know the
"go" till you know the "no." God gives the power of the Holy Spirit to those who
obey Him.

- Where have you experienced the restraint of the Holy Spirit in your
  life?
- How does the Holy Spirit lead us to change our lives? Why does
  this include doing some things and not doing other things?

PRACTICE THIS Spend time in reflection, asking God to reveal to you the areas
in which He is calling you to obedience. Ask Him to lead you to faithfulness in
those areas beginning today.

PRAY OVER THIS

Likewise you younger people, submit yourselves to your elders.
Yes, all of you be submissive to one another, and be clothed with
humility, for "God resists the proud, but gives grace to the humble."

1 PETER 5:5

PONDER THIS When people are filled with pride, do you know what happens to them? They do not receive the grace of God because God gives grace to the humble. When a person is full of pride, grace is withdrawn, and God sets up a barricade against that person. God resists the proud. Now that's bad enough, but go down to verse eight. First Peter 5:8 says, "Be sober, be vigilant; because your adversary the devil walks about like a roaring lion, seeking whom he may devour." Can you imagine an individual like this? Devoid of the grace of God; God resisting him; Satan circling to devour him. That's what pride does. Nothing puts a person more out of the reach of Satan than genuine humility.

- How can you know if you are driven by pride or humility?
- How does following Jesus lead us to humility?

PRACTICE THIS Consider the areas of pride in your life. Take intentional and prayerful steps toward humility in these places today.

PRAY OVER THIS

Now all these things happened to them as examples,
and they were written for our admonition.

1 CORINTHIANS 10:11A

PONDER THIS In the wilderness, when the children of Israel were coming out of Egypt and going to Canaan, they lived in sin, they fell into idolatry, and God destroyed many of them. First Corinthians 10:11a says, "Now all these things happened to them as examples, and they were written for our admonition." God does certain things as examples. God says, "You want to know how I feel about murmuring? There's an example. You want to know how I feel about hypocrisy and superficiality in the Church? There is an example." God does these things sometimes as examples. Will we learn today?

- What examples of God's people from the Bible help you learn how to follow God?
- What are some things you have learned not to do from the examples of others?

PRACTICE THIS Write out an example from the Bible that you can learn from in order to follow God rightly. Write out what happened in the biblical account and what takeaways you might learn from that account.

PRAY OVER THIS

But there was a certain man called Simon, who previously practiced
sorcery in the city and astonished the people of Samaria, claiming
that he was someone great, to whom they all gave heed, from the
least to the greatest, saying, "This man is the great power of God."

ACTS 8:9-10

PONDER THIS Here was a man who was using sorcery. Sorcery is just another word for witchcraft. And witchcraft is alive and well in the world today. Witchcraft is alive and well in America, in your city, and in many churches today. You may say, "Oh, no." Yes, and many people are dazzled by this. They fail to understand that there is supernatural power in the things they see. Simon was not just an illusion; he was in league with the devil. You may ask if I believe that there's anything to witchcraft. Absolutely. Do I believe that some of these people have supernatural power? Beyond the shadow of any doubt. We must be careful that the power we are drawn to is of God and not of the devil.

- Have you ever seen anything that might have been accomplished by the devil's power and not by God's?
- How can you know the difference between something that is done by God's power and something done according to the devil's power?

PRACTICE THIS Take time to consider the types of supernatural things that have made the greatest impact in your life. Consider how you know these things were from God, or how you might recognize if they were not.

PRAY OVER THIS

And when Simon saw that through the laying on of the
apostles' hands the Holy Spirit was given, he offered them
money, saying, "Give me this power also, that anyone
on whom I lay hands may receive the Holy Spirit."

ACTS 8:18-19

PONDER THIS There are people who claim to be believers in Jesus, but they don't believe the doctrines of the Bible. They don't necessarily believe Jesus is the only way to Heaven. They believe in astrology. They believe in reincarnation. These things are emphatically taught against in the Word of God. We have today a generation of people who are "very spiritual" but do not believe the faith that was once for all delivered to the saints.

But the reality is we better get a bulldog grip on God's Word and God's truth. Thousands of churches are filled with moral people who had spiritual experiences but were not born again. Simon the sorcerer said he believed. But Peter said, "You have neither part nor portion in this matter, for your heart is not right in the sight of God" (Acts 8:21).

- How can you know your faith is truly faith in Jesus and not in someone or something else?
- How does clinging to God's Word help you make this distinction?

PRACTICE THIS Make a list of things you believe that come from Scripture. As you are able, note specific references that show you these things are real.

PRAY OVER THIS

Now about that time Herod the king stretched out
his hand to harass some from the church.

ACTS 12:1

PONDER THIS Have you ever watched a painter put his colors on canvas? He's splashing the colors on that canvas and he's mixing this. He says, "I think a little more yellow, yeah." And you watch and you think, "Man, that guy's so good; how does he do that?" But then he will reach in, and he'll get some colors and he'll go, "Shoosh!" And you think, "Oh no, you ruined it!" He put some big old splashy thing on it, and you think, "Mister, you really messed up—let's see how you're going to get out of this." And then, suddenly it just comes together. It's a masterpiece!

Sometimes we look at what God does, as He puts His colors on the canvas and we say, "Lord, you're really doing good." And then suddenly God just goes, "Shoosh!" And we think, "Lord! You have messed things up." Have you ever felt that way? That may have been how the Early Church felt when Herod began his attack. "God, how did You let this happen?" Just because things are not making sense to you, do not think that they don't make sense. And just because you can't see God working doesn't mean He is not.

- Do you remember a time you felt like God was not working but later recognized that He was?
- How can these moments, both from our own experience and as recorded in Scripture, help us to remain faithful to God when it is hard to see how He is working?

PRACTICE THIS Write down an area in which you are looking for God to work, but you're not seeing it yet. Take time to pray over this, asking the Lord to give you continued faithfulness as you wait for Him.

PRAY OVER THIS

But there was a certain man called Simon, who previously practiced
sorcery in the city and astonished the people of Samaria, claiming
that he was someone great, to whom they all gave heed, from the
least to the greatest, saying, "This man is the great power of God."

ACTS 8:9-10

PONDER THIS Don't be deceived or dazzled by the power of false religion.
It is real. Pharaoh's magicians performed miracles when Moses performed
miracles of God. As we think about counterfeit Christianity, it is important that
we not be dazzled by it. If some magician, some soothsayer, some astrologer,
some necromancer, or fortune-teller comes and does things that you cannot
understand, don't go trailing after him because you say, "Well, I know it's real!"
That is the point. It is real. That doesn't mean to follow it; it means to flee from
it. Just because there is a sign or a wonder, does not mean the thing is from
God. We should always come back to the Scripture to see what it says about
such signs and about how God reveals Himself. The things of God always point
back to God.

- What are some examples you know of signs or wonders that are
  not of God?
- How can you seek to prepare yourself to know if things you see in
  the world are of God or not?

PRACTICE THIS Spend time reading through Acts 8:9-25 to see the difference
between the signs Simon performed and those of the apostles. Consider how
this might help you discern the truth about signs you witness in the world.

PRAY OVER THIS

Repent therefore of this your wickedness, and pray God if
perhaps the thought of your heart may be forgiven you. For I see
that you are poisoned by bitterness and bound by iniquity.

ACTS 8:22-23

PONDER THIS Do you know why so many churches have trouble? They are inhabited by bitter people who are in bondage. These people have met religion, but they've never met Jesus. They have never been broken at the foot of the cross. They've never laid their pride in the dust. They have come into a church, not for what they can give, but for what they can get. The Spirit of God is not in these people, and they are troublemakers everywhere they go because their religion has never satisfied them and it never can. They are disillusioned, they have unfulfilled desires, they got into religion for the wrong reason, and they never have satisfaction. Everywhere they go, they're like Simon, full of bitterness and full of bondage. As Jesus reminded, those who know Him are not characterized most by bondage but by freedom.

- What are some wrong reasons people might seek God today?
- How can you know you are seeking Jesus for the right reasons?

PRACTICE THIS Make a list of your most prominent desires right now. Assess if these things point to a life that honors God or one that seeks selfish gain.

PRAY OVER THIS

Peter was therefore kept in prison, but constant prayer
was offered to God for him by the church.

ACTS 12:5

PONDER THIS I heard about a young lawyer who just got his degree and opened up his brand spanking new law offices. He didn't have any clients, but he had his sign out front. One day, he heard footsteps in the hallway and thought his first client was coming. So, he picked up the phone like he was busy. He said, "Hello, yes, no, I'm sorry I can't, perhaps next Thursday. I have a heavy corporation case coming up on Wednesday but perhaps we can arrange it." And he put the phone down. By this time the man he heard coming was standing in front of his desk. The lawyer said, "Yes sir, what may I do for you?" The man replied, "Well, I'm from the telephone company and I came to hook up your telephone." Many times, our prayers are that way—we're trying to impress somebody else but we haven't connected with God. The people in today's passage weren't trying to impress anybody else. They were desperate. Their prayer was unto God.

- Would you say you more often pray for God to hear or for others to hear?
- What might be some characteristics of these two kinds of prayers?

PRACTICE THIS Spend time today praying to God. Be honest with Him, sharing your heart and praying for Him—and not anyone else—to hear.

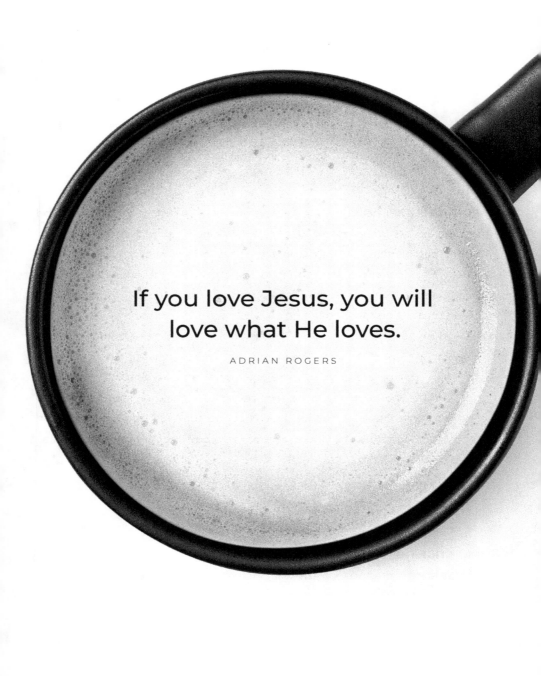

If you love Jesus, you will love what He loves.

ADRIAN ROGERS

PRAY OVER THIS

And He commanded us to preach to the people,
and to testify that it is He who was ordained by
God to be Judge of the living and the dead.

ACTS 10:42

PONDER THIS You ought to share your faith. If you have no desire to share your faith, there is reason to assess if you have really been changed by Jesus. You've heard people say "Keep the faith." Not only should you keep it, but you ought also to give it away. And if you have no desire to give it away, perhaps you ought to give it up. If you knew the cure to cancer, you'd want to share that, wouldn't you? The best news this world has ever known is the saving Gospel of our Lord and Savior Jesus Christ. I can give you this testimony: from the day I gave my heart to Jesus Christ to this very moment, there has always been a desire in my heart to share Him. That's one of the ways I know my faith is real. I've not always shared Him as I ought. I've not always been wise. I've not always been diligent. But there has always been, down in the recesses of my heart, a desire to share the Lord Jesus Christ. Do you have this same desire?

- How would you rate your own desire to share Jesus with others?
- What obstacles make this difficult for you?

PRACTICE THIS Ask God to show you your true heart for sharing Him with others. Ask Him to help you be honest with Him and with yourself, recognizing that it is of no benefit to try to convince yourself of falsehood in this area.

2

PRAY OVER THIS

Him God raised up on the third day, and showed Him openly, not to all the people, but to witnesses chosen before by God, even to us who ate and drank with Him after He arose from the dead.

ACTS 10:40-41

PONDER THIS Where did Peter get confidence in the message he preached? Some may have asked, "Are you sure you're not hallucinating? Peter, are you sure He wasn't a ghost?" Peter would have likely replied, "A ghost!? We ate and drank with Him. We touched Him."

Many have questioned if this was all a lie. Men may live for a lie, but no man will willingly die for a lie. People tell lies to get out of trouble, not to get into trouble. These people, with no hope of personal gain, knew beyond a shadow of a doubt that Jesus was alive, and they were convinced of His virtuous life. They were convinced of His vicarious death. They were convinced of His victorious resurrection.

- What gives you confidence in sharing Jesus with others? How have you experienced Him personally?
- What are some things that cause you to question the message about Jesus? How might you submit these things before God?

PRACTICE THIS Make a list of things that give you confidence in Jesus and things that make you hesitant to share about Him with others. Ask God to give you further confidence in the true and evidenced message of the Gospel.

3

PRAY OVER THIS

And beginning at Moses and all the Prophets, He expounded
to them in all the Scriptures the things concerning Himself.
LUKE 24:27

PONDER THIS The Old Testament, without the Lord Jesus Christ, would be a dead-end road leading to nowhere. And yet, as you take a step back and look at the whole Bible, you see Jesus everywhere.

An artist took the Constitution of the United States, and he painted the letters very carefully and shaded each letter. Once he was done, as you looked at the Constitution of the United States of America, you could read it as the framers intended it to be, but if you stepped back and looked at it, you would see that the artist had so shaded the letters that there was a portrait of George Washington. That's how we read the Old Testament in relation to Jesus. You'll find all the laws and ceremonies and practices, but as you step back, there He is: Jesus the Son of God.

- What are some ways you have seen Jesus throughout the Old Testament?
- How do these things give you further confidence in who He is?

PRACTICE THIS Take time today to look up some examples of practices or accounts in the Old Testament that point to Jesus either directly or indirectly.

4

PONDER THIS True faith goes beyond evidence and becomes its own best evidence. If you try to figure God out, you will die and go to Hell without having God figured out. Nothing will hold anything beyond its own capacity. In other words, you can't put two gallons of liquid in a one-gallon jug. Do you think that you can cram God into your mind? Your mind doesn't have the capacity to contain God. For God to be worthy of worship, He must be greater than our mentality. If we could understand God fully and know everything about Him, we wouldn't need God. The good news is we don't have to understand Him to know Him.

When I was a little boy, my dad used to go off to work. I didn't know where he went or what he did, but I knew he was my dad, and I knew him personally, and I loved him. You don't have to understand how God runs the mighty universe to put your faith and trust in Him. Someone once asked Mrs. Albert Einstein, "Do you understand the theory of relativity?" She said, "No, but I understand Dr. Einstein." Even though it is impossible to understand Him fully, by faith you can know the Lord Jesus Christ.

- What are some ways you have sought to understand God fully?
- How has this brought you frustration or disappointment?

PRACTICE THIS Write out several things you don't understand about God. Take time to review this list and thank God that you can know Him, even though you cannot fully comprehend Him.

PRAY OVER THIS

To Him all the prophets witness that, through His name,
whoever believes in Him will receive remission of sins.

ACTS 10:43

PONDER THIS When it comes to sharing your faith, not only is there the witness of the soul-winner but there is also the witness of the Scriptures. The Scriptures give witness to the truth about Jesus. He fulfilled the prophecies of the Old Testament. There are more than 300 prophecies in the Old Testament that were directly fulfilled by the Lord Jesus Christ. There are some people who see these Scriptures fulfilled and say, "Well, that's only because they've rigged it. Jesus and His apostles arranged for Him to fulfill these prophecies." If we really dig into it, we find that theory is quite impossible. Yet, the reality is, we cannot convince others to believe. We must only be faithful to present the truth, and the Scriptures give witness to that truth.

- What are some prophecies Jesus fulfilled that stand out to you?
- How might you learn more about these fulfillments to share them with others?

PRACTICE THIS Take time this week to research some of the prophecies Jesus has fulfilled and the historical evidence that supports these fulfillments.

PRAY OVER THIS

While Peter was still speaking these words, the Holy
Spirit fell upon all those who heard the word.

ACTS 10:44

PONDER THIS Do you know what Holy Spirit conviction is? It's when the Holy Spirit of God speaks to you and the Holy Spirit says, "That's true." How do you know Jesus is the Son of God? How do you know the Scriptures are true? How do you know those who say Jesus has transformed their lives are really transformed? Because the Holy Spirit of God convicts and confirms it.

I've had people tell me, "You would make a good salesman." I don't know whether I would or not. But I don't want to be a salesman when it comes to the Gospel. I'm not just trying to argue you into signing on the dotted line. I want the Holy Spirit of God to convict you of these things that I've preached, and the Holy Spirit of God will. I'm not dependent upon eloquence, logic, or personal magnetism. All is in vain unless the Spirit of the Holy One comes down.

- When have you experienced the conviction of the Holy Spirit?
- How does this give you boldness to share the truth with others?

PRACTICE THIS Take some time to write down some of your experiences in being convicted by the Holy Spirit.

7

And He answered and said to them, "Have you not read that He who made them at the beginning 'made them male and female,' and said, 'For this reason a man shall leave his father and mother and be joined to his wife, and the two shall become one flesh'?"

MATTHEW 19:4-5

PONDER THIS The highest relationship in human relationships is not parent-child. The highest relationship is husband and wife. God says we are one flesh. We leave father and mother, but we cleave unto our mate. This is God's plan for us. Parents are not the supreme commitment. Now, you're to honor your parents, and if your parents are old and feeble and in need, it's your responsibility to take care of them. The Bible says if you don't do it, you're worse than a nonbeliever. But your parents are not your supreme commitment, and your children are not your supreme commitment, according to the Bible. Mate to mate is higher than parent to child or child to parent.

- Based on today's text, is there anything you need to do to reprioritize the relationships in your life?
- What are some ways you have seen others wrongly prioritize the relationships in their lives? How does each relationship get what it needs when all are prioritized rightly?

PRACTICE THIS If you are married, prayerfully reflect on the ways you might prioritize your relationships rightly. If you are single, take time to pray for the relationships in your church.

PRAY OVER THIS

Husbands, love your wives, just as Christ also loved
the church and gave Himself for her.
EPHESIANS 5:25

PONDER THIS The Bible says a husband is to love his wife as Christ loved the Church, and that is unconditional love. It is not performance-based love: "But God demonstrates His own love toward us, in that while we were still sinners, Christ died for us" (Romans 5:8). "For when we were still without strength, in due time Christ died for the ungodly" (Romans 5:6). When you have unconditional love as Christ has for the Church, let me tell you what it's going to do for your home: It's going to give security in the place of fear. It's going to give peace in the place of guilt. And it's going to give joy that will replace anger. This kind of love is an act of the will. How does God love us? Do you think God loves us romantically? Do you think God loves us because we're lovely? No, God loves us as an act of His will.

- Would you say you regularly love as an act of the will? Why or why not?
- What makes this difficult?

PRACTICE THIS How might you practically show love to someone as an act of will this week? Take steps to actually do this.

9

Not that I speak in regard to need, for I have learned
in whatever state I am, to be content.
PHILIPPIANS 4:11

PONDER THIS What is contentment? Contentment is an inner sufficiency that keeps us at peace despite outward circumstances. In the New Testament, the word *contentment* has the idea of being self-contained. While in the Philippian jail, Paul said: "I have learned in whatever state I am, to be content" (Philippians 4:11). The idea means, "I'm self-contained; I don't have to look at circumstances to find my peace." When the space shuttle goes up, they put everything on board that people are going to need because there's no 7-Eleven in the neighborhood up there. It is self-contained, it has everything on board. In the same way, Christians have this self-containment. To be clear, this is not at all because we can find what we need in ourselves, but because the Spirit of God has come to live within us. Our contentment is found in Him.

- How have you experienced the "self-contained" contentment that is found in your relationship with Jesus?
- What does it look like to seek contentment in your circumstances instead of in something else that is passing away?

PRACTICE THIS Take a walk today to prayerfully consider where you find your contentment. Ask God to lead you to seek contentment in Him alone.

PRAY OVER THIS

Now godliness with contentment is great gain.

1 TIMOTHY 6:6

PONDER THIS Covetousness is wrong. This doesn't mean it's wrong to have godly ambition or to have things. But covetousness is so deceptive, it is so debasing and so destructive. Paul summed up our point in today's text: "Now godliness with contentment is great gain." In 1 Timothy 6:7, he went on to say: "For we brought nothing into this world, and it is certain we can carry nothing out." It has been said, "You never saw a hearse with a U-Haul behind it." We all get caught up in having more and believe the lie that one more thing or one more achievement will bring us contentment. Yet, Jesus didn't even have the most basic things. He said: "Foxes have holes and birds of the air have nests, but the Son of Man has nowhere to lay His head" (Matthew 8:20). But He wasn't discontent. When we are found in Him, we can find true contentment that doesn't exist anywhere else.

- Why is covetousness opposed to godliness?
- How can you find contentment in Jesus today, no matter what else is going on?

PRACTICE THIS Make a list of the reasons you have contentment available in Jesus today.

PRAY OVER THIS

Wives, likewise, be submissive to your own husbands, that
even if some do not obey the word, they, without a word, may
be won by the conduct of their wives, when they observe your
chaste conduct accompanied by fear. ...Husbands, likewise,
dwell with them with understanding, giving honor to the
wife, as to the weaker vessel, and as being heirs together of
the grace of life, that your prayers may not be hindered.

1 PETER 3:1-2, 7

PONDER THIS My home is solidly built on Jesus Christ. Joyce knows she's not number one in my life. She knows God is first in my life. I know God is first in her life. I don't mind that because I know she loves me with a stronger, deeper, purer love by putting God first than she could if she made me first. It is God who makes us together. In our dating life, growing up as high school sweethearts, we would conclude our dates in prayer. On the first night of our honeymoon we kneeled beside the bed and gave our home to Jesus Christ. Every day we pray together at breakfast and pray for all our children, and grandchildren, and for various other things. Our home is built on prayer. It began with prayer. It continues with prayer. You'll never have a successful home apart from God.

- How have you seen the principle described in today's devotion play out in daily life?
- How are homes and families healthier when they put God first, before anyone else in the family?

PRACTICE THIS Consider the practices you might put in place to make God number one in your home. Take steps toward implementing these practices today.

PRAY OVER THIS

Let your conduct be without covetousness; be content
with such things as you have. For He Himself has
said, "I will never leave you nor forsake you."

HEBREWS 13:5

PONDER THIS The secret of satisfaction, of true contentment, is God Himself. If you told the man on the street that the fear of the Lord is the beginning of wisdom and the secret of satisfaction, he would laugh at you. Hebrews 13:5 says, "Let your conduct be without covetousness; be content with such things as you have. For He Himself has said, 'I will never leave you nor forsake you.'" The word *conduct* literally means "behavior." The first secret of family contentment is God Himself. It is important to note we can't just say we are content with God. We must also follow up with our behavior.

- Does your behavior indicate you are content in God?
- Where might you be seeking contentment outside of God? What might you need to change?

PRACTICE THIS Make a list of the most frequent ways you spend your time. What does this say about where you seek contentment?

PRAY OVER THIS

Blessed is every one who fears the LORD, who walks in His ways.

PSALM 128:1

PONDER THIS A wise man looked back on his life and asked himself, "If I could do it all over again, what would I do differently with my family?" He said, "I would love my wife more in front of my children. I would laugh with my children more at our mistakes and our joys. I would listen more, even to the youngest child. I would be more honest about my own weaknesses and stop pretending perfection. I would pray differently for my family. Instead of focusing on their faults, I would focus more on what I need to change. I would do more things with my children. I would be encouraging and bestow more praise. I would pay more attention to little deeds and words of loving-kindness. And finally, if I could do it all over again, I would share God more intimately with my family, using every ordinary thing that happened to point them to God." For many of us, at the end of our lives, we will recognize that the things that matter now may not be as important as they seem in the moment. We should ask God to help us reprioritize our lives for His glory.

- If today were the last day of your life, how would you spend it?
- How does the way we spend our lives show what is important to us, no matter what we say?

PRACTICE THIS Take time today to think about what needs to change in the way you spend your life. Seek to implement that change moving forward.

14

PRAY OVER THIS

"Be angry, and do not sin": do not let the sun go down on your wrath.
EPHESIANS 4:26

PONDER THIS Have you ever had a splinter in your finger? Maybe it's down deep enough and you see it as a little dark spot and say, "Well, I could get that out, but I don't know." You could get a needle and pick it out or say, "Well, maybe it'll work its way out," and just leave it there. It seems to be all right. And then one morning you wake up and you've got this incredible pain and this thing is throbbing, it is festered, and it is infected because you didn't get it out. The Bible says, "Do not let the sun go down on your wrath." Don't ever go to sleep, husband and wife, back-to-back, angry and pouting. Sometimes it's hard to make up. If we aren't careful, our anger can be like that splinter. It may start small, but if we let it go, it can grow into a significant problem.

- Why is it difficult to forgive quickly?
- How have you seen a difference in your life when you were more willing to offer forgiveness to those closest to you?

PRACTICE THIS Take time today to consider who you need to forgive. What steps will you take toward forgiveness?

15

PRAY OVER THIS

When you eat the labor of your hands, you shall be happy, and it shall be well with you. Your wife shall be like a fruitful vine in the very heart of your house, your children like olive plants all around your table. Behold, thus shall the man be blessed who fears the LORD.

PSALM 128:2-4

PONDER THIS There is nothing more important for a father than integrity. Now you might fail in a lot of different ways, but oh, if you just simply fear God and live with integrity! You cannot teach what you do not know. And you cannot come from where you've not been. You cannot give what you do not have. You must fear God. You must walk in integrity.

What do you want to be remembered for? Do you know what I want my kids to remember me for? I want them to say, my dad feared God. My dad walked in the ways of God. We can be sure that our children will remember our character, whether good or bad. If we walk in the fear of the Lord, we can be sure that we will live with integrity and display character worth remembering.

- What do you remember most about your father?
- What showed you that he lived with high character or a lack thereof?

PRACTICE THIS What would those closest to you say about your integrity? What needs to change for you to live with godly character?

PRAY OVER THIS

Who can find a virtuous wife? For her worth is far above rubies.

PROVERBS 31:10

PONDER THIS A diamond catches and reflects light, but a ruby has an inner glow. The beauty of a ruby is on the inside. And that's what God is talking about when He speaks of the value of a virtuous wife. Look at Proverbs 31:30, and you'll see what He's talking about: "Charm is deceitful and beauty is passing, but a woman who fears the Lord, she shall be praised." Now there's nothing wrong with beauty, but virtue far exceeds beauty. The word *virtue* here really means "moral strength." The Bible says that because of her moral strength, her husband can trust her. Proverbs 31:11a says, "The heart of her husband safely trusts her." What does that mean? It means she's going, to be honest, she's going to be wise, she's going to be loyal, and she's going to be prudent.

- Who comes to mind when you think about godly women in your life?
- How do they exhibit the qualities of godly virtue?

PRACTICE THIS Take time today to reach out and encourage the women you know who exhibit these qualities regularly. Make a phone call or send a text message to let them know.

PRAY OVER THIS

She also rises while it is yet night, and provides food for
her household, and a portion for her maidservants.

PROVERBS 31:15

PONDER THIS She is getting up to have a quiet time with the Lord. And the Bible goes on to say, in verse 30, that she is one who fears the Lord. I cannot tell you the times that I have awakened to find my wife already awake singing hymns to our Lord or walked in to find her on her knees studying and preparing her heart for the day. I think that's the exact picture our Lord has here. You may think if you didn't have the distractions or responsibilities of the modern world that you could do the same. While we have different responsibilities and distractions, we also have more luxuries than the people of this day. These include washers and dryers and stoves and refrigerators, and we wouldn't want to trade places for anything. But here is a woman of godly worship, who is getting up early to have her quiet time with the Lord. The fact is, it was a priority for her. Is it for us?

- How important is time in the Word and prayer to your daily routine?
- What might change if you made this a higher priority?

PRACTICE THIS Commit to regular time spent with the Lord each day this week. Take notice of how your life is impacted by this commitment.

18

> **PRAY OVER THIS**
>
> And the LORD God said, "It is not good that man should be
> alone; I will make him a helper comparable to him."
>
> **GENESIS 2:18**

PONDER THIS The word *helper* here is a noun, not a verb. God was not just saying He was going to give Adam some help. God could have simply given Adam a friend to help him pick fruit. But that's not the idea. The idea is someone who was going to cooperate with him. Someone who would become a part of a team with him. Someone who would make him more than he could have been without that person. Someone to help Adam to reach his full potential. Adam could not be what he ought to be without Eve, any more than I could be what I ought to be without my wife, whom God has given to me. Joyce has been this helper to me throughout our married life and our ministry.

- How have you seen the best marriages you know function in the way discussed in today's devotional?
- If you are married, how has your spouse helped you be who God made you to be?

PRACTICE THIS If you are married, take time to encourage your spouse by pointing out the ways God has blessed you through him or her. If you are not married, take time to encourage a married couple that exhibits these godly qualities.

19

Her husband is known in the gates, when he
sits among the elders of the land.

PROVERBS 31:23

PONDER THIS The woman described in Proverbs 31 is to her husband a helpmeet—a completer, an enhancer. This verse says her husband is known in the gates. The gates were the place of commerce in this day. This was like her husband being known in city hall or in the courthouse square. Her husband is a well-known citizen, but because God is extolling the wife here and not the husband, the implication is very clear that he is what he is because she is what she is. Likewise, I know I am what I am today, not only because of God, but because of my precious wife. I know that beyond any shadow of a doubt. And that's what this verse is saying. Her husband is known in the gates. She is a woman who is behind her husband, encouraging her husband at every step.

- Why is it important that wives learn to encourage their husbands?
- Do you know of a couple who mutually encourage and appreciate one another in a godly manner?

PRACTICE THIS Take time this week to show your appreciation to someone who is good at encouraging others.

20

PONDER THIS This passage describes a woman who has control of her tongue. She opens her mouth with wisdom and on her tongue is the law of kindness. Do you know why this is? Do you know why she can talk with such dignity, poise, and grace? Because she's already been up early in the morning; she's had her quiet time with God. Her life is well-ordered because her heart is at peace with God. When you lash out at others, it reveals more about you than anyone else. If you're one who is continually lashing out, you're a person who is not at peace with yourself. And if you're not at peace with yourself, it's because you're not at peace with God. And if you're not at peace with Him, it is because you have not had quality, priority time with Almighty God.

- Have you experienced the peace that comes from continual and regular time spent with God?
- When you are not at peace with God, have you found it more difficult to control your anger and your tongue?

PRACTICE THIS Make a commitment each day this week to spend dedicated time with God, so that you might grow in relationship with Him and find peace in your spirit.

PRAY OVER THIS

For the husband is head of the wife, as also Christ is head
of the church; and He is the Savior of the body.

EPHESIANS 5:23

PONDER THIS Philippians chapter 2 tells us that the Lord did not consider it a thing to be grasped to be equal with God, but made Himself of no reputation and took on the form of a servant in obedience. And the Bible says, "Therefore God has highly exalted Him" (Philippians 2:9). Jesus took the low way and God exalted Him. The devil took the high way and God brought him down and will bring him down to the very pit. We are never more like Jesus than when we have submissive spirits. We are never more like the devil than when we have rebellious spirits. Submission is not inferiority. The Bible teaches in 1 Corinthians 11:3, "But I want you to know that the head of every man is Christ, the head of woman is man, and the head of Christ is God." Husbands are called to be the heads of their wives and their families in the same manner that Jesus led through servanthood.

- How does this idea of submission contrast with the way of the world?
- What would change in your life if you sought to lead others through servanthood?

PRACTICE THIS Take an opportunity this week to serve someone else in a specific way as a means of following Jesus.

22

PONDER THIS God made husbands and wives different so that He might make them one. God gave you one nature and God gave your wife another nature. God gave husbands masculinity and responsibility that they are to assume. In that responsibility, you may give your wife authority, but you can never get rid of your responsibility. You are to let your wife know that she is number one. You move in to protect your wife from internal traumas, so that you can present her without spot or wrinkle, to make her a more radiantly beautiful Christian. And then, husbands, once you have done that, then you move in to encourage her, nourish her, and cherish her. It is up to the husband to take the initiative. All of us must practice what God's Word says, that there might be harmony in the home.

- What do you think it looks like to share authority but take responsibility as we've discussed today?
- What responsibilities has God given you? Are there any ways you have sought to relinquish those wrongly?

PRACTICE THIS Make a list of responsibilities you feel God has given you. If you are failing to honor God in any of these responsibilities, consider what needs to change.

23

PRAY OVER THIS

A merry heart makes a cheerful countenance, but
by sorrow of the heart the spirit is broken.
PROVERBS 15:13

PONDER THIS Good, wholesome laughter is a gift from God. Abraham Lincoln once said that God must have meant for us to laugh, or else He would not have made so many mules, parrots, monkeys, and human beings. God wants us to laugh. God gave Sarah a little child, and God led Sarah to name that child Laughter; we call his name Isaac. The name *Isaac* means "laughter." In Genesis 21:6, "Sarah said, 'God has made me laugh, and all who hear will laugh with me.'" God's gift of a little boy brought such joy that Abraham and Sarah named the child Laughter. We should cherish the gift of wholesome laughter in our homes; it brings cheer to one another and glory to God.

- Have you ever thought of laughter as wholesome or unwholesome?
- What might be some examples of unwholesome laughter?

PRACTICE THIS Take time this week to spend time with another person, speaking about things that bring cheer and wholesome laughter.

PRAY OVER THIS

A wrathful man stirs up strife, but he who is
slow to anger allays contention.
PROVERBS 15:18

PONDER THIS All anger is not bad. Jesus was angry, but He was angry at the right things. The Bible says in Ephesians 4:26a, "Be angry, and do not sin." The Bible warns us to be slow to anger because we do often sin in our anger. (See James 1:19.) Proverbs 14:17 says, "A quick-tempered man acts foolishly." Proverbs 18:13 says, "He who answers a matter before he hears it, it is folly and shame to him." Proverbs 29:20 says, "Do you see a man hasty in his words? There is more hope for a fool than for him." Be slow to anger. The way to control your anger is to control your words. Consider Proverbs 15:1a, "A soft answer turns away wrath." Controlling our anger begins with controlling our speech. One angry word builds the next word and that builds the next word, until it gets worse and worse. We must learn to be slow to speak and slow to anger.

- What might be an example of righteous anger?
- How can even righteous anger turn to sin if we are not careful?

PRACTICE THIS Make a list of things that you have anger or passion about today. Consider what is of God and what is not. Ask Him to help you let go of any anger that is not honoring to Him.

PRAY OVER THIS

Husbands, love your wives, just as Christ also loved
the church and gave Himself for her.
EPHESIANS 5:25

PONDER THIS Did you know Jesus never makes me do anything? Husbands, you are going to be in severe difficulty if you think that when the Bible says you are the head, you read that as, "I am the boss." "I am the dictator." No. Jesus is not the dictator of the Church; He is the head of the Church. If the Church, as His bride, refuses to follow, then she is going to reap repercussions, but He never forces us to do anything. Any husband who takes the attitude of a dictator is going to see that his home is in severe trouble. He is seeking to use the Bible as a club saying, "I am the head. Submit." This is not the way of Jesus and cannot be our way either.

- Who do you know who you would say is a great leader?
- What makes that person a leader you want to follow?

PRACTICE THIS Consider the positions of influence and leadership you have been given. How will you move toward Christ-honoring leadership?

26

PRAY OVER THIS

For the love of money is a root of all kinds of evil, for which
some have strayed from the faith in their greediness, and
pierced themselves through with many sorrows.

1 TIMOTHY 6:10

PONDER THIS Every now and then a graduation commencement speaker will tell the graduates, "Make all the money you can as long you make it honestly." That's the worst advice I've ever heard. If you're trying to make all the money you can, then you're going to be making money when you ought to be doing something else. You're going to be making money when you ought to be praying or going to church or spending time with your children. No one should have a goal to make all the money he or she can. Sure, we must provide for our families, but when we determine that we're going to be rich, we put ourselves in a very vulnerable position.

- What would you say is the difference between making a living as we should and chasing riches?
- How can you guard against the love of money in your life?

PRACTICE THIS Assess your current priorities. Where might you be pursuing money inappropriately? What needs to change?

PRAY OVER THIS

Without counsel, plans go awry, but in the multitude
of counselors they are established.

PROVERBS 15:22

PONDER THIS Notice in verse 22, "in the multitude of counselors" this wisdom is established. If I had it to do over again, I would have more family counsels. We had family worship, but I would bring the family together. We would sit down, and I would listen to each person, and we would, as a family, say everything we had belonged to us equally. We would share the amenities and the responsibilities, and we would learn to make decisions together. We would make a family budget and we would stick to it. We would make decisions as a family about discipline and many other things. The parents are the head of the family, but there is wisdom in doing these things together.

- How have you experienced the truth that plans are established in the multitude of counselors?
- How does living this way help us to rely less on ourselves and more on God?

PRACTICE THIS Where do you currently need wisdom? Spend time praying about this area and seek wisdom from a trusted advisor this week.

PRAY OVER THIS

For this reason a man shall leave his father and mother and
be joined to his wife, and the two shall become one flesh.
EPHESIANS 5:31

PONDER THIS It is not your love that sustains your marriage, it is your marriage that sustains your love. Marriage is a commitment. The Bible says you are to be joined. A "no-fault" divorce is an impossibility. What happens many times is that 10 percent of a marriage is in trouble and the other 90 percent goes down the drain because of a lack of commitment.

Somebody says, "I owe it to myself to be happy." What do you mean you owe it to yourself to be happy? When you were at the marriage altar, you made a vow. You owe it to God to keep your vow. You owe it to your spouse, and you owe it to your children. The one-flesh union of marriage must go beyond our personal preferences.

- If you are married, what kinds of sacrifices have you had to make for the sake of your spouse? If you are not married, how have you witnessed married couples make these types of sacrifices?
- How are all followers of Jesus called to sacrifice for the sake of others?

PRACTICE THIS Consider an area in which you need to lay down your rights and preferences this week. Take steps to sacrifice to serve someone else.

The way to lose the next victory is to fail to give God the proper praise for the last victory.

ADRIAN ROGERS

①

PRAY OVER THIS

Ask, and it will be given to you; seek, and you will
find; knock, and it will be opened to you.

MATTHEW 7:7

PONDER THIS Prayer is God's way of causing us to be dependent upon Him. If God just gave us what we needed without our asking, we would cease to be dependent on Him. Prayer is a way of binding us to Him. Asking God for what we need ought to be just as natural as breathing. Don't get the idea you can only ask God for spiritual things, and you take care of the secular things. Can you imagine Jesus dividing His life into the secular and the sacred? Everything is important to God. You may say, "Well, this is beyond God," or "This is too small for God to deal with." No! Can you think of anything too big or too small for God to notice? Ask Him for any desire of your heart. You may say, "What if I want something that I shouldn't?" You can still pray about it. You can say, "God, I want something You don't want. Fix my want-er." Pray about everything.

- How easy or difficult do you find it to pray to God about everything?
- What are some obstacles that keep you from praying to God about everything?

PRACTICE THIS Make a list of everything that is weighing on your mind this week. Take time to pray about everything on this list, no matter how big or small.

2

PRAY OVER THIS

Ask, and it will be given to you; seek, and you will
find; knock, and it will be opened to you.

MATTHEW 7:7

PONDER THIS When should you stop asking, stop seeking, and stop knocking about a particular matter? There are three reasons to stop. Number one, you stop asking when you have what you asked for; when God gives it to you, you don't have to keep on asking. Number two, you stop asking when, though you don't have the answer in your hand, you have the answer in your heart. I had a very big prayer that God put in my heart once. But God said, "Now Adrian, you're asking Me to do something I'm not going to do, but what you really need is this, and I've heard your prayer." I didn't have what I requested in my hand, but I had it in my heart. Thirdly, you stop asking when God says no. Paul asked God to take away a thorn in the flesh. But God said, "My grace is sufficient for you" (2 Corinthians 12:9a). Sometimes God simply says no, and we must trust Him.

- Is there anything you need to stop asking for?
- Is there anything you need to start asking for?

PRACTICE THIS Make a list of the most pressing things you pray for regularly. Ask God to show you if He's already answered in one of the forms we considered today. Respond in obedience to Him.

PRAY OVER THIS

"Bring all the tithes into the storehouse, that there may be food in My house, And try Me now in this," says the LORD of hosts, "If I will not open for you the windows of heaven and pour out for you such blessing that there will not be room enough to receive it."

MALACHI 3:10

PONDER THIS Do you know why you don't obey the Word of God? You don't believe it. Consider today's text. There's not a person in the Church who doesn't want Heaven opened and God pouring out such blessings that we can't even contain them all. All of us want that, but not all of us tithe. Why? Because we don't believe the promise. If you believed the promise, you would tithe. We always show what we believe by our actions. Doesn't everyone want Heaven opened and doesn't everyone want a blessing? We simply don't believe the Word of God.

- Where do you recognize that you don't believe the Word of God?
- What evidence does your life give for your belief or lack thereof?

PRACTICE THIS Ask God to reveal in areas in which you have not shown belief in and obedience to His Word. Take steps toward obedience today.

4

PONDER THIS Faith is confidence that goes beyond emotions. Emotions are the shallowest part of your nature. Faith is the deepest work of God, and God doesn't do the deepest work in the shallowest part of you. Don't live your life under the tyranny of emotions. It feels good to feel good and there is nothing wrong with feeling good. But feelings are fickle.

When I go to preach, I always try to look like I'm having a good time and I feel good. But sometimes I don't. Surprised? Maybe I didn't get any sleep last night. Maybe I got an upset stomach. Maybe I've got a dull headache when I come up here, but it's time to preach and I'm going to preach. Other times you think it's going to be a good service, but nothing seems to go right. The preacher's tongue gets tied up. And the ushers won't ush. And the choir can't hit the notes. And you think, "Good night! God is light-years from this place." Yet Heaven comes down. Our emotions had nothing to do with that.

- When was a time you felt like everything was going right but didn't see the spiritual fruit you hoped for? When was a time everything felt wrong, but you saw God move powerfully?
- What does this teach you about what God can do, no matter how you feel?

PRACTICE THIS Take time in prayer today to ask God for faith in Him that goes beyond your feelings, whether they are good or bad.

5

PRAY OVER THIS

By faith we understand that the worlds were framed
by the word of God, so that the things which are seen
were not made of things which are visible.

HEBREWS 11:3

PONDER THIS Every three or four months there is some new article in the newspaper about the origin of the Universe. Every now and then a scientist will say some good words about God. That doesn't give me any more faith in God. A little more faith in the scientist, maybe, but not in God. What is science? Science is the study of phenomena now existing. God asked Job this question in Job 38:4a, "Where were you when I laid the foundations of the earth?" How do we understand everything we see in creation? By faith.

You may say, "Well, that takes a lot of belief." Well, it takes more to believe nothing times nobody equals everything. That's what many believe. No wonder the Bible says, "The fool has said in his heart, 'There is no God'" (Psalm 14:1a). God is the supreme fact and the man who denies it is the supreme fool. Faith is not contrary to reason, it's simply beyond reason. To go in the laboratory to try to prove God would be like tearing a piano apart trying to find a tune.

- What are some ways people seek to prove (or disprove) God today?
- What are some ways you've sought proof of God outside of the faith described in the Bible?

PRACTICE THIS Take time today in prayer to ask God to give you faith in Him and His Word beyond what you can see or prove.

6

PONDER THIS Faith is the heart's response to the character of God. When your eye is right, it responds to light. When your ear is right, it responds to sound. When your heart is right, it responds to God and that response is called faith. That's the reason the Bible says, "Beware, brethren, lest there be in any of you an evil heart of unbelief in departing from the living God" (Hebrews 3:12). Unbelief never comes out of the head. Unbelief comes out of the heart. A lack of faith shows what is in our hearts. Faith is the dynamic of spiritual worship. Faith honors God and God honors faith. Are you honoring Him through faith?

- How have you experienced the reality of faith as a response to the character of God?
- What are some ways your life might show a lack of faith, no matter what you say you believe?

PRACTICE THIS Make a list of ways your faith is manifest in your life. Make another list of ways your life shows a lack of faith. What needs to change? Take those things before God in prayer.

7

PRAY OVER THIS

By faith Abel offered to God a more excellent sacrifice than Cain,
through which he obtained witness that he was righteous, God
testifying of his gifts; and through it he being dead still speaks.

HEBREWS 11:4

PONDER THIS What did Abel offer? "Abel also brought of the firstborn of his flock" (Genesis 4:4a). Abel's offering was based on a blood atonement and this pointed forward to Jesus. Religion is what sinful people do for a holy God. The Gospel is the Good News of what a holy God has already done for sinful man.

Where did Abel get the idea of bringing a blood offering to Almighty God? When Adam and Eve sinned against God, they tried to clothe themselves with fig leaves. What is that? The fruit of the ground. What did God do? God came into the Garden of Eden and made them coats of animal skin. How do you get coats of skin? Blood must be shed. This sacrifice foreshadowed the blood of Jesus that would be shed as the ultimate sacrifice.

- Why was it necessary for Jesus's blood to be shed?
- What other Old Testament examples can you think of that point forward to the shed blood of Jesus?

PRACTICE THIS Make a list of some Old Testament references to sacrifices. Consider the ways these accounts pointed to Jesus.

PRAY OVER THIS

And according to the law almost all things are purified with
blood, and without shedding of blood there is no remission.

HEBREWS 9:22

PONDER THIS Pavlov, the Russian psychologist, did experiments in what we call "conditioned response." He had his dogs, and he would ring a bell, feed the dogs, ring a bell, feed the dogs, ring a bell, feed the dogs. He conditioned the dogs so that all he had to do was ring a bell and they'd begin to drool. They began to salivate because they knew that the bell meant food. What was God doing in the Old Testament with all the sacrifices, beginning with the skins that clothed Adam and Eve and continuing with Abel's offering? He was conditioning His people. When they saw the blood, they were reminded repeatedly that sin meant death. Therefore, God's people were ready for the death of the Lord Jesus Christ upon the cross. For, "without shedding of blood there is no remission."

- As you read God's Word, how do the Old Testament sacrifices help you look for the coming sacrifice of Jesus?
- How does it change your perspective of the Old Testament to read it in this way?

PRACTICE THIS Take time in prayer to thank God for the sacrifices of the Old Testament that continually pointed to the ultimate sacrifice of Jesus.

PRAY OVER THIS

And Enoch walked with God; and he was not, for God took him.

GENESIS 5:24

PONDER THIS Faith is not guessing at the will of God. Faith is hearing from God through the Word of God, learning the will of God, and believing God. You don't name it and claim it; God speaks, and you believe it. Without faith it's impossible to please God (Hebrews 11:6).

You want to walk with God? Walking with God is not just about coming to church. It's not only learning the facts. Would you like for God to be more real to you than the person sitting next to you? This walk with God begins with faith. Enoch walked with God because he believed God.

- How does the Word of God reveal the will of God?
- What would it look like for you to walk with God in faith this week?

PRACTICE THIS Write a list of things you know to be the will of God according to His Word. Reflect on this list throughout the week.

PRAY OVER THIS

He has shown you, O man, what is good; and what
does the LORD require of you but to do justly, to love
mercy, and to walk humbly with your God?"

MICAH 6:8

PONDER THIS Sometimes we come to church, and we act differently.
Sometimes this is appropriate. Obviously, when somebody is preaching, we
want to be quiet. When we sing, we want to join together. But don't change
your personality. A Christian is perfectly natural and naturally supernatural.
God has made us with intention, and we are to bring our whole selves into
the church. There's a time to be still. But the Bible also says shout unto the
Lord. There's a time to cry, but also a time to laugh. There are times when we're
exuberant in our worship and times when we are to be on our face with the
Lord. But in all of this, we're to be natural. Faith is not something that we put on
when we come to church. We are to walk with God 24 hours a day, seven days
a week, 365 days a year. It is a constant walk.

- What are some ways you are tempted to act differently with
  others in the church?
- What would it look like for you to walk with God in every moment
  of life?

PRACTICE THIS Ask God to show you the areas of life in which you might be
living falsely with Him or with others. Ask Him to help you live authentically in
every moment of life.

11

By faith Noah, being divinely warned of things
not yet seen, moved with godly fear.
HEBREWS 11:7A

PONDER THIS God warned Noah of the flood. But Noah had never seen a flood. In fact, Noah had never even seen rain. Genesis 2:5-6 says, "...before any plant of the field was in the earth and before any herb of the field had grown. For the Lord God had not caused it to rain on the earth, and there was no man to till the ground; but a mist went up from the earth and watered the whole face of the ground." Noah didn't have evidence of the flood, but He did have evidence of God and His faithfulness.

When Noah believed God, he feared God. Fear and faith are inseparably linked. Fear sees God's power, holiness, and justice. Faith sees God's lovingkindness, grace, and mercy. Therefore, the fear of God is not a cringing dread of God. It is love on its knees.

- What evidence is there in your life that you fear God in an appropriate way?
- How does a right fear of God lead to living faithfully before God?

PRACTICE THIS What is something you know God is calling you to do? Obey Him without delay. Fear God that you might walk faithfully before Him.

PRAY OVER THIS

By faith Enoch was taken away so that he did not see death,
"and was not found, because God had taken him"; for before
he was taken he had this testimony, that he pleased God.
HEBREWS 11:5

PONDER THIS When Enoch walked with God, he walked with God at a time called "the days of Noah." Violence, vice, and wickedness were so rampant that God decided He was going to destroy the world with a flood. In the days of Noah, Enoch walked with God. In a day of demonic force, he walked with God.

You might be tempted to say, "Pastor, it's easy for you because you're a preacher. You don't know where I work. You don't know what my house is like. It's hard for me to walk with God." The reality is, it's impossible for any of us to walk with God in our own strength. Think about a power plant. Somebody says, "That plant generates power." But in the truest sense, it releases power. The power is in the atomic energy that is released. In the same way, the power that's in my life is from God who is releasing His power into me to walk the Christian life day by day. I would not be faithful were it not for the Lord in me. Enoch walked with God. If it's God who walks with you, then you do not have to generate the power. The power comes from Him.

- Would you say you are more reliant on yourself or on God for daily power?
- What are some practical ways you can depend on God for power each day?

PRACTICE THIS Write out your schedule for the week. Consider practical ways you can depend on God's power rather than your own as you walk through this week.

13

PRAY OVER THIS

The Lord is not slack concerning His promise, as some count slackness, but is longsuffering toward us, not willing that any should perish but that all should come to repentance.

2 PETER 3:9

PONDER THIS Why has Jesus not come in our day and our age? God's waiting for more people to be saved. Peter wrote that many would say, "Where is the promise of His coming? For since the fathers fell asleep, all things continue as they were from the beginning of creation" (2 Peter 3:4). Peter continued on, "But, beloved, do not forget this one thing, that with the Lord one day is as a thousand years, and a thousand years as one day. The Lord is not slack concerning His promise, as some count slackness, but is longsuffering toward us, not willing that any should perish but that all should come to repentance" (2 Peter 3:8-9).

It could be that the reason Jesus didn't come yesterday is because God wants you saved today. It could be that God is keeping the door open one more time. But remember, in Noah's time the flood did come. And even now the raging waters of God's wrath are furiously pounding against the dam of His mercy. He has promised that one day Jesus Christ will come, and it will be too late for many as it was too late in Noah's day.

- Have you made sure you have valued God's grace and not dismissed His patience?
- How should this reality motivate us to tell others about Jesus?

PRACTICE THIS Have a conversation with someone this week about God's patience evidenced by the delayed coming of Christ.

14

PRAY OVER THIS

So Noah, with his sons, his wife, and his sons' wives, went
into the ark because of the waters of the flood.

GENESIS 7:7

PONDER THIS Religion that does not begin at home does not begin. Have you ever thought, "My loved ones are the hardest ones to witness to"? Do you know why they are the hardest ones to witness to? Because they know you. Would you go and say, "Forgive me for the life that I have lived in front of you? I'm a Christian, but I have been a poor example." They'll be watching you. Then later on go back and say, "Would you forgive me for something else? ...I haven't shared with you the most important thing on Earth to me. Would you forgive me for not sharing Jesus with you?" This type of humility gives you an open door to share the Lord Jesus Christ with your loved ones. Noah had faith and that faith was for the saving of his household.

- In what areas are you convicted of the way you have lived with and before your family members?
- Who do you need to ask forgiveness from in this regard?

PRACTICE THIS Take concrete steps to ask forgiveness from a family member this week as the Lord leads you.

PRAY OVER THIS

By faith Abraham obeyed when he was called to go out
to the place which he would receive as an inheritance.
And he went out, not knowing where he was going.
HEBREWS 11:8

PONDER THIS Abraham was a pagan and an idolater. He lived in a place called Ur of the Chaldees. When God spoke to him, he enrolled in the school of faith—2000 years before Christ. Furthermore, he was 75 years of age when he enrolled in this school. Don't tell me you're too evil and don't tell me you're too old. If Abraham became the father of those who believed, (See Romans 4:16-17.) can you not step into this wonderful, glorious life of faith also?

Think about it. A man over 70 years of age. He was in a strange land. He was settled there. He had a beautiful wife, a business, and family nearby. But he left it all to go to a country he had never seen, and he was marching under sealed orders. God didn't tell him where he was going or how long it was going to take him to get there. God didn't tell him what he was going to do when he got there, how long he would stay, or what would happen to him. God just said, "Get up and go." And Abraham left and enrolled himself in the school of faith.

- How does today's passage encourage you that it's never too late to start fresh with God?
- Where have you believed the lie that you were too evil or too old to receive grace from God?

PRACTICE THIS List ways you've believed you were too far from God. Submit these before Him in prayer, trusting that He will receive you as He did Abraham.

PRAY OVER THIS

Now faith is the substance of things hoped
for, the evidence of things not seen.
HEBREWS 11:1

PONDER THIS There is an invisible world. There is a world that is more real than this world, and all the heroes of the faith were people who could see the invisible. Most of us only see what is before us—our cars, our houses, our jobs. We never get a vision. We never look upward. We never look onward. But even in the material world, the people who make a mark—the explorers, the novelists, the artists, the creators, inventors—all of these have the ability to see the invisible. Before I ever preached in this pulpit, I would come out here when it was sheer dirt and stand up here and preach. I know that may sound funny to you, but God put a dream in my heart of what the future would look like.

Faith begins with a vision. Faith is setting your affection on something that is bigger than what most of us are living for. God wants to give each of us that vision if we will look to Him.

- Are your sights typically set more on the things you can see or the vision God has for you?
- What are some practical ways you might set your eyes toward the things God has for you in life?

PRACTICE THIS Make a list of your goals in life, both short- and long-term. Consider if these things are aligned with seeking God's vision for your life.

17

PRAY OVER THIS

By faith Abraham, when he was tested, offered up Isaac, and
he who had received the promises offered up his only begotten
son, of whom it was said, "In Isaac your seed shall be called."
HEBREWS 11:17-18

PONDER THIS God is going to test your faith by asking you to do something that may surprise you. The test is often not in giving up wrong things and bad things, but in giving up good things. It would be relatively easy if God only asked us to give up bad things. Most of us don't have trouble trying to give up lying, stealing, cheating, or pride to show that we love Him. But that's not what God is asking. God had given Abraham a possession, a wonderful son. God had also given to Abraham a promise that He would make Abraham into a great nation. And that promise was going to come through the gift of Isaac. But now God seemed to be asking for all of it back.

Are you able to give your blessings back to God? The question is not if you are willing to give up your sins for God. Are you willing to give your blessings back to God? That's what Abraham was asked to do.

- How hard do you find it to give up good things God has given you?
- Why is it important to be obedient when God asks you for something?

PRACTICE THIS Take time to reflect on the good thing God might be calling you to give up. How will you respond?

PRAY OVER THIS

...concluding that God was able to raise him up, even from the dead, from which he also received him in a figurative sense.

HEBREWS 11:19

PONDER THIS When we were children, we use to have a saying, "Finders keepers; losers weepers." Did you ever say that? God says, "Keepers weepers; losers finders." Lose your life for Mine and you will find it. (See Matthew 16:25.) The Bible says in Hebrews 11:19, Abraham was "concluding that God was able to raise him (Isaac) up, even from the dead…" The word *concluding* literally means "considered." It means "to reckon." It means "to calculate." It's the Greek word we get our word "logistics" from and our word "logic" from. Abraham was saying, "God, You gave me this boy. I can trust You with him. You have a purpose. I can trust You. You made a promise, then I reckon on it. God, You're going to keep Your word. You cannot lie. I don't have to understand. I don't have to run it past the judgment of my own knowledge." And God gave him back his son by providing another way. In response, Abraham called the name of that place, "Jehovah-Jireh," meaning, "God will provide." (See Genesis 22:14.)

- How do you regularly count on the promises of God?
- How does knowing and studying the promises of God change the way we look at daily life?

PRACTICE THIS Write out a promise of God you are counting on to be true. How should you live today in light of this promise?

PRAY OVER THIS

By faith he [Abraham] dwelt in the land of promise as
in a foreign country, dwelling in tents with Isaac and
Jacob, the heirs with him of the same promise.
HEBREWS 11:9

PONDER THIS I am sometimes asked by young pastors about the approach they should have when taking a position at a new church. Here is what I tell them: "When you go to a church, you must be able to do two things: number one, you must be prepared to spend the rest of your life there, and number two, you must be ready to leave in the next 15 minutes." Both are true. You can't only say, "Lord, I'm building a nest." You need to pray, "Lord, if I'm building a nest, put a thorn in it. I am ready to go." Trust and obey, for there's no other way to be happy in Jesus. God gives you the choice. If you do not obey what you know, don't ask God for more light. God is not going to give it to you.

Are you having a faith problem? If you're having a faith problem, you're probably really having an obedience problem. Is there a confession that you need to make? Is there restitution that you need to perform? Is there a gift you need to give? Is there a testimony you need to offer? Is there a place you need to go? Obey! Do you want faith? First, you must hear from God, but then you must obey God.

- Where is God currently calling you to obey Him?
- How will you respond this week?

PRACTICE THIS Take concrete steps toward obeying God in whatever way He has called you this week.

PRAY OVER THIS

For he [Abraham] waited for the city which has
foundations, whose builder and maker is God.

HEBREWS 11:10

PONDER THIS Abraham had a pilgrim character. Now, that doesn't mean he was a dropout. Abraham was in business. He had a family. He taught. He even had to go to war several times. But Abraham was not molded by this world.

What are your personal goals? Is your goal to make enough money to retire and have a nice house, to live in ease and have certain things? Or are you more concerned about your spiritual walk? Do you want your children to be successful and famous? Or are you more concerned about the character of your children growing in Christ and the kingdom of Heaven? Would you leave your present job and take a lesser job for less pay if it were better for the character of your children? Is your goal to impress other people? Would you rather be with the rich and the famous, or the godly and the pure? Most of us are so squeezed in by this world, and yet we wonder why we don't have faith. Abraham was a man to whom this world meant very little because "he waited for the city which has foundations, whose builder and maker is God." He had a pilgrim character.

- Be honest with yourself. What are your goals for your life?
- Do your goals align closer with the kingdom of God or the kingdom of this world?

PRACTICE THIS Write out the goals you have for your life. Be honest and do not hold back. Pray over this list. Ask God to help you shift your focus and priorities to pursue His Kingdom over the kingdom of the world.

PRAY OVER THIS

Concluding that God was able to raise him [Isaac]
up, even from the dead, from which he [Abraham]
also received him in a figurative sense.

HEBREWS 11:19

PONDER THIS Abraham took Isaac and started up Mount Moriah to offer his son. How was he able to do that? Hebrews 11:19 says he was "concluding that God was able to raise him up, even from the dead, from which he also received him in a figurative sense." In Abraham's mind, Isaac was dead for three days. From the day that God said, "Abraham, take him and offer him," until the day that Abraham got him back, he considered his son dead. In this way, Abraham received Isaac from the dead.

Now, what is the Gospel that you and I preach? Christ died for our sins, He was buried, and was raised again on the third day. (See 1 Corinthians 15:3-4.) God the Father received Jesus back literally. In this, we see that Isaac prefigured Jesus.

- How are you encouraged in your faith when you see examples like Isaac, who pointed to the coming work of Jesus?
- Why do examples like this matter in our faith and life?

PRACTICE THIS List any other examples you know from the Old Testament where events or individuals foreshadowed the life of Christ.

22

PRAY OVER THIS

Then on the third day Abraham lifted his eyes and saw
the place afar off. And Abraham said to his young men,
"Stay here with the donkey; the lad and I will go yonder
and worship, and we will come back to you."

GENESIS 22:4-5

PONDER THIS Abraham and Isaac came to a point beyond which the others couldn't go. The others were told to stay back while they went to commune together. This reminds us of the darkness of Gethsemane where Jesus left Peter, James, John, and the other disciples and went alone to commune with His Father as He faced Calvary. In Genesis 22:7, Isaac looked at his father. In Abraham's hands were a torch and a knife. Isaac could read his father's face. He began to realize what was about to happen. Think of what must have been going through Isaac's heart as he saw his father go up without a lamb to that place of sacrifice. Think of what must have been in Abraham's heart.

When my first son was born, I ceased to think so much of the love of Jesus, and I thought more of the love of the Father. Though both are infinite in their love, I thought how it must have moved the Father's heart to give His only Son to die upon the cross. Think how much the Lord Jesus suffered. Think how much God the Father suffered. But they both did so willingly, for our sake.

- How are you reminded of the Father's heart for you?
- How does it change your perspective to think of the Christian life not solely as a duty to be lived out, but as a relationship with the perfect loving Father?

PRACTICE THIS Spend some time today reflecting on the Father's love. Spend time on a prayer walk or write out a prayer of adoration to your Father.

PRAY OVER THIS

And Jacob gave Esau bread and stew of lentils; then he ate and
drank, arose, and went his way. Thus Esau despised his birthright.

GENESIS 25:34

PONDER THIS The birthright was a special blessing that belonged to the
firstborn son. It linked everything in Isaac's family to the blessing God had given
to Abraham. God gave a blessing to Abraham. Abraham gave the blessing to
Isaac. Isaac was to give the blessing to his son, and so forth. The birthright was
to follow on not only through Isaac, Jacob, and Jacob's sons—the twelve tribes
of Israel—but also on to Jesse and David, all the way to Joseph and Mary, and
on to Jesus. The birthright was a promise that included provision. It included
possessions. It included protection.

Now here's the ironic thing: According to Genesis 25, the birthright already
belonged to Jacob. God said that the older would serve the younger (Genesis
25:23). The second son that came out of the womb would have the birthright.
And here's Jacob trying to connive and get what is already his. So, he said to
Esau, "Okay, friend, you want the stew; I want the blessing. We'll just make a
trade. Deal?" And they shook hands and Esau ate the stew and Jacob said, "I've
put one over on him. I now have the birthright." But it was already his.

- What "birthright" belongs to you if you are a follower of Jesus?
- What are some ways you work to earn from God, even though He's
  already given you what you need in Jesus?

PRACTICE THIS Look back at the ways you said you seek to earn favor from
God. Make a corresponding list of the ways God has already provided all you
need in Jesus.

PRAY OVER THIS

When Esau heard the words of his father, he cried with
an exceedingly great and bitter cry, and said to his father,
"Bless me—me also, O my father!" But he said, "Your brother
came with deceit and has taken away your blessing."

GENESIS 27:34-35

PONDER THIS Isaac's family was dysfunctional. There was favoritism. There were two brothers that hated one another. There was a dad who was caught up in what he could see and feel, a mother who was scheming, one son who was shady, and another son who was heartbroken all together in this one family. But God was at work in this family.

You may say, "My family is a mess." Good news. God is still God. I want you to see what God did. Hebrews 11:20 says, "By faith Isaac blessed Jacob and Esau concerning things to come." Despite the dysfunction, God was still at work. A wise man once said, "God does not change us in order to love us; God loves us in order to change us." God loves your family. God loves you. You may say, "My family is one royal mess." Hang on! God is not done yet.

- What in your life or family seems too messy for God to redeem?
- How are you encouraged by the account of Isaac's family members and the work God did in their lives?

PRACTICE THIS Take time in prayer to submit your mess before God. Confess to Him the things that seem irredeemable in your life. Ask Him to work in your mess.

PRAY OVER THIS

And He [the Angel of the Lord] said, "Let Me go, for the day breaks."
But he [Jacob] said, "I will not let You go unless You bless me!"

GENESIS 32:26

PONDER THIS Have you ever watched wrestlers? My eldest son was a wrestler. I have two grandsons who are wrestlers. Do you know what muscle is most important to a wrestler? His thighs. His legs. That's where his strength is. If you take away his leg, he can't begin to wrestle. The Angel of the Lord took away Jacob's strength (v. 25). How was he going to wrestle anymore? And the Angel (the preincarnate Christ) said: "Let Me go." But Jacob replied: "I will not let you go, not until you bless me." Now if this was the Lord, why did He say: *"Let Me go?"* It was because the Lord didn't want him to let go. You may be thinking, "That doesn't make sense." Oh, yes, it does.

When studying the Bible, you find out that many times God will act as if He wants to get away from us when He wants us to pursue Him with all our hearts. Do you remember on the Road to Emmaus when two disciples were going there after the resurrection, and Jesus appeared in His resurrected body? He walked with them, and their hearts were burning within them. Luke said Jesus made as if He would go further, and they said, "Oh no, don't. Spend the night with us here," and He did. (See Luke 24:28-29.) In our moments of greatest uncertainty or difficulty, God calls us to pursue Him with all our hearts.

- When was a time you felt like you were pursuing God?
- How do times of struggle or difficulty lead you to pursue Him further?

PRACTICE THIS Consider one thing you need to do to pursue God. Take action today.

PRAY OVER THIS

Then Isaac called Jacob and blessed him, and charged him,
and said to him: "You shall not take a wife from the daughters
of Canaan. Arise, go to Padan Aram, to the house of Bethuel
your mother's father; and take yourself a wife from there of the
daughters of Laban your mother's brother. May God Almighty
bless you, and make you fruitful and multiply you, that you may
be an assembly of peoples; and give you the blessing of Abraham,
to you and your descendants with you, that you may inherit the
land in which you are a stranger, which God gave to Abraham."

GENESIS 28:1-4

PONDER THIS Isaac was a man who was shaken. He was a man who came to his senses. He was a man who came back to the Word of God. God had brought great conviction to his heart, and he was shaken to the core.

There are some of us who need a similar awakening. We should assess where we are and look at our families. We should ask where the path we are headed on will eventually take us. Ask, if your family is going to change, who's going to change it? Where does God want to wake you up to be part of the solution? God knows how to discipline you, and He will for your good. (See 1 Corinthians 11:31-32.) God wants to wake you up, for your sake and the sake of those around you. Will you respond?

- Where might God want to wake you from your spiritual slumber?
- How might you best position yourself to receive this awakening?

PRACTICE THIS Dedicate time to sitting in silence and asking God to reveal the areas in which you have been spiritually asleep. Ask Him for next steps in response.

PRAY OVER THIS

By faith Isaac blessed Jacob and Esau concerning things to come.

HEBREWS 11:20

PONDER THIS Isaac loved God in his youth but got away from God. He messed up his family, and then came back to God. There are two lessons here. Number one: Never mistake the moment for the man. This is what we see with Isaac trying to bless the wrong son. This was not the true Isaac. The true Isaac was the one we read about in Hebrews 11. When God came to write about his life, God did not write about his life through the lens of his failures. Aren't you glad God remembers our iniquities against us no more? Aren't you glad God does not mistake the moment for the man? God knew Isaac loved Him, and Isaac came back to God. That can happen to you too. You can be a person of God and get away from God and mess up your family, but you can also come back to the will of God. Where is He calling you back today?

- What are some moments from your life that you hope aren't taken as "the whole story" about you?
- Where is God calling you back to Himself today? How will you respond?

PRACTICE THIS Take some time to journal about a low moment in your life that God used as a means of redemption over time.

PRAY OVER THIS

Now when He saw that He did not prevail against him,
He touched the socket of his hip; and the socket of
Jacob's hip was out of joint as He wrestled with him.

GENESIS 32:25

PONDER THIS Did you know God likes broken things? People throw broken things away, but God rarely uses anything until He first breaks it. David said in the Psalms: "The sacrifices of God are a broken spirit, a broken and a contrite heart—these, O God, You will not despise" (Psalm 51:17). Some of us are not being used by God because we've never been broken. If God breaks you and you become broken bread and poured out wine, He will use you. God took a little boy's lunch and broke it and fed the multitudes. Mary took an alabaster box of ointment and broke it and lavished her love upon the Lord Jesus Christ. The prophet Jeremiah said: "Break up your fallow ground, and do not sow among thorns" (Jeremiah 4:3). You'll never have the crop you ought to until you put the plow in, until the old clods are broken. Even the Lord Jesus Christ took the bread at the last supper and said: "This is My body which is broken for you." People throw broken things away. God uses broken things for His glory.

- What are the "broken things" in your story?
- How have you seen God use even what is broken in your life?

PRACTICE THIS Share the way God has redeemed broken parts of your life with another person this week.

PRAY OVER THIS

My God, My God, why have You forsaken Me? Why are You so
far from helping Me, and from the words of My groaning?

PSALM 22:1

PONDER THIS When Jesus Christ went to the cross, He was the sin-bearer. He who knew no sin, God made to be sin for us. And my sin, your sin, all sin was placed upon the Lord Jesus Christ. Habakkuk 1:13 says that God's eyes are too pure to look upon sin. God turns His face from sin. The Lord Jesus Christ became the sin-bearer for us, and He had to suffer the penalty. The penalty for sin is to be forsaken by God. Jesus on the cross said, "My God, my God why have you forsaken me?" (Matthew 27:46b).

He who had been in the bosom of eternity past was forsaken by God the Father. King David, who wrote this psalm, said in Psalm 23:4, "Yea, though I walk through the valley of the shadow of death, I will fear no evil; for You are with me; Your rod and Your staff, they comfort me." When Jesus Christ died, He walked that lonesome valley all by Himself, so that we would not.

- How does it humble you to remember Jesus was forsaken by God so you would not be?
- How should this motivate us to tell others of the great love of Jesus?

PRACTICE THIS Share with someone about the love of Jesus that was poured out on the cross.

PRAY OVER THIS

When I was with you daily in the temple, you did not try to
seize Me. But this is your hour, and the power of darkness.

LUKE 22:53

PONDER THIS In this verse, Jesus referred to the power of Satan. Hell had a holiday and demons taunted and tormented the Lord Jesus when He was on the cross. God-forsaken, attacked by Satan, and abused by men, Jesus suffered, bled, and died for you at the holy hand of God, the hateful hand of man, and the hellish hand of Satan.

That's the agony of the cross. How can we be unmoved? How can we ignore such love? How can we go idly on our way when Jesus Christ paid that price for us? You may wonder, "Did He really take my hell? He was only there for six hours on the cross." But in six hours, Jesus suffered everything you'd suffer for eternity. He, being infinite, suffered in a finite period, what you as a finite being would suffer in an infinite period. The sins of the world were distilled upon Jesus and eternities were compressed upon the Lord Jesus. No one ever suffered like Jesus, and it was for your sake.

- What stands out to you about the fact that Jesus suffered for your sake?
- How does it change your perspective of God to remember He willingly sent Jesus to suffer so you would be restored to Him?

PRACTICE THIS Make a list of ways you know Jesus suffered. Prayerfully reflect over this list and thank God that this was done for your sake.

PRAY OVER THIS

And the King will answer and say to them, "Assuredly,
I say to you, inasmuch as you did it to one of the
least of these My brethren, you did it to Me."

MATTHEW 25:40

PONDER THIS When you do something for one of the brothers of Jesus, it's just like you have done it unto Jesus because His friends are our friends. If you love Jesus, you're going to love what Jesus loves. And if you don't love the brethren, certain conclusions are in order.

The late, great Vance Havner was a Baptist preacher from North Carolina, full of wisdom. Here's what he said: "When I see a bird that looks like a duck, quacks like a duck, paddles in water like a duck, and prefers the company of ducks, I conclude it must be a duck!"

When you see people who live like the world, dress like the world, act like the world, and prefer the company of the world rather than the company of God's people, they're of the world! If you love the Lord Jesus Christ, you're going to love what Jesus loves, and Jesus loves the Church. He loves the brethren. His friends are our friends—"...as He is, so are we in this world" (1 John 4:17b).

- What evidence does your life give that you are "of Jesus"? "Of the world"?
- What changes is God calling you to make to move closer to Jesus today?

PRACTICE THIS Consider the changes you feel God leading you to make. Take concrete steps toward change today.

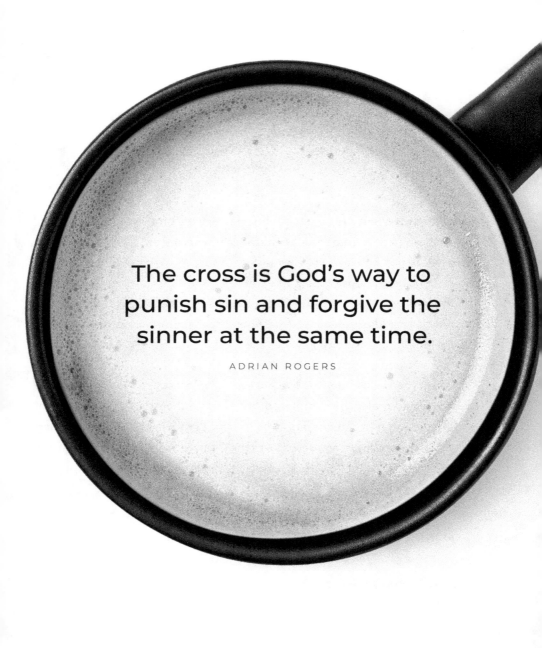

The cross is God's way to punish sin and forgive the sinner at the same time.

ADRIAN ROGERS

1

PRAY OVER THIS

...and all drank the same spiritual drink. For they drank of that
spiritual Rock that followed them, and that Rock was Christ.

1 CORINTHIANS 10:4

PONDER THIS The Israelites were in a barren land. They were dying of thirst, and Moses said, "God, what shall I do?" God replied, "Take with you the elders of Israel. Take a rod, go to this rock, and strike the rock with the rod. When you do, water will come from the rock." (See Exodus 17:5-6, author's paraphrase.)

Now, what is all of this about? It's no stretch to say this was a glorious illustration of our salvation. First Corinthians 10:11a says, "All these things happened to them as examples." And 1 Corinthians 10:4 says, "...all drank the same spiritual drink. For they drank of that spiritual Rock that followed them, and that Rock was Christ." That rock pictured the Lord Jesus Christ, the Rock of Ages, stricken for us. Isaiah 53:4b says, "Yet esteemed Him stricken, smitten by God, and afflicted."

Jesus, the Rock of Ages, was smitten for us. And because Jesus was smitten for us, out of His side came forth water. That water represented the Holy Spirit, which is the water of life. Because Jesus hung in agony and bled upon that cross and died for us, out of His side has come the refreshment of the Holy Spirit that is in God's people right now. He was stricken and smitten, that we might be refreshed.

- What difference does it make that Jesus is the Rock of Ages who was stricken for you?
- How do these types of connections between the Old and New Testaments help to build your faith?

PRACTICE THIS Read back through the account in Exodus 17:1-7. Reflect on how this is a picture of the salvation that was to come in Christ.

2

PONDER THIS People are known by the enemies they have. Every now and
then someone will say something like: "Oh Pastor Rogers, we love you so much.
Everybody loves you." When I hear this, I laugh because everybody doesn't love
me. And that doesn't break my heart. I don't expect to be loved by everybody,
nor should you. We cannot be popular with a world that crucified our Lord. If
His friends are our friends, His enemies are our enemies. That doesn't mean
we're not to love our enemies. Jesus loved His enemies. He prayed for those
who crucified Him. I don't mean we are to be filled with hate and spite. But the
reality is that some people are enemies of the cross of Jesus Christ. Paul said, "I
tell you weeping that there are enemies" (Philippians 3:18, author paraphrase).

- Who would you classify as your enemies?
- What does it look like to practically love our enemies?

PRACTICE THIS Take an inventory of your life. Where are you hating the things
Christ hates? Where are you loving the things that He hates? What needs to
change?

PRAY OVER THIS

Love has been perfected among us in this: that we may have boldness
in the day of judgment; because as He is, so are we in this world.

1 JOHN 4:17

PONDER THIS Once I was reading the *Houston Chronicle* and came across a picture of a woman who had her ear on the chest of a man. And there was a caption under the photo that explained the man had received a heart transplant, and the heart that was beating in his chest was the heart of this woman's son. She was listening by putting her ear to his chest to hear her son's heart beating. When I read that, I thought, "Would to God that He could put His ear on my chest and hear the heartbeat of His Son."

If God Almighty puts His ear to your chest, and Jesus is in there, you're going to have a heartbeat for missions and evangelism. Jesus said, "As the Father has sent Me, I also send you" (John 20:21b). And why was He sent? Luke 19:10: "...for the Son of Man has come to seek and to save that which was lost."

- What evidence does your life give that you have the same "heartbeat" as Jesus?
- Why must this be true of us if we are genuinely following Him?

PRACTICE THIS Make a list of the things your heart "beats for." Be honest with yourself, recognizing that change can only come through honest assessment.

4

PRAY OVER THIS

Now Amalek came and fought with Israel in Rephidim.
And Moses said to Joshua, "Choose us some men and
go out, and fight with Amalek. Tomorrow I will stand on
the top of the hill with the rod of God in my hand."

EXODUS 17:8-9

PONDER THIS The victory over your flesh is a God-given victory. Paul wrote in Galatians 5:16, "Walk in the Spirit, and you shall not fulfill the lust of the flesh." If I've learned one thing in all my Christian life it is this: holiness is not the way to Christ; Christ is the way to holiness. Now, I'm not just playing with words. Paul did not say, "If you will not walk in the flesh, then you can walk in the Spirit." He said to walk in the Spirit as the means to keep from walking in the flesh.

Victory over your flesh is a God-given victory. That's the only way you're going to come out of Egypt, through the wilderness, and into Canaan. There's an Amalek within you that stands to try to keep you from living in victory. But thank God, there is a victory. When you take the staff of God, which is the Word of God, through the power of God, the Spirit of God, and you hold it high, He will give you victory.

- Where do you currently need to fight against your own flesh?
- How will you depend on God to give you this victory?

PRACTICE THIS Journal the ways you are currently fighting against the flesh. Write out the ways you will depend on God for victory in these areas.

PRAY OVER THIS

For dogs have surrounded Me; the congregation of the wicked
has enclosed Me. They pierced My hands and My feet.
PSALM 22:16

PONDER THIS The entire Bible is about the Lord Jesus Christ. The Word of God is written to help you to love the God of that Word and His Son who is Jesus Christ. When you do that, it will lead you to worship. Worship is the bottom line; it is the highest attainment you can reach. We're not saved primarily so we'll miss Hell and go to Heaven. We're saved to worship God. Salvation is more than having our sin forgiven. It is coming to a relationship where we can know God intimately and personally for ourselves.

When you study Psalm 22, you're going to come away loving God more and loving the Word of God more than perhaps any other chapter in the entire Bible. You cannot read Psalm 22 and go away not loving the Bible and not loving the Lord Jesus Christ. As you read Psalm 22, you'll have to say it's all about Jesus.

- How does today's verse remind you of Jesus?
- What are some other Old Testament passages you know that point to Jesus?

PRACTICE THIS Read Psalm 22 completely. Make note of the places where you see a direct connection to Jesus.

6

PRAY OVER THIS

He who did not spare His own Son, but delivered Him up for us
all, how shall He not with Him also freely give us all things?

ROMANS 8:32

PONDER THIS I have two sons. If you were to ask me, "Will you give me one of
your sons so that I might butcher and torture him?" I would say no, absolutely
not! You might ask, "What if it might save me and I could be forgiven?" I still
wouldn't do it. The reality is, I don't love you that much. I don't love anybody that
much. But God so loved the world that He gave His only begotten Son. He did
not spare Jesus. Jesus had my sin, your sin, our sin upon Him. Consider this. Do
you think God will spare you if you don't receive Jesus if you don't put your faith
where God has put your sin? If there were ever a time when God would have
been tempted to be lenient upon sin, it was when that sin was upon the Lord
Jesus Christ. But Jesus suffered at the holy hand of God as the only means by
which we can be saved.

- How does it impact you to dwell on the truth that God gave His
  Son up for you?
- What do we communicate to God if we seek salvation in some
  way outside of the provision He has made in Jesus?

PRACTICE THIS Spend time today dwelling on the reality that God has given
up His only Son for you.

7

PRAY OVER THIS

What shall we say then? Shall we continue in sin
that grace may abound? Certainly not! How shall
we who died to sin live any longer in it?

ROMANS 6:1-2

PONDER THIS What is the doctrine of identification? It is to be identified with Jesus who gave Himself for you. When Jesus was crucified when Jesus faced that agony, that passion upon the cross, not only was Christ on that cross, but since He was your substitute, you were on that cross. Since He died for you, the old person you used to be died with Him, and now you have become one with Him in His death. You are no longer in Adam. Now you are in Christ. You are now identified with Christ. Everybody in the world is either in Adam or in Christ. Because of the crucifixion of Jesus Christ, when Jesus died, the old man or woman that you used to be died with Him.

- What does it mean that every person is either in Adam or in Christ?
- How does your life look different because you are in Christ?

PRACTICE THIS What gives you confidence that you are "in Christ"? If you are not confident, how is God calling you to respond to Him today?

8

PRAY OVER THIS

Likewise you also, reckon yourselves to be dead indeed
to sin, but alive to God in Christ Jesus our Lord.

ROMANS 6:11

PONDER THIS *Reckon* is a bookkeeping term. It does not mean to think, feel, or guess but speaks of something that you can count on—a matter of fact. *Reckoning* in the context of this verse means "acting" by faith on what you know to be a fact. The fact is that Christ died for you, and you died with Him and you must reckon on it. You may ask, "Well, what does that mean?" If you're saved, you already know how to reckon. That's how you got saved. You believe Jesus Christ died for your sins and put your faith where God put your sins—on Jesus. Were you there when it happened? Did you see it with your eyes? No, but you know it to be true, and you reckoned on it for salvation. In the same way, you reckon for sanctification. As you receive the Lord Jesus, so walk in Him. We're not told to feel it. We're not even told really to understand it. But we are told to reckon on it.

- What would it look like for a person to reckon on the fact of Jesus's death and resurrection daily?
- What might this specifically look like in your life?

PRACTICE THIS Make a list of things that might take place in your life if you reckoned on Jesus each moment.

PRAY OVER THIS

But You, O LORD, do not be far from Me; O My Strength, hasten
to help Me! Deliver Me from the sword, My precious life from
the power of the dog. Save Me from the lion's mouth and
from the horns of the wild oxen! You have answered Me.

PSALM 22:19-21

PONDER THIS I took a course in criminology. I went to Rayford Prison in Florida where people are electrocuted. I went into the room where the electric chair is and sat down. I put my hands on the arms where the electrodes are and my legs where they would be strapped down. And I thought, what a terrible thing it must be to be electrocuted or to be put to death by injection.

But there is no execution like crucifixion. In six hours, the eternities were compressed. In six hours, the sins of the world were distilled, and Jesus, the Son of God, died at the holy hands of God, the hateful hands of man, and the hellish hands of Satan. Why? Because He loves us.

- How does it affect you to know Jesus died in one of the worst possible ways for your sake?
- How does this grow your love for Him?

PRACTICE THIS Take time today to praise God for sending Jesus to die in your place in an unimaginable way.

PRAY OVER THIS

They will come and declare His righteousness to a
people who will be born, that He has done this.

PSALM 22:31

PONDER THIS Who were the people that would be born? Lift your hand. Hold it up. Say, "I'm the one that He's talking about." David, looking down through the centuries, looked at the death, burial, and resurrection of our Lord and Savior Jesus Christ. And then he said, "It is for a people that will be born" who will say, "He has done this." Do you know what "he has done this" means literally? It is finished. Second Chronicles 4:11a says, "Then Huram made the pots and the shovels and the bowls. So Huram finished doing the work that he was to do." Now, where it says he "finished the work," it's exactly the same word used here in the phrase "he has done this." It is the Hebrew word *ossa*, which means in one word, "it is finished." And when Jesus, the Son of God, bowed His head upon Calvary's cross, He said in one Greek word, *tetelestai*, which means, "It is finished."

- What has Jesus finished for you?
- How would you explain this complete work of Jesus to another person?

PRACTICE THIS Have a conversation with another person today, sharing the finished work of Jesus for sinful people.

PRAY OVER THIS

For Christ also suffered once for sins, the just for the
unjust, that He might bring us to God, being put to
death in the flesh but made alive by the Spirit.

1 PETER 3:18

PONDER THIS We have a problem. God is holy; He's "the just." We are unholy;
we are "the unjust." How could God, who is holy, punish sin and love the sinner
at the same time? That's the problem that was solved by Calvary. God was, in
Christ, reconciling the world to Himself. Here the doctor not only makes a house
call, leaves Heaven, and comes to Earth, but the doctor Himself makes the
patient well by taking the patient's sickness. He dies: "the just for the unjust."
The judge not only adjudicates the criminal guilty, but also steps from behind
the bench, stands in the place of the accused, and takes the punishment upon
Himself. You'll never understand the cross until you understand the principle of
substitution. Jesus Christ died for us.

- What does it mean for you that Jesus is your substitute?
- Do you rely on Jesus as the perfect substitute, or are you still
  working to earn your own way before God? What needs to
  change?

PRACTICE THIS Make a list of the ways Jesus is your perfect substitute.

12

PRAY OVER THIS

Yet it pleased the LORD to bruise Him; He has put Him to grief.

ISAIAH 53:10A

PONDER THIS When Jesus Christ suffered as our substitute, He took the full force of the Father's wrath. The fires of God's wrath burned themselves out on the Lord Jesus Christ on Calvary. No one ever suffered like the Lord Jesus. He, the Son of God, who had been in the bosom of the Father for all eternity, was not only abandoned by the Father but also became the object of the Father's loathing and wrath. All the sin of the world was distilled into that cup He drank.

How could Jesus suffer an eternity of hell on the cross? The reason is this: He, being infinite, suffered in a finite period what we, being finite, would suffer in an infinite period. The eternities were compressed upon Jesus. The sins of the world were distilled upon Jesus. We cannot begin to imagine the emotional suffering of the Lord Jesus Christ. No wonder He lay there prostrate on the ground with red blood and black dirt on His face, saying, "Father, if there be some other way, please! Let this cup pass from Me." But the silence from Heaven said, "There is no other way." So, the dear Savior said, "Then not My will, but Thine be done."

- What does it tell you of Jesus's love for you that He denied His own will to rescue you?
- Where is God calling you to follow His will instead of your own?

PRACTICE THIS Consider where God is calling you to follow His will over your own and act in accordance with that conviction today.

PRAY OVER THIS

Hear me when I call, O God of my righteousness! You have relieved
me in my distress; have mercy on me, and hear my prayer.

PSALM 4:1

PONDER THIS Many of us want to use God like our spare tires rather than our steering wheels. We want to wait until we have spiritual blowouts and see if God will come and help us rather than doing as Jesus taught us to do by seeking first the kingdom of God and His righteousness. (See Matthew 6:33.) Why does God allow us to have problems? To cause us to do exactly what Jehoshaphat did: to seek Him!

Did you know that if we never had problems, most likely we would not seek God? When are the times you've grown the most? Be honest. When everything was fine? Likely, the times God was the nearest, dearest, and most real to you—the times when you agonized in prayer and found God to be faithful—were when you were going through trouble. That's what David said: "Thou hast enlarged me when I was in distress" (Psalm 4:1b, KJV).

- How do you relate to this picture of the spare tire versus the steering wheel? Which are you more likely to view God as in your life?
- How have you seen your dependence on God grow in difficult times? What can that teach you?

PRACTICE THIS Journal about a difficult time when you grew in dependence on God. Write about the unique blessings that came out of that time.

14

PRAY OVER THIS

So they rose early in the morning and went out into the Wilderness of Tekoa; and as they went out, Jehoshaphat stood and said, "Hear me, O Judah and you inhabitants of Jerusalem: Believe in the LORD your God, and you shall be established; believe His prophets, and you shall prosper."

2 CHRONICLES 20:20

PONDER THIS If you're in the middle of a problem, begin to praise God, because He says, "The battle is not yours, it's Mine." You do have a part in the battle. Your part is praise. And you can't hide until the battle is over and then praise the Lord. You may think, "Lord, when You've done it all, and when You've given me the victory, then I'm going to praise You." But God says, "You're not going to have any victory until you start praising until you start singing." You may naturally respond, "I can't sing and praise yet because I don't have any victory yet."

We are to give praise that comes not after the victory, but before the victory. Why is this? That is ultimate faith—when we begin to praise God before we see the answer. It's our way of saying, "God, we don't know how You're going to do it. That's none of our business to know. But You're bigger than this problem. And, therefore, I praise You."

- What makes it difficult to praise God before He gives victory in a situation or if He never gives victory at all as we wish?
- Why is God worthy of praise, no matter the outcome of our circumstances?

PRACTICE THIS Make a list of ways God has provided for you and given you victory in the past. Consider how you might recall these instances as a catalyst for praise in future difficulties.

15

PRAY OVER THIS

And if Christ is not risen, then our preaching is
empty and your faith is also empty.
1 CORINTHIANS 15:14

PONDER THIS I heard of a time back when haircuts were 50 cents, back in the olden days. A preacher went into the barbershop and got a haircut, and he started to pay the barber. The barber said, "No, that's all right. You're a pastor. I'm not going to charge you." The pastor said, "No, I want to pay." The barber said, "No, I will come listen to you preach, and I'll take it out in preaching." The pastor said, "I don't have any 50-cent sermons." The barber said, "That's okay. I'll come twice." I want to tell you that a sermon that does not affirm the resurrection of Jesus Christ is a profitless, worthless exercise in futility.

- Why are Christian preaching and the Christian faith empty if Christ has not been raised from the dead?
- How would you answer another Christian who says the reality of the resurrection doesn't matter very much?

PRACTICE THIS Journal a list of ways the resurrection impacts our lives each day as Christians and gives us hope for the future.

16

PRAY OVER THIS

Yes, and we are found false witnesses of God, because
we have testified of God that He raised up Christ, whom
He did not raise up—if in fact the dead do not rise.

1 CORINTHIANS 15:15

PONDER THIS Were the disciples liars? Were they deceivers? If so, why? Why would they deceive? Why would they lie? What gain did they have if Jesus Christ was still in the grave? They died as martyrs. They were tortured, they were persecuted, they were burned at the stake, they were eaten by lions, they were stoned, they were crushed, and they were humiliated.

Hypocrites and martyrs are not made of the same stuff! People tell lies to get out of trouble, not to get into trouble. A man may live for a lie, but few if any men will willingly die for a lie. The disciples said, "We have seen Him! We have touched Him!" Are you going to tell me Simon Peter was a con man? That John the apostle was a crook? That the apostle Paul who wrote most of the New Testament was a known perjurer, deceiver, and a false witness? Of course not. But if Christ is still in the grave, preaching is profitless, faith is foolish, and the disciples would have been deceivers.

- How does the willingness to die for the truth of the Gospel give witness to the credibility of the Gospel to the world?
- Is there something or somewhere that you would consider "too far" to go for the Gospel? How might you submit this before God?

PRACTICE THIS Take time today to ask God what you are holding back from complete submission to Him. Ask Him to help you let that go.

PRAY OVER THIS

But now Christ is risen from the dead, and has become
the firstfruits of those who have fallen asleep.

1 CORINTHIANS 15:20

PONDER THIS I was at a funeral. The beautiful flowers were there. I walked around looking at the flowers, and I saw one beautiful bouquet. You could tell it was done by the grandchildren. This was an elderly man, a saint on this earth, a dear member of the church. And on the floral offering, it said, "To Pop-Pop."

And I stood there, as is the pastor's habit as people come by, and I saw that precious widow, who'd walked with her husband for more than half a century and was a lady of great faith. She was not in despair. She walked up and laid her hand on his sleeve and touched him, patted it a couple of times, and turned and walked away. And I thought to myself, "Is that it? Is that all there is to life? Pop-Pop is gone? Her husband is gone?" No! Death does not have dominion! Christ is risen! Those who have fallen asleep in Christ have not perished. He is alive.

- How have you experienced the hope that comes from Christ when losing a loved one?
- How does the resurrection give us hope not just for the future, but for today?

PRACTICE THIS Make a list of the ways the resurrection provides hope for followers of Jesus.

18

PRAY OVER THIS

So it was, while they conversed and reasoned, that
Jesus Himself drew near and went with them.

LUKE 24:15

PONDER THIS Jesus met the two disciples on the way to Emmaus and He challenged them with the Word of God. It's important to note that Jesus sought them. "So it was, while they conversed and reasoned, that Jesus Himself drew near." And He's done that so many times for you and me. Jesus did not seek them to condemn them or even to condone them but to claim them and comfort them. And just as the Lord Jesus sought us when we were lost—we didn't seek Him; He sought us, and we love Him because He first loved us— so He sought these men. Now these men, evidently, were already believers, although they were backslidden and discouraged. If Jesus would seek us when we were outright sinners, surely, He will seek us when we're saved and away from Him. At some point, every backslidden and confused Christian is met by Jesus in this way—not to be condemned or condoned, but to be comforted and claimed.

- How has Jesus sought after you before you knew Him and after you came to know Him?
- How has He called us to likewise seek after others who are far from Him?

PRACTICE THIS Intentionally seek after someone who doesn't know Jesus this week for the sake of having a Gospel conversation.

PRAY OVER THIS

And beginning at Moses and all the Prophets, He expounded
to them in all the Scriptures the things concerning Himself.

LUKE 24:27

PONDER THIS If you read the Bible and you don't find Jesus, you've missed the point. Go back. Standing somewhere in the shadows you'll find Jesus. He'll be there in prophecy. He'll be there in precept. He'll be there in parable. He'll be there in poetry. He Himself challenged the people of His day when He was talking about the Old Testament, "Search the Scriptures...these are they which testify of Me" (John 5:39). I've been preaching long enough to know the Bible becomes a wonderful book to you when you find Jesus in it. Whether it's the Old Testament or the New Testament, you'll find Jesus there. There's no lasting joy without Jesus. He's the one you need. God has engineered it that you're not going to have joy without Jesus, and you're not going to know Jesus apart from the Scriptures.

- How have you come to know Jesus more through the Scriptures?
- What are some "unlikely places" you've found Jesus in the Bible?

PRACTICE THIS Read Luke 24:13-32. Reflect on the way Jesus revealed Himself to these disciples through the Scriptures.

20

> **PRAY OVER THIS**
> Therefore a man shall leave his father and mother and be
> joined to his wife, and they shall become one flesh.
> **GENESIS 2:24**

PONDER THIS The Bible says a husband is to love his wife as Christ loved the Church. Is Jesus Christ committed to the Church? Or, when we fail, does Jesus say, "So long. I want a divorce from you. I no longer want to be your Lord, your Savior"? No! The Lord stays with us, and He has said, "I will never leave you nor forsake you" (Hebrews 13:5b). Praise God for that.

You want me to tell you what a perfect husband is? A perfect husband is a man who does not demand a perfect wife. You want me to tell you what a perfect wife is? One who does not demand a perfect husband. Have you ever thought that your spouse's failures may be God's gift to you to help you develop character? His or her lateness may be God's gift to help develop your patience. God knows what He's doing. None of us is perfect. What a shame to let 90 percent of a good marriage go down the tubes because of a 10 percent problem. There needs to be a lifetime commitment. To be *joined* in today's text means "to be glued together, welded together." You are one flesh.

- How has Christ loved you? How can this be applied to marriage?
- If you are married, what are the areas in which you might have an impossibly high standard for your spouse? What needs to change?

PRACTICE THIS If you are married, have a conversation with your spouse about the ways you might have held an unrealistic expectation and discuss changes you want to pursue moving forward in God's grace.

PRAY OVER THIS

No longer do I call you servants, for a servant does not know
what his master is doing; but I have called you friends, for all
things that I heard from My Father I have made known to you.

JOHN 15:15

PONDER THIS In marriage, there must be a lasting commitment, but there must also be loving communication. Many marriages get into difficulty because the husband and the wife don't learn how to communicate. Again, let's go back to the analogy of Christ and the Church. Does Jesus Christ communicate with the Church? Yes, He does. He's given us His Word. He speaks to us. He has sent His Spirit into our hearts. He whispers to our being that we belong to Him. We have the most intimate relationship with the Lord Jesus Christ, who said, "No longer do I call you servants, for a servant does not know what his master is doing." He has given His Spirit to share His heart and life with us. Most husbands and wives who fail in their marriages have not learned to communicate.

- What are some ways you've seen communication as an obstacle in your own marriage or marriages of those close to you?
- What would it look like to communicate with those around you in the manner Jesus communicates with you?

PRACTICE THIS Make a list of ways Jesus communicates with you. Consider how you might follow some of these same principles in communicating with others.

22

PRAY OVER THIS

Now concerning the things of which you wrote to me: It
is good for a man not to touch a woman. Nevertheless,
because of sexual immorality, let each man have his own
wife, and let each woman have her own husband.

1 CORINTHIANS 7:1-2

PONDER THIS God has set some definite boundaries for the physical act of marriage. And without these boundaries, a nation, a city, and a family cannot exist. Can you imagine what it would be like to play or watch a football game without any rules or boundaries? Imagine the fullback gets the ball, and he goes up through the stands with it. A lot of folks would get hurt.

God has given us some boundaries not to harm us, but to help us and protect us. Inside these boundaries, sex is a wonderful gift of God. You'll never improve on God's plan. God's plan is for a man and a woman in the bounds of holy matrimony, and only in the bounds of holy matrimony, to be one flesh. God's plan in sex is to bring a man and a woman, in the sanctity of marital love, to a sense of oneness in which they become one flesh.

- Where have you experienced the goodness of God's boundaries in any area of life?
- What about in the area of sex?

PRACTICE THIS Make a list of boundaries God has set for His people. Write out some reasons the world might push against these, and then write the ways these are actually good boundaries set by God.

"Be angry, and do not sin": do not let the sun go down on your wrath.

EPHESIANS 4:26

PONDER THIS Years ago, many people collected trading stamps in a little book with the hope that the stamps would gain value over time. That's the way a lot of marriages falter. If your spouse hurts you, put it in the book. Late for dinner, put it in the book. Forgot your anniversary, put it in the book. After a while, you don't deal with things as they come up. And one day, there's an explosion. A husband or wife comes to cash in all the stamps, and both spouses wonder, how did all of this happen? But they have failed to do what the Bible says—to deal with things as they come up when they're small and can be addressed. One trading stamp is not so big. It can be dealt with. Don't let the sun go down on your wrath! And when you do address these things as they come up, stick to the subject. Don't attack one another; attack the problem.

- Have you experienced times when you "cashed in" your collection of hurts with another person? What was the result?
- What difference has it made for you when you have addressed individual problems as they arose instead of saving them up over time?

PRACTICE THIS Have a conversation with someone who you have saved up hurts from. By God's grace, clear the air in that relationship as much as it depends on you.

24

PRAY OVER THIS

So then, my beloved brethren, let every man be
swift to hear, slow to speak, slow to wrath.

JAMES 1:19

PONDER THIS Sometimes Joyce and I will be in a disagreement. We'll be sitting at the kitchen table, and it will get tense. She'll say to me, "Adrian, you're wrong." "Not me." "Yes, you're wrong." "No, I'm not wrong." One, two, three, four, and on and on the conversation goes. Often, one of us will say, "Well, let's just stop for a while."

I go in my study and try and prepare a sermon. Ha! Try to read. Try to do something else. But I can't do it. So I say, "Lord, did You see what went on in there?" He says, "Yeah, you were wrong." "Me?" "Yeah, you! You were wrong!"

"Okay, Lord." And I have to go back: "Honey, I was wrong. Forgive me." She says, "I forgive you." And we hug and kiss and make up.

Prayer will do that. Be honest with God and let Him speak to you. He will show you what is true.

- How have you seen the value of prayer in tense moments?
- How have you seen God restore your relationships when you have come to Him in prayerful humility?

PRACTICE THIS Set aside time today to pray and ask God to reveal any wrongs for which you need to apologize.

PRAY OVER THIS

Husbands, likewise, dwell with them with understanding, giving
honor to the wife, as to the weaker vessel, and as being heirs
together of the grace of life, that your prayers may not be hindered.

1 PETER 3:7

PONDER THIS The Bible says here, "Husbands, dwell with your wives according to understanding" or knowledge. We could translate it this way: Live together in the same house with good sense.

What does it mean to live with a car according to knowledge? You get a new automobile. What do you do? You read the manual. You see what kind of oil it takes, what kind of fuel it takes, what the air pressure in the tires needs to be. You watch the gauges, and the gauges indicate the needs of that car. If you want that car to work well, you have to understand the car. With our spouses, God's Word is the manual. And wives (or husbands) are constantly sending signals. But many of us don't read the manual, and we pay no attention to the signals. Many of us pay more attention to our automobiles or other possessions than we do to our spouses. This is not living together according to knowledge and understanding.

- What are some things the Bible teaches about the best way to live with a spouse?
- How have you seen the impact of living according to the Bible's way in your own family situation?

PRACTICE THIS Take time this week to encourage your spouse or to encourage another married couple you know.

26

PRAY OVER THIS

Her children rise up and call her blessed; her
husband also, and he praises her.

PROVERBS 31:28

PONDER THIS Husbands, do you know what it means to give your wife honor? To give honor means to set something aside as having great value. Somehow you have to get across to your wife that you value her, that she is of worth to you, that she is important to you, and that she is God's priceless gift.

One of the ways to do this is to tell her how much you value and appreciate her. Thank her and give her honor for all the ways God has blessed you through her. Let the children know that you honor her. Let your children hear you praise their mother. This is one of the finest things you can possibly do and one of the clearest ways you can be a blessing to your wife.

- Who might you honor in your life—whether your spouse or someone else?
- How does speaking well of another honor both the person and the Lord?

PRACTICE THIS Ephesians 5:33 says for husbands to love their wives and for wives to respect their husbands. Consider how you might show love or respect to your spouse today; act on this.

PRAY OVER THIS

And these words which I command you today shall be in your
heart. You shall teach them diligently to your children, and
shall talk of them when you sit in your house, when you walk
by the way, when you lie down, and when you rise up.

DEUTERONOMY 6:6-7

PONDER THIS Did you know Thomas Edison was sent home from school because his teacher said he was too dumb? Do you know what his mama said? His mama said, "I know my boy and he is not stupid. He's smart. I'll teach him myself." And she did. The problem was that the teacher couldn't realize how smart the boy was, not that he was dumb. You see, every child is different. Parents know the unique proclivities in their children. See your child as unique before God and learn to communicate with your child creatively. Your child is made in God's image. God has gifted you with the ability to discover the best way to communicate spiritual truth to your child. Do not neglect to disciple your children in the unique ways that only you can.

- What are some of the unique things about the children in your life?
- How might you disciple the children in your life according to their unique attributes?

PRACTICE THIS Brainstorm ways you might disciple children in your life according to their unique makeup. Decide on some first steps and take action.

28

PRAY OVER THIS

Then they brought little children to Him, that He might touch them;
but the disciples rebuked those who brought them. But when
Jesus saw it, He was greatly displeased and said to them, "Let the
little children come to Me, and do not forbid them; for of such is the
kingdom of God. Assuredly, I say to you, whoever does not receive
the kingdom of God as a little child will by no means enter it." And He
took them up in His arms, laid His hands on them, and blessed them.

MARK 10:13-16

PONDER THIS When a child disobeys his parents, do you know what that child has done? He's sinned against God. It's not primarily you he's sinned against; he's sinned against God. We are making a mistake if our primary goal in disciplining our children is to make them sorry for what they've done to us. We are missing an opportunity for discipleship. We should say, "Listen, Daddy's (or Momma's) heart is broken because God doesn't want us to behave that way." Now, be careful. You cannot be the Holy Spirit. You can pray for repentance in that child's heart, you can try to lead that child to repentance, but remember the Holy Spirit must do that. But you should continually pray for and guide that child to repentance.

- What is the danger of only drawing your children's attention to human hurt but never to the hurt they cause God?
- What are some ways you might make the connection to repentance for your children?

PRACTICE THIS Spend some time writing out ideas for how you might effectively communicate the idea of repentance to your children (or children close to you) in ways they might understand. Help them receive correction according to God's grace.

PRAY OVER THIS

Let this mind be in you which was also in Christ Jesus, who,
being in the form of God, did not consider it robbery to be
equal with God, but made Himself of no reputation, taking the
form of a bondservant, and coming in the likeness of men.

PHILIPPIANS 2:5-7

PONDER THIS Jesus stepped out of Heaven and went from sovereignty to slavery. He humbled Himself. He became obedient. Satan, in contrast, in his pride said, "I will ascend. I will be like the Most High." He thought, "I'm going up, up, up, up." But God said, "No, you're going down, down, down, down, down." Jesus stepped out of glory and humbled Himself. It is, for this reason, the Bible says, "Therefore God also has highly exalted Him and given Him the name which is above every name, that at the name of Jesus every knee should bow" (Philippians 2:9-10a).

Many of us fight for our reputation. Jesus laid aside His reputation. We like to talk about how we came from nothing to something. Every now and then, you'll have an evangelist who will travel from place to place. Maybe God saved him in prison and his message is, "From the Prison to the Pulpit." I'm glad for that, but Jesus came from something and made Himself of no reputation for our sake.

- How does it affect you to remember that Jesus made Himself nothing out of something for your sake?
- How does this compare to the way you live daily and the goals you pursue for yourself?

PRACTICE THIS Consider how you might practice humility this week and prayerfully take action in that regard.

30

PRAY OVER THIS

And the second is like it: "You shall love your neighbor as yourself."

MATTHEW 22:39

PONDER THIS Most of us have never really accepted ourselves. We're still struggling and trying to make ourselves acceptable. But we can't. Just accept by faith that God has accepted you and be at peace. That is real peace.

I hear people say you're not supposed to love yourself. No, that's wrong. You're to love yourself. You're not to love your faults. I'm not talking about egotism. May I ask you a question? Does God love you? Is it all right for you to love what God loves? What does the Bible say? We are to love one another as we love ourselves. Now, if you don't love you, you can't love me. See? How do we love ourselves? We understand we are what we are by the grace of God. We have been born of God. We're going to God. We have that peace.

- Do you love yourself as described in today's devotion?
- How can you love yourself in this way while still honoring God? Why is it not sinful to love yourself in this way?

PRACTICE THIS Write out a list of ways God loves you. Consider how you are to love yourself so that you can display true love to others.

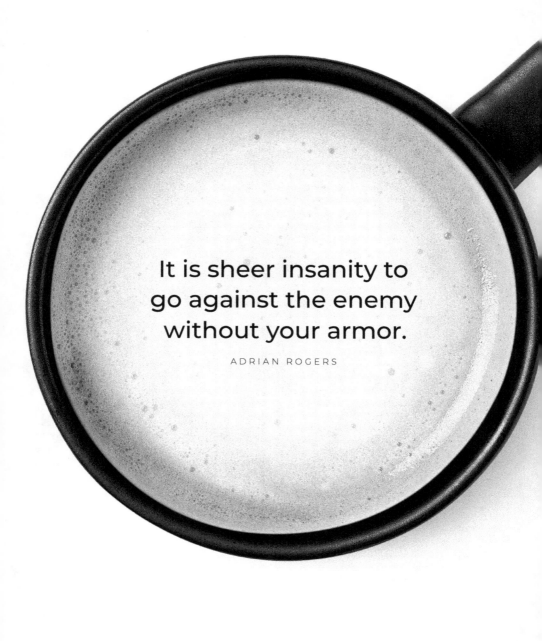

It is sheer insanity to go against the enemy without your armor.

ADRIAN ROGERS

PRAY OVER THIS

A new commandment I give to you, that you love one another;
as I have loved you, that you also love one another.

JOHN 13:34

PONDER THIS Love is not giving others what they deserve but giving them what they need. A well-known preacher went into an airport restaurant. The waitress came out and being unfriendly said, "What do you want?"

"I'd like some breakfast." So he gave the order. She came out again with a bad look, slapped the food down, and said, "You want anything else?" He said, "No, ma'am. That's fine. Thank you." She turned and went away. He ate his breakfast, filled out the check, and left a $20 bill on the table.

He started to leave, and the waitress said, "Hey, you left some money on the table." He replied, "Don't they tip around here?" She said, "Wait a minute. You left a $20 tip after the way I treated you? Why would you do that?" He said, "I could tell you were hurt. You must have some problem, and I thought I would show you some love." She began to cry. "You don't know the problems I've had. I left a child today sick. Coming to work, my old car broke down. The boss got all over me for being late." And this conversation gave the man an opportunity to share the Gospel with her. Do you know what that is? That's Christ-like love. That is not giving her what she deserved; it was giving her what she needed, and what she needed right then was love.

- How has God shown you even more love in Christ than the example in today's devotion?
- How might you display this love to others?

PRACTICE THIS Take action to show love to someone else by giving not what is deserved but what is needed.

2

PONDER THIS Take your Bible and read the first two chapters. You won't find any devil there. Read the last two chapters of the Bible and you won't find any devil there. Habakkuk 2:14 gives this promise, "For the earth will be filled with the knowledge of the glory of the Lord, as the waters cover the sea." The reason that everything's such a mess today is things are out of place. Think about it. The Church is the bride, but the bride belongs with the groom. We're not yet with Him. Jesus is the King, and the King belongs on the throne. He's not yet ruling. The devil is a criminal; he belongs in prison. He's not yet there. But one day soon, the bride's going to be with the Groom. One of these days the King's going to be on the throne, and one of these days the devil's going to be in prison. What a day that will be. That is the day we are to watch and hope for.

- How does it shape your daily perspective to remember that Jesus has promised to return and rule forever?
- What would you do differently today if you truly believed that?

PRACTICE THIS Make a list of ways you might live differently if you truly believed Jesus could return soon. Take action to make changes to align with this list today.

PRAY OVER THIS

And I saw the beast, the kings of the earth, and their
armies, gathered together to make war against Him
who sat on the horse and against His army.

REVELATION 19:19

PONDER THIS In Revelation 19, the battle is set. Here is the Antichrist and his armies. They have come to make war on Heaven's King. But this is laughable. Jesus, followed by the armies of Heaven, is coming this time, not *for* His Church, but this time *with* His Church after the seven years of the Great Tribulation. Here's the Antichrist, this braggart, with his followers, speaking blasphemies, ready to make war with Jesus. And the battle ensues, the moment of anticipation has come, but it's over with two words. Jesus says, "Drop dead." He destroys them with the sword that goes out of His mouth. (See Revelation 19:21.) His word, the same word that spoke them into existence, will speak them into oblivion.

- How often do you reflect on the power of God's Word?
- How does the reminder that Satan is no match for Jesus change the way you view the problems you are facing today?

PRACTICE THIS Take time today to read Genesis 1 and John 1; reflect on the truth and power of Jesus as God's Word.

4

PRAY OVER THIS

For the Lord Himself will descend from heaven with a shout, with the voice of an archangel, and with the trumpet of God. And the dead in Christ will rise first.

1 THESSALONIANS 4:16

PONDER THIS When I was a little boy, near our house there used to be a scrap yard. There were all kinds of metals in that scrap yard, and there was a great magnet on a crane that would move steel and iron from one place to another. If you were to take one of those great magnets and sweep it across the ground, not every piece of metal would rise. Only those made of iron would rise. Why is that? Because the iron has the same nature as the magnet. If you have the same nature as Jesus Christ, when He comes again, you're the one going up, whether you're beneath the ground or on top of the ground. You're the one going up. If you've been Heaven-born, you will be Heaven-bound because you share the nature of our Lord and Savior Jesus Christ.

- What confidence do you have that you are "of the same nature" as Jesus?
- How does sharing that nature change the way you live each day?

PRACTICE THIS Take time to read Galatians 5:22-25 to learn about the fruit of having the same nature as Jesus. Reflect on where this fruit (or lack thereof) is found in your life and respond to God appropriately.

5

PRAY OVER THIS

Then we who are alive and remain shall be caught up
together with them in the clouds to meet the Lord in
the air. And thus we shall always be with the Lord.

1 THESSALONIANS 4:17

PONDER THIS In ancient weddings, the groom would take the initiative. He would go to the father of the bride's house, negotiate for the bride, and pay a price for the bride. This was called the betrothal. The young man and woman would have a cup of wine over which a betrothal blessing had been given, and they would drink from that cup together. And then he would go back to his father's house to prepare a place for her, and she would stay back and begin to prepare for the wedding. The groom would set the date for the wedding in conjunction with his father. Eventually, he would come with a torchlight parade, and there would be one who would go before him, shouting, "Behold, the bridegroom comes!" And the bride would gather her things and be ready.

And that's what's going to happen with Christ's Church. We're the bride of Christ, and we're going to be in a secluded place with our Lord. Suddenly, perhaps before we even finish this day, there will be a shout and Jesus will return. Are you ready?

- How do passages like 1 Thessalonians 4:13-18 help us be ready for Jesus' return?
- What does it look like to prepare yourself daily for Jesus' return?

PRACTICE THIS Look over your schedule for the week. What would you do differently if you knew Jesus was coming back this week? Take action to align your life with this promised coming reality.

PRAY OVER THIS

Then she made a vow and said, "O LORD of hosts, if You will
indeed look on the affliction of Your maidservant and remember
me, and not forget Your maidservant, but will give Your
maidservant a male child, then I will give him to the LORD all
the days of his life, and no razor shall come upon his head."

1 SAMUEL 1:11

PONDER THIS Do you know why so many parents' prayers are unanswered? People say, "Well, I pray for my child, and God just doesn't seem to hear my prayer." Let me ask you a question. What are you praying for your children? What is your desire for your children? Think about it. Are you praying for health? Success? Popularity? Fame?

There are many people who feel it would be a tragedy if God were to make a missionary out of their child. I can remember people talking to my parents, to convince them to discourage me not to go into the ministry because they thought it would be a waste. Many don't equate ministry with "being something" in the way they hope for their children. How many of you are praying, "God make my son important. Make my daughter famous"? We must regularly examine our priorities.

- If you are honest, what are your greatest priorities for your children or the children you are close to in your life?
- How do these compare to God's priorities for them?

PRACTICE THIS Take time today in prayer, submitting the children in your life to God. Ask Him to lead them according to His priorities and not your own.

7

PRAY OVER THIS

"For this child I prayed, and the LORD has granted me
my petition which I asked of Him. Therefore I also have
lent him to the LORD; as long as he lives he shall be lent
to the LORD." So they worshiped the LORD there.

1 SAMUEL 1:27-28

PONDER THIS If our desire is for godly children, then our goal will be to live as godly parents. Have desires for your children. Have goals for yourself. Say, "By God's grace, I will be a magnificent mom like Hannah was, a woman of grace." Hannah prayed, "Lord, I want him to serve You."

Do you know what Joyce and I do every morning that we're together? We sit at the breakfast table and hold hands, and we pray for each of the children and the grandchildren by name. We've done this for many days, morning, and evening, over and over again. We're not praying that they're going to be rich. We're not praying that they're going to be famous. We are praying that they will know and love God with all their hearts. That's what we want from the Lord.

- When you look at the goals you have for your children, are you certain they are worthy goals?
- Who do you need to submit before the Lord today, recognizing that He is in control, and you are not?

PRACTICE THIS Write out a list of desires you have for loved ones in your life. Submit these desires before God. Commit to praying God's will for your loved ones.

PRAY OVER THIS

And she said, "O my lord! As your soul lives, my lord, I am the woman who stood by you here, praying to the LORD."

1 SAMUEL 1:26

PONDER THIS In May we take time to remember our mothers. Abraham Lincoln said, "All that I am, or ever hope to be, I owe to my angel mother." I talked and prayed with the past President of the United States, George Bush, about his personal salvation, and his relationship with Christ, and he looked me in the eyes and said, "I want to tell you, my mother was the most godly person I've ever known." He told me about the influence his mother had on his life. Augustine, that great believer, and theologian, was a renegade boy, but he could not escape the prayers of his mother, Monica. John and Charles Wesley, out of whose hearts and minds came the Methodist church, had a mother whose name was Susanna. If you want to know who the mother of Methodism is, it was Susanna. She raised those children for Jesus Christ. And I've read what Dr. Billy Graham had to say about his godly mother.

There is nothing greater than raising a baby for Jesus Christ. Never underestimate the power of a mother.

- What is the most significant impact your mother has had on you?
- What impact might you be having on those closest to you, whether or not you are a mother?

PRACTICE THIS Take time in prayer to thank God for your mother or someone else in your life who pointed you toward Him.

PRAY OVER THIS

Seventy weeks are determined for your people and for your holy
city, to finish the transgression, to make an end of sins, to make
reconciliation for iniquity, to bring in everlasting righteousness,
to seal up vision and prophecy, and to anoint the Most Holy.

DANIEL 9:24

PONDER THIS In this text, Daniel said that God was going "to finish the transgression," not a transgression, but *the* transgression. To whom was Daniel speaking? Israel. What is the transgression of Israel? It was the rejection of Israel's Messiah. But one day, thank God, that rejection will be over. Israel's transgression will be in the past.

Further, God's going to make an end of sins, because there can be no end of sins without Messiah. There is no forgiveness of sin apart from the Lamb of God who takes away the sin of the world. There's coming a time when the Jews shall turn in faith to Jesus Christ and trust Him. Romans 11:26 says, "And so all Israel will be saved, as it is written: 'The Deliverer will come out of Zion, and He will turn away ungodliness from Jacob.'"

- How are you comforted by the promises of God throughout Scripture?
- How can you see today's text pointing to the coming of Christ?

PRACTICE THIS Find a time today to talk with another person about the promises of God that have been fulfilled in the Bible and throughout history.

10

> ## PRAY OVER THIS
>
> Now as He drew near, He saw the city and wept over it, saying, "If you had known, even you, especially in this your day, the things that make for your peace! But now they are hidden from your eyes."
>
> **LUKE 19:41-42**

PONDER THIS In Luke 19, Jesus wept on the Mount of Olives. Do you know why Jesus wept? Luke 19:41-42 says, "Now as He drew near, He saw the city and wept over it, saying, 'If you had known, even you, especially in this your day, the things that make for your peace! But now they are hidden from your eyes.'" No wonder Jesus wept. The prophet Daniel gave the precise day. Jesus said, "If you'd only known the things that belong to you on this your day." The Israelites had been given a very specific warning, but they refused to see it. We must be careful that we also don't miss the warnings of God that we have received. God has been gracious to reveal Himself to us; we must be careful not to ignore Him.

- What are some warnings God has given us in the Bible?
- What will the consequences be if we don't heed these warnings?

PRACTICE THIS Ask God to show you ways you might have ignored His Word. Ask Him to give you a repentant and obedient heart to move forward in a way that honors Him.

PRAY OVER THIS

For you yourselves know perfectly that the day of
the Lord so comes as a thief in the night.

1 THESSALONIANS 5:2

PONDER THIS We don't know when Jesus is coming again. We may have a feeling that we are living on the edge of eternity, and we can be sure that Jesus's return is two thousand years nearer than it's ever been before. While we may consider the time between His ascension and return to be slow, He will never be late. God is not in a hurry. Second Peter 3:8b says, "with the Lord one day is as a thousand years, and a thousand years as one day." Peter goes on to say, "But the day of the Lord will come" (2 Peter 3:10a). We have also been given the reason for the delay. God in mercy is holding back this day. "The Lord is not slack concerning His promise, as some count slackness, but is longsuffering toward us, not willing that any should perish but that all should come to repentance" (2 Peter 3:9). We can be sure that Jesus is coming. The question is, will we be ready?

- What would you do differently if you knew Jesus was coming back today?
- How can you prepare now for the return of Jesus?

PRACTICE THIS Make a list of ways living in light of Jesus's return should change your day-to-day habits. Take action regarding some of these things this week.

12

PRAY OVER THIS

And to give you who are troubled rest with us when the Lord
Jesus is revealed from heaven with His mighty angels.

2 THESSALONIANS 1:7

PONDER THIS Eternity is going to be a homecoming. Can you imagine a family that gathers for a homecoming? They're all there with a sumptuous meal on the table and there's a lot of laughter, happiness, and joy. But then somebody says, "Where's Susan? Has anybody seen Susan? Susan is not here." If one little child or another member of the family were missing, wouldn't that spoil the homecoming?

Likewise, when we're caught up, not one will be lost. This reminds us of the words of the hymn, "How Firm a Foundation," which says, "The soul that on Jesus hath leaned for repose I will not, I cannot, desert to his foes; that soul, though all hell should endeavor to shake...I'll never, no never, no never forsake!" On that day, we will worship Jesus in fullness, and the homecoming will be like nothing we've experienced.

- How often do you consider what life will be like with Jesus and the Church after we're fully united with Him?
- How should this change the way we think about others in the Church now?

PRACTICE THIS Who will be at this glorious homecoming that you need to be restored with? How will you take steps toward that restoration this week?

13

PRAY OVER THIS

Let no one deceive you by any means; for that Day will not
come unless the falling away comes first, and the man of sin is
revealed, the son of perdition, who opposes and exalts himself
above all that is called God or that is worshiped, so that he sits
as God in the temple of God, showing himself that he is God.

2 THESSALONIANS 2:3-4

PONDER THIS Jesus said, "He who has seen Me has seen the Father" (John
14:9b). The Antichrist can say the same thing. He is of his father, the devil. Just as
Jesus Christ was God in human flesh, the Antichrist will be the devil in human
flesh and he will be able to say, "He who has seen me has seen my father."

Satan desires worship, and he will receive that worship through the
Antichrist. In 2 Thessalonians 2:4, the Apostle Paul tells us that the Antichrist
will sit in the temple considering Himself as God. The devil has always wanted
to be worshipped, and all people were made to worship. The question for us is
who and what will we worship?

- What are some markers that tell us what people worship in their
  lives?
- Though you may never say you worship anything other than God,
  what in your life would you have the hardest time letting go of if
  God asked you to? What might this indicate?

PRACTICE THIS Make a list of things you consider to be of the highest value
in your life. Spend time reflecting on this list and seeking to submit each item
before the Lord.

14

PRAY OVER THIS

And this gospel of the kingdom will be preached in all the world
as a witness to all the nations, and then the end will come.

MATTHEW 24:14

PONDER THIS What will determine the time Jesus is going to come and take the Church? It will be when His bride is complete. That will be when the fullness of the Gentiles has come in. Perhaps there's a service tonight in the mountains of North Carolina. Perhaps there's a little country church there with a fill-in preacher who's stepped in for the pastor who is ill. He's doing what a lot of preachers would do on short notice—he's just trying to explain how to be saved, and he's using John 3:16. Maybe there are not more than forty people there in that little church building, and this layman is trying to share what Christ has done for him using John 3:16. And as he does, tears fall out of his eyes, with a trembling voice and no homiletical beauty at all, he simply tells how God loved the world and gave His Son. He says that if people would repent of their sins and trust Jesus, they'll be saved. And a little girl steps out and comes forward to give her hand to that preacher and her heart to Jesus. And that may be the last soul that'll ever get saved before Jesus comes. It could be today. And God says, "Gabriel, that's it! Marshal the troops. Jesus, it's time! My Son, go and claim your bride. She is complete."

- According to today's verse, what must happen before Jesus will return?
- Considering this truth, how is the Church directly involved in bringing about the return of Christ?

PRACTICE THIS Consider who God has put on your heart to share the truth of the kingdom with. Make time to have that conversation today.

15

PRAY OVER THIS

Know therefore and understand, that from the going forth of
the command to restore and build Jerusalem until Messiah the
Prince, there shall be seven weeks and sixty-two weeks; the street
shall be built again, and the wall, even in troublesome times.

DANIEL 9:25

PONDER THIS I don't know what this does for you, but when I study this passage, it helps me see every world event through the lens of God's Word. It encourages me when I see how God so meticulously and wonderfully pinpointed the exact, precise time when Messiah would come. Daniel, so long before Jesus ever came to this Earth, prophesied the crucifixion of Jesus and the destruction of Jerusalem. Isn't the Bible a wonderful book? It tells me God is in control and gives me hope for the Jewish nation that I love. God has a great and glorious future for His people; He has not forgotten them. Paul, in Romans 11, reminded us: "I say then, has God cast away His people? Certainly not! For I also am an Israelite, of the seed of Abraham, of the tribe of Benjamin. God has not cast away His people whom He foreknew" (Romans 11:1-2a). Paul went on to promise: "Even so then, at this present time there is a remnant according to the election of grace" (Romans 11:5).

- Does it encourage you to read God's prophecies and to see them fulfilled?
- How should this give us confidence in every promise God has made that has not yet been fulfilled?

PRACTICE THIS Is there something particular you are praying about that you know is within God's will? How do His sure promises speak into your situation?

16

PRAY OVER THIS

Remember the former things of old, for I am God, and there is no other; I am God, and there is none like Me, declaring the end from the beginning, and from ancient times things that are not yet done, saying, "My counsel shall stand, and I will do all My pleasure."

ISAIAH 46:9-10

PONDER THIS In 1870, a bishop named Milton Wright heard a person prophesy that one day men may fly like birds. When this bishop heard that, he said, "That's preposterous." He said, "Flight is reserved for the angels, and I beg you not to repeat your statement lest you be guilty of blasphemy." Thirty-three years later, Wilbur and Orville Wright, the sons of this bishop, made their wonderful flight at Kitty Hawk.

Thomas Watson, who was the chairman of IBM said in 1943, "I think that there's a world market for maybe five computers." Then in 1977, Ken Olsen, who was the president, chairman, and founder of Digital Equipment said, "There's no reason anyone would want a computer in their home." Looking back on these statements today, they seem silly. Though the predictions of men are never certain, we can remember that God's prophecies will always come to pass.

- What are some prophecies of man you know that did not come true?
- What examples do you know of God's prophecies that have been fulfilled?

PRACTICE THIS Take time today to thank God that His prophecies always come true and His promises never fail. Reflect on a specific promise of God that is dear to you.

17

PRAY OVER THIS

Wisdom calls aloud outside; she raises her voice in the
open squares. She cries out in the chief concourses, at the
openings of the gates in the city she speaks her words.
PROVERBS 1:20-21

PONDER THIS The invitation of wisdom is a public invitation, not just to a chosen few. God loves all people and wisdom speaks to all people. The voice of the Bible is for whosoever will come. Some people join secret societies to gain certain knowledge—things other people are not supposed to know. But if it's so good, you ought to give it away to everybody. Jesus said He had done nothing in secret (John 18:20). Friend, if it's wonderful and good, it ought to be public and for anyone. I'm so grateful that the Lord God loves the whole wide world.

Do you know what the Bible says? In Matthew 10:27, Jesus said, "Whatever I tell you in the dark, speak in the light; and what you hear in the ear, preach on the housetops." Let the whole world know that Jesus saves and that the invitation of wisdom is a public invitation. We hear people say, "Keep the faith." Not only should you keep it, but you also ought to give it away. As far as I'm concerned, if you don't want to give it away, you ought to give it up, because what you have is not real. You'll never convince me that you know the real joy of the Lord Jesus if you do not want to share it.

- Why must our faith be one we long to give away?
- How has God "given away" the truth about Himself? How has that changed your life?

PRACTICE THIS Select a specific person to whom you want to give the faith away. Take action toward sharing the truth of the Gospel with that person.

PONDER THIS Who are the simple in this verse? The word *simple* here comes
from a root word that means "open." This person is just open to everything—
easily led. We might also call this person gullible. He or she does not stop to think
things through. There are many people today who could be characterized as
simple. They never stop to think about the great issues of life. They just want to
have a good time, and they never stop to think. They don't consider if something
honors God or dishonors God. They just don't think serious thoughts. Proverbs
22:3 says, "A prudent man foresees evil and hides himself, but the simple pass
on and are punished." They never stop to think there's death and judgment to
face or that there's Hell to shun and Heaven to gain. The prudent avoid evil but
the simple walk directly toward it.

- If you honestly assessed your life, would you say you are simple or
  wise according to the Bible's descriptions?
- How might you gain wisdom if you have lived simply to this point?

PRACTICE THIS Create two lists: one containing the wise aspects of your life
and one containing the simple. Submit this list before God, asking Him to give
you the wisdom that only comes from Him.

19

PRAY OVER THIS

He who is often rebuked, and hardens his neck, will
suddenly be destroyed, and that without remedy.
PROVERBS 29:1

PONDER THIS God gives us all spiritual direction. That is seen in the fact that He says we are, "often rebuked." That means God speaks to us time and again. Do you know that it would be more than justice requires if God only spoke to us one time? Because we're all sinners, God doesn't owe us anything. But God has spoken one time, two times, three times, and over and over again. We are "often rebuked."

God does strive, God does knock, God does rebuke, and God does call over and over again. How does He do it? One way God may speak to us is through His Holy Spirit. The Bible teaches that the Holy Spirit is a still small voice God has given to reprove us and bring us to Him. That longing to know God, that sensitivity to the things of God, that urge to get right with God? That's God's Holy Spirit bringing you, drawing you, and wooing you to Jesus Christ.

- How have you experienced God speaking in your life?
- How does this show His mercy and grace?

PRACTICE THIS Take a walk sometime this week in prayer. Rather than speaking to God continuously, spend most of this time listening to God.

PRAY OVER THIS

And do not grieve the Holy Spirit of God, by whom
you were sealed for the day of redemption.

EPHESIANS 4:30

PONDER THIS Did you know it is possible for God to give up on a person? Did you know that God will not always send His Holy Spirit to talk to a person? The Bible says in Genesis 6:3a in a solemn warning, "My Spirit shall not strive with man forever." Now God is infinitely patient, but there comes a time when the Holy Spirit can be so insulted, so sinned against, that you cross a deadline and God's gentle, precious Holy Spirit, no longer speaks to your heart. Did you know you cannot be saved unless the Holy Spirit of God draws you to Jesus Christ? Did you know man's preaching can never save anybody? Did you know that even the truth of the Word of God cannot save you unless the Holy Spirit of God makes that truth real to your heart? Jesus said, "No one can come to Me unless the Father who sent Me draws him" (John 6:44a). The Spirit of God must draw you to Jesus Christ. But there comes a time when the Holy Spirit of God may be so blasphemed that He will no longer speak to your heart.

- What warning do you receive from today's devotion?
- What needs to change in your heart in response to this warning?

PRACTICE THIS Identify what you need to put aside to better hear the Spirit of God today; take action so that you can hear His voice.

PRAY OVER THIS

For it is impossible for those who were once enlightened, and
have tasted the heavenly gift, and have become partakers of
the Holy Spirit, and have tasted the good word of God and the
powers of the age to come, if they fall away, to renew them
again to repentance, since they crucify again for themselves
the Son of God, and put Him to an open shame.

HEBREWS 6:4-6

PONDER THIS This passage tells us it is impossible to renew some people to repentance. It is absolutely, totally, one hundred percent impossible that these people could ever repent and get right with God. Who are they? These are people who were enlightened; their eyes were opened. These are people who have tasted the power of the Word of God. The writer was not talking about people who have been saved and then lose their salvation. He meant people who come to the very brink of salvation, who with their eyes wide open, crucify Jesus again, so to speak. They refuse Christ, they trample the precious blood of the Lord Jesus Christ beneath their feet. And they know what they're doing—they do this after they know the truth.

- What warning is there in this passage?
- What good news is there for those who read this passage and are struck by the truth?

PRACTICE THIS Take time this week to share the truth of the Gospel with another person. Pray that God will do what only He can.

22

PRAY OVER THIS

It is appointed for men to die once, but after this the judgment.

HEBREWS 9:27

PONDER THIS Is there a chance after death? Absolutely not. There are some people who teach and preach that we have a second chance—after we die—to get right with God. That is false, that is heresy, and I do not want to leave that hope to you. If you want to be saved, you may be saved. If you need to be saved, Christ can save you. And whosoever will is able to come, but I want to tell you with all of the urgency, emergency, function, and unction of my soul, you will not come to the judgment of God and be able to throw yourself on the mercy of the court and say, "God I now believe; have mercy, God. Please save me." If you want mercy, you may have it. If you want grace, you may have it. If you want forgiveness, you may have it. But you must have it in this life. The Bible says now is the accepted time. Today is the day of salvation. The Bible says it is appointed for man to die once; after this, there is not a second chance, there is judgment.

- What is the urgency of today's verse?
- Have you turned to Christ for salvation? If not, how do you need to respond? If so, why should you be compelled to share with others?

PRACTICE THIS Make a list of people you will pray for regularly to come to know Christ. Pray that these people will not reject the opportunity to know Christ in this life.

PRAY OVER THIS

For the love of money is a root of all kinds of evil, for which
some have strayed from the faith in their greediness, and
pierced themselves through with many sorrows.

1 TIMOTHY 6:10

PONDER THIS Money is neither good nor bad. It's either master or servant—however, we make it. But the love of money is the root of all kinds of evil.

When a man says, "I will haste to get rich; rather than seek God, I will seek the things of this world," it warps his life and distorts his values. It's amazing what the love of money and the things of this world will do to someone. Those who chase money lose their discretion. No matter how much they have in the bank, they are impoverished if the goal of their lives is to be rich and famous.

- How have you personally experienced the danger of the love of money?
- How can we guard against this each day?

PRACTICE THIS Prayerfully brainstorm ways you can guard against an improper love of money and seek to put some of these practices into action this week.

24

PRAY OVER THIS

Remember therefore from where you have fallen; repent
and do the first works, or else I will come to you quickly and
remove your lampstand from its place—unless you repent.

REVELATION 2:5

PONDER THIS What is a backslider? A backslider is not an unsaved person. No unsaved person can be a backslider. When Christians use the term *backslider* we're not talking about the lost, we're talking about the saved. You must go somewhere in order to slide back; that is, you must have known the Lord before you can backslide away from Him. A lost person is just lost. The backslider is a saved person who's out of fellowship with God.

If there was ever a time when you loved the Lord Jesus Christ more than you love Him at this moment; if there was ever a time when He meant more to you, when prayer was sweeter to you, when worship was more real to you, when your service was more effective for the Lord Jesus Christ; if there was ever a time like that when it was more than it is now, you may be backsliding.

- What might be some evidence that you are backsliding in your fellowship with Christ?
- What are some ways to guard against this each day?

PRACTICE THIS Spend dedicated time in prayer, asking God to reveal where you might have backslidden and to renew your fellowship with Him.

PRAY OVER THIS

So David sent and inquired about the woman. And someone
said, "Is this not Bathsheba, the daughter of Eliam, the wife
of Uriah the Hittite?" Then David sent messengers, and took
her; and she came to him, and he lay with her, for she was
cleansed from her impurity; and she returned to her house.

2 SAMUEL 11:3-4

PONDER THIS There are three individuals sitting in the seat where you are right now: the person you are at this moment, the person you could be for God and for good, and the person you could be for evil. Now, many of us do not realize the propensity for evil that's in our hearts. Many do not realize the depths, the depravity, to which they could go as children of God. You say, "Not me, preacher." Are you better than David? David is one of the greatest men that ever lived, but David got casual about his walk with the Lord. He just assumed that God was going to keep on giving him victory. He let down his pursuit of the things of God and became idle and lazy. He was casual, then he was careless, and then he was compulsive.

- What can we learn from David's example?
- How does God use accounts like David's to keep His people from the danger of sin?

PRACTICE THIS Reflect on any areas in which you might have let down your pursuit of the things of God. Take action today to draw nearer to the Lord, confessing anything you need to confess.

26

PRAY OVER THIS

He who hears you hears Me, he who rejects you rejects
Me, and he who rejects Me rejects Him who sent Me.

LUKE 10:16

PONDER THIS No man is prepared to serve the Lord until he's first heard the Lord. One of the marks of all true Christians is that they have heard the Lord. Notice in today's verse, Jesus put "he who hears" in opposition to those who are false witnesses. Now, what did Jesus say in John 10? Jesus said in John 10:27, "My sheep hear My voice, and I know them, and they follow Me." The Lord doesn't know anyone unless they've heard His voice. "My sheep hear My voice, and I know them." You cannot be a Christian without hearing the voice of the Lord Jesus Christ. Have you heard His voice?

- Have you heard the voice of the Lord?
- If yes, how so? If not, how might you seek to hear Him?

PRACTICE THIS Take time to listen to the voice of the Lord today. Do this through Bible reading or listening to Him through prayer.

PRAY OVER THIS

Do not boast about tomorrow, for you do not
know what a day may bring forth.

PROVERBS 27:1

PONDER THIS There is nobody so bad he or she cannot be saved. There is no one so good he or she need not be saved. There are many, however, who are going to be lost because of their self-righteous attitudes. They never repent of their sin. They never receive Christ as their Savior. But I'm going to tell you why I believe most people hear me or any other Gospel preacher, and then go out but are still lost. It's not because they rebel against God or disbelieve, and it's not because they're self-righteous. I believe most of the people who hear the Gospel message and remain unsaved are lost because of procrastination. They know that they need to be saved, and they say, "One of these days I'm going to get saved." But they keep putting it off. Why? Well, they got by yesterday without Jesus, they got by the day before without Jesus, and the day before that, and so on. So, they assume that tomorrow will be like yesterday. This is a dangerous assumption and one no one should make.

- How have you been guilty of procrastinating in your faith?
- What is God calling you to do today? How will you respond?

PRACTICE THIS Take action to respond in obedience to God in an area in which you have procrastinated.

28

PRAY OVER THIS

He who covers his sins will not prosper, but whoever
confesses and forsakes them will have mercy.

PROVERBS 28:13

PONDER THIS David tried to cover up his sin by having Uriah killed. Today's verse reminds us that those who cover their sin will never prosper. Oh, would to God that as soon as David committed that sin with Bathsheba, he had said, "Oh my God, what have I done? God, forgive me. God, have mercy. God, I'll bring a sacrifice and make restitution. God, have mercy." God would have had mercy, God would have forgiven him, and God would have cleansed him. It still would have been a terrible sin, but the Bible says to "Agree with your adversary quickly, while you are on the way with him, lest your adversary deliver you to the judge, the judge hand you over to the officer, and you be thrown into prison" (Matthew 5:25). That means if you've done wrong, quickly confess it. As soon as you know, confess it, and don't let that sin build up in your heart. But instead, David spent a year without confessing that sin.

- When was a time you had an opportunity to confess sin but instead sought to hide it?
- How can we learn from these times so that we respond differently in the future?

PRACTICE THIS Confess before God any sin that is lingering in your life today.

PRAY OVER THIS

The backslider in heart will be filled with his own ways,
but a good man will be satisfied from above.

PROVERBS 14:14

PONDER THIS In the beginning of 2 Samuel 11, David had become casual about the things of God. He had been blessed so much—God had been so good to him, and David had enjoyed victory after victory—that he no longer had to fight. He could just sit back, coast, and take it easy. David had put off the armor, but the Bible warns that we are to endure difficulties as good soldiers of the Lord.

Many of us gave our hearts to the Lord Jesus as children. We meant business and our heart belongs to Him. But I wonder if there are not some of us who need to say, "Lord Jesus, I have gotten casual about this thing. I have taken for granted what I did as a child or as a young person. But now today, Lord Jesus, I present the most precious thing I have—my life, my soul, my all—to you anew and afresh like I have never ever done it before."

- In what ways have grown casual about your relationship with the Lord?
- How is He calling you to respond?

PRACTICE THIS Consider your life and relationship with Christ. Respond to Him with renewed commitment today.

30

PRAY OVER THIS

Seek the LORD while He may be found, call upon Him while He is near.

ISAIAH 55:6

PONDER THIS Somebody told a parable of the devil and his demons who were planning how to damn the world. One of the demons cleverly said, "Tell the people there's no God. Then they won't prepare to meet God." The devil said, "That won't work. Only fools don't believe in God. That'll only damn a few." Another said, "Let's tell them the Bible is not the Word of God." The devil said, "Some will believe that. But the Bible has such self-authenticity about it, and the fulfilled prophecy reveals the truth of the Bible. It will be hard to get men not to believe the Bible's the Word of God." A devil said, "Let's deny the deity of Christ and fill pulpits with liberal preachers who pretend to preach the Bible, but never preach the blood atonement, the Virgin Birth, and the full deity of Christ." The devil said, "That's a good plan, and I'll see to it that I have some preachers like that. But I need something more." Finally, a demon known for his wickedness said, "Here's my plan. We will admit there's a God. We will admit the Bible is the Word of God. We will tell people Jesus Christ is the Son of God. And we'll tell them they need to be saved. *But not today*." A cheer went up in the halls of Hell. Satan said, "With that tool, I will be able to damn the souls of millions."

- Regarding spiritual things, what are you tempted to believe you can put off until tomorrow?
- In what way is God giving you a sense of urgency today?

PRACTICE THIS Consider the things of the faith you may be putting off. Respond to God without delay.

31

And not only that, but we also glory in tribulations,
knowing that tribulation produces perseverance.
ROMANS 5:3

PONDER THIS For several centuries, a village was known for its exquisite and fragile porcelain. Especially striking were its urns, which were as high as tables and as wide as chairs. They were admired around the globe for their strong form and delicate beauty. Legend has it that when each urn was finished, there was one final step. The artist broke it and then put it back together with gold filigree. An ordinary urn was then transformed into a priceless work of art. What seemed finished wasn't complete until it was broken.

Men throw broken things away. But God never uses anything until He first breaks it: "A broken and a contrite heart—These, O God, You will not despise" (Psalm 51:17b). God is trying to break your life for eternal good.

- How has God used the broken things in your life to build godly character?
- How has your faith grown stronger through the hardship you have faced?

PRACTICE THIS Journal today about some of the ways God has used the broken things in your life to build stronger character and faith in Him.

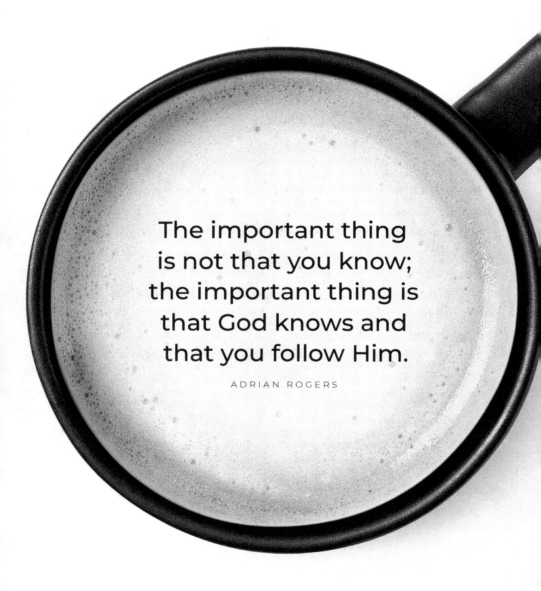

The important thing
is not that you know;
the important thing is
that God knows and
that you follow Him.

ADRIAN ROGERS

1

PRAY OVER THIS

However, when He, the Spirit of truth, has come, He will guide
you into all truth; for He will not speak on His own authority, but
whatever He hears He will speak; and He will tell you things to come.

JOHN 16:13

PONDER THIS How does God speak? How does God reprove? He does so by His Holy Spirit. There have been times when you've been driving along in your car, doing dishes, maybe you've been out on the football field, or just about to go to sleep, and you feel the Spirit of God speaking to you. When you come to Christ, God speaks to you and you know you're a sinner, you know you're doing wrong, you know you need to be saved, and God's Holy Spirit is gently but strongly speaking to your heart. He spoke to mine when I was a teenage boy, before I came to the Lord Jesus Christ. There's no way to describe it except that the dear precious Holy Spirit of God was speaking. And if God's Holy Spirit is speaking to you today, I beg you, I plead with you, listen to the Spirit of God.

- When has the Holy Spirit spoken to you?
- How have you verified the voice of God through His Word? Why is it important that we do this?

PRACTICE THIS Spend time in the Bible today, asking God to speak to you through His revealed Word.

June

2

PRAY OVER THIS

And even as they did not like to retain God in their
knowledge, God gave them over to a debased mind,
to do those things which are not fitting.

ROMANS 1:28

PONDER THIS Three times in the first chapter of Romans, God speaks of giving people up: "God gave them up" (Romans 1:24); "God gave them up" (Romans 1:26); and "God gave them over" (Romans 1:28). The old-time preachers used to call that, "When the lights go out on the road to Hell." This is when the Holy Spirit of God no longer speaks to a man. In Genesis 6:3a, God said before the flood, "My Spirit shall not strive with man forever." Don't get the idea that the Holy Spirit's conviction is going to stay in your heart and in your life if you continually reject Him. You may come to a place of sudden destruction in your spirit as well as in your mind, a place in which the Holy Spirit of God no longer speaks to you and God no longer draws you. God has given us this warning in advance as a means of His grace. We must respond while we can.

- The idea of God giving us over to ourselves should give us fear, but that fear has a purpose. What is the goal of this godly fear?
- What is the role of those who know Christ in warning others to listen to God's conviction while they can?

PRACTICE THIS Ask God today who He is calling you to speak with about the offer of His forgiveness. Ask Him for wisdom and next steps in obedience in this regard.

PRAY OVER THIS

Is it not lawful for me to do what I wish with my own things?
MATTHEW 20:15A

PONDER THIS In Matthew 20, Jesus told a parable to teach us that it is His prerogative to choose to save people who come to Him late in life. The thief on the cross was saved in the eleventh hour. Just before he died, he turned to Jesus and said, "Lord, remember me when You come into Your kingdom" (Luke 23:42). Still, you shouldn't deliberately deny Christ and say to yourself, "I'll get saved in the eleventh hour," because you may never get to the eleventh hour. You may die tonight. You may die tomorrow. Your heart may become hardened. But what does Jesus say? He says it is never too late to start and it is always too soon to quit. The workers in Matthew 11 came into the vineyard even in the eleventh hour, which was as soon as they were called. It is better to start and to serve lovingly all day, but it is never too late to start.

- How does today's passage remind you that no one is without hope when it comes to trusting Christ?
- Who have you given up hope on? How does today's devotion challenge you to keep praying?

PRACTICE THIS What is something God has called you to do but you have put off? Respond with action today.

4

PRAY OVER THIS

He who is often rebuked, and hardens his neck, will
suddenly be destroyed, and that without remedy.

PROVERBS 29:1

PONDER THIS God has called me to proclaim that He loves you with an infinite love. He has spoken to you over and over again, and He's speaking to you today. But God says, "If you continue to harden your neck, you'll be destroyed." And when you are, there'll be no second chance. It will be without remedy, without hope. I looked this verse up in several different translations, and they all mean the same thing: no hope, without a second chance, without a remedy, without a cure.

But why would God rebuke you? Because He loves you so much, and He wants to save you today. You may ask, "Pastor Rogers, would Jesus save me today?" Yes. "Pastor Rogers, are you sure?" Yes, I'm sure, if you'll call upon Him." You say, "What if I've crossed the deadline?" If you call upon Him, you haven't.

- How might you use the message of today's devotion to encourage someone in the truth?
- How does God's rebuke always give us hope? Why is it worse to not have His rebuke?

PRACTICE THIS Consider where God is rebuking you currently. Respond to Him in obedience as He is prompting you.

PRAY OVER THIS

For "whoever calls on the name of the Lord shall be saved."
ROMANS 10:13

PONDER THIS Let me give you good news. Anybody who wants to be saved can be. The man who crosses the deadline has no desire to be saved, but if you have a desire to be saved, the Holy Spirit of God is working in you. And if you want to be saved, you can be saved. And I thank God that the Bible says, "For 'whoever calls on the name of the Lord shall be saved.'" And if you were to show me one time or one place where anybody asked Jesus to save them and He didn't save them, I'd close my Bible and never preach again. I promise you on the authority of the Word of God, He'll save you today if you trust Him.

- What reason does today's verse give to continue inviting people to trust Christ?
- Who have you given up on that God is calling you to continue to pursue with the Gospel?

PRACTICE THIS Reach out to a person you've stopped pursuing with the Gospel. Remember that you don't know how God might be working in that person's life, even today.

PONDER THIS A while back, I received a letter from a man. He said, "Forgive me for taking so long to write this letter, but I want to tell you how God used you in my life." He continued, "It was on Merritt Island where you used to pastor. I was a long-haired surfer going down the road with my surfboard, and you stopped and picked me up. It was a hot day. And you talked to me about Jesus. I laughed at you. I made it as if it had no impact on me at all. You let me out. I went on my way, but I was never, ever able to forget what you said to me until I gave my heart to Christ. Jesus saved me, and now I am the pastor of a very wonderful church, and I just want to thank you." After some thought, I vaguely remembered picking that boy up. You see, sometimes the things we do we don't put in the books, and the things we think we have done God does not put in the books. But you will be wise to let God keep the books.

- Has anyone ever told you a way God used you, even if you didn't know it at the time?
- How does this reality encourage you to continue in faithfulness, no matter the outward response?

PRACTICE THIS Are there people who have encouraged you in the Lord that you've never told? Call them, text them, or write them a letter today to thank and encourage them.

7

Jesus said to him, "I am the way, the truth, and the life.
No one comes to the Father except through Me."

JOHN 14:6

PONDER THIS There used to be a time when you would preach on the inerrancy of the Word of God, the Virgin Birth, or the bodily resurrection and someone would say, "I don't agree with that." And you could discuss the matter and philosophize. You could take the Word of God and other sources and go back and forth trying to determine what is true and what is not true. But that's not so today. Today you might say, "I believe in the Virgin Birth. I believe in the absolute sinless deity of the Lord Jesus Christ. I believe in His vicarious death upon the cross." But with our culture's view of tolerance, you would not be argued with. They would say, "That's wonderful. That's your truth. Now let me tell you my truth." And you soon realize there is no fixed standard for anybody's truth. All truths today are considered equal. But that's not what the Bible says, and we are called to be faithful to God's truth.

- Where in your life have you encountered the idea that absolute truth does not exist?
- Why is it easy to fall into this way of thinking if we are not careful?

PRACTICE THIS Take time to write out some statements that are true about God and the world.

8

PONDER THIS Some years ago, a woman was waiting for an airplane. She went to a shop and bought a bag of cookies and sat down. Soon a man came and sat down beside her. The cookies were in between the two of them, unopened. The man reached over, opened the cookies, took one out, and began to eat it. She thought, "What unmitigated gall and nerve that he would do that!" In response, she reached in, got one, ate it herself, and gave him a dirty look. He smiled, reached in and got another. They traded back and forth until one cookie was left in the bottom and with a smile; he broke it in half, took one half, and left her the other half. She thought as she got on the plane, "I've never seen a person as arrogant as that man was." But when she opened her purse, there was her bag of cookies unopened.

Sometimes we judge others because of our sheer ignorance. (See Romans 14:4.) Another reason we unmercifully judge other people and fail to tolerate them is that we're insensitive. We don't love as we ought. But Jesus did not come to condemn. He came to save. As John 3:17 says, "For God did not send His Son into the world to condemn the world, but that the world through Him might be saved."

- When was a time you assumed the worst about another person but found out you were wrong?
- What are some ways you can remind yourself that God is the only right judge of people?

PRACTICE THIS If appropriate, reach out to a person you've misjudged and apologize. If this is not appropriate or possible, journal about this circumstance.

PRAY OVER THIS

When we had sailed slowly many days, and arrived with
difficulty off Cnidus, the wind not permitting us to proceed,
we sailed under the shelter of Crete off Salmone.

ACTS 27:7

PONDER THIS Why would God take almost an entire chapter in the Bible to tell us about a ship in a storm? Because it is more than history. The Holy Spirit has taken this story and made an incredible illustration with a great spiritual application for all of us because life is like a voyage. Sometimes the sea is calm, sometimes the wind blows softly, sometimes the sun is shining, and thank God for those times. Maybe that's where you are right now, just sailing along, and if you are, enjoy it. It's a gift of God. But sometimes the wind rises, the sky darkens, and we find ourselves amid a terrible storm. And that's the way life is. This chapter is an illustration of every human being sailing between two eternities. Sometimes things are good and sometimes things are bad. But God is in control of it all.

- If you compare your life to being at sea, what are the wind and waves like currently?
- How have you seen God work in seasons of good and bad "weather"?

PRACTICE THIS Read Acts 27. Take time today to thank God for the season He has you in and for the confidence you can have that He is working in your life.

PRAY OVER THIS

Now when much time had been spent, and sailing was now
dangerous because the Fast was already over, Paul advised them,
saying, "Men, I perceive that this voyage will end with disaster
and much loss, not only of the cargo and ship, but also our lives."
Nevertheless the centurion was more persuaded by the helmsman
and the owner of the ship than by the things spoken by Paul.

ACTS 27:9-11

PONDER THIS The question arose regarding whether to continue or not. Those leading the ship said, "What does everybody want to do?" Now there was a crowd on that boat, and Paul was outvoted. Despite Paul's warning, they said, "Let's sail." But we should recognize that majority support doesn't make a thing right. Morality is not set by the majority, but by God.

Twelve spies went out to spy out the land in Joshua's day. Ten said, "It can't be done." Only two said, "It could be done." The ten were wrong, and the two were right. Later, the people of Israel didn't have a king and they wanted a king. They should have been a theocracy, ruled by God, but they wanted a monarchy. They said, "How many of you want a king?" And they all voted for a king. They got Saul. God gave them what they wanted, but after a while, they didn't want what they got. The majority was wrong. What is most important is what God is calling us to do, not what gains the most favor.

- When was a time you felt led to go against the crowd in God's name?
- What makes this so difficult?

PRACTICE THIS Consider today where God might be calling you to go against the crowd for His sake. Take action toward faithfulness in this area.

PRAY OVER THIS

Then, fearing lest we should run aground on the rocks, they
dropped four anchors from the stern, and prayed for day to come.

ACTS 27:29

PONDER THIS In this verse, the sailors prayed in essence, "Oh! If I just had some light; if I just knew what to do!" But they had rejected God's light. And now they found themselves in darkness. The sailors of that day didn't have the modern instrumentation that we have today. They sailed by the stars, the sun, the moon, the land, and the shore. But the Bible tells us in Acts 27:20 that the storm was so fierce, all these things had disappeared. They were gone! What do you do, dear friend, when the stars go out of your night and the sun disappears out of your day? These sailors were in suffocating darkness, wishing for the day. And their hopes vanished.

- What are some of the things you might be tempted to turn toward when you lose your spiritual bearings?
- Why is it important that we heed God's guidance in these situations and not reject it, as these men did?

PRACTICE THIS Is there anywhere God is leading you that you haven't obeyed? Act in obedience today.

12

PRAY OVER THIS

Therefore I urge you to take nourishment, for this is for your survival, since not a hair will fall from the head of any of you.

ACTS 27:34

PONDER THIS In Acts 27:30-32, there were some sailors aboard a ship with Paul during a fierce storm who said, "We'll get in that lifeboat. We'll get off this big ship and we'll escape." These men sought a form of escapism built upon selfishness. Don't do it! You may say, "I'll outrun or drown out my problems." No, they can swim. You're the one who is going to drown.

There were others who were working, throwing everything overboard. They couldn't see which way to go. Do you know people like that? This was a storm they'd been warned about, to begin with, and now they were facing the consequences of their actions. That's how the godless sometimes go through storms.

But what about the godly? Paul called the men together and encouraged them. He gave a good message from God. Just as in this account, there are three classes in America: those who are afraid, those who don't know enough to be afraid, and those who know their Bibles.

- Which of these categories would you count yourself in? Why?
- How can you remain encouraged and encourage others in the middle of life's storms?

PRACTICE THIS Encourage someone you know is having a tough time today.

13

PRAY OVER THIS

We do not look at the things which are seen, but at the
things which are not seen. For the things which are seen are
temporary, but the things which are not seen are eternal.

2 CORINTHIANS 4:18

PONDER THIS The Bible teaches there is a visible material world and an invisible spiritual world. These two co-exist side by side. We would be foolish to deny there is an unseen spiritual world just because we cannot see it with our physical eyes. A blind man would be foolish to deny the radiant splendor of a sunset simply because he cannot see it.

If you were to take my great-grandfather and bring him back to this world and tell him this room is full of music, sports, drama, action, automobiles crashing, and news from all over the world, he'd say, "No, that's not true, you're telling a lie." But we know it is true. If we turn on the TV, it could draw these images out of the air. We cannot see them because we're not tuned in, but we know they're there. This gives us a wonderful illustration of another world in this age in which we live that our great-grandfathers did not have.

Jesus is here now, but unless you have your antennae up and tuned into station J-E-S-U-S, you may not know it. You may say, "These people are conjuring up things and talking about things that are not reality." But there is more to life than what you can touch, what you can taste, what you can smell, what you can see, and what you can hear.

- How have you experienced the unseen spiritual reality of the world?
- How does this reality exist in support of God and in opposition to Him?

PRACTICE THIS Spend time today reflecting on the reality of the unseen spiritual world.

14

PRAY OVER THIS

For our light affliction, which is but for a moment, is working
for us a far more exceeding and eternal weight of glory.

2 CORINTHIANS 4:17

PONDER THIS One time I was in serious danger; thankfully that danger passed. But in that danger, I went to the Word of God and read, "I shall not die, but live, and declare the works of the LORD" (Psalm 118:17). God took that word right off the page and gave it to me. But the strange thing was, several days after, I received three letters, one from down in Mississippi, one from Georgia, and another from Memphis. They all said in some manner, "Adrian, were you in difficulty? Were you in trouble? God laid on my heart that I should pray for you." What a blessing it was to get these letters and know the angel of the Lord encamps around those who fear Him.

God is good and He protects His own. We, in times of fear and persecution, can say, "Lord, open my eyes to see the angels that are encamped around me and protecting me." Nobody and nothing can get to you except through God's angels. If God allows something, He will allow it for your good and for His glory.

- What are some ways God has worked in your life that you couldn't see with your physical eyes?
- How do these moments serve to build your faith?

PRACTICE THIS Spend time praying today for someone God lays on your heart. Reach out and encourage that person by saying, "I'm thinking about you and praying for you."

PRAY OVER THIS

So the LORD said, "I will destroy man whom I have created
from the face of the earth, both man and beast, creeping
thing and birds of the air, for I am sorry that I have made
them." But Noah found grace in the eyes of the LORD.

GENESIS 6:7-8

PONDER THIS We've come to a day in which a man's word means absolutely nothing, whether it's a treaty between nations, a marriage contract, a business agreement, or a political speech. In Genesis 6, we read that people's hearts were wicked continually before the Lord. And it had reached such a level that God said, "I'm sorry that I made them! I'm going to have to judge the Earth." (See Genesis 6:6-7.) The same sins that produced the flood in Noah's day have reached up to Heaven today.

But what did Jesus say the days of Noah were like? He said they were, "eating and drinking, marrying and giving in marriage" (Matthew 24:38a). They were going on with the same old routine of life. The problem in our society is that we're standing right on the threshold of imminent judgment, but nobody seems to care. We just yawn in the face of God. In these dangerous days, we need to thank God we have His amazing grace. Genesis 6:8 says, "But Noah found grace in the eyes of the LORD."

- What are signs that the world gives no thought to the things of God?
- How have you received grace like Noah?

PRACTICE THIS Take time today to journal about the process of your "finding grace in the eyes of the Lord."

PRAY OVER THIS

Then the Lord said to Noah, "Come into the ark, you
and all your household, because I have seen that you
are righteous before Me in this generation."

GENESIS 7:1

PONDER THIS In order to be saved from the wrath of God, you have to get on board the good ship of grace. If you don't get on board, you're going down. You will not be an unsinkable saint. Genesis 7:1 says, "the Lord said to Noah, 'Come into the ark, you and all your household.'" But Noah had to take that step of faith. Noah had to come into the ark, and that one step of faith is all it took to put Noah in the ark. God said to Noah and to Noah's family, to his sons and his daughters-in-law, and to his wife, "Come into the ark!" And Noah responded in effect, "Just as I am, I come, I come." Likewise, we must respond to God, "Just as I am without one plea, but that Thy blood was shed for me. Oh, Lamb of God, I come to Thee! I come."

- How was the ark a picture of God's grace that would be revealed in Jesus?
- How do we "enter" into Christ as the ark that saves us from God's wrath?

PRACTICE THIS Talk with someone today about the similarities between the ark and Christ as our savior.

PRAY OVER THIS

For the husband is head of the wife, as also Christ is head
of the church; and He is the Savior of the body.

EPHESIANS 5:23

PONDER THIS The word *head* here speaks of leader. The husband is the head of the wife, that is, he is the leader. But he's not the dictator. The husband is not some sort of a top sergeant, to be beating his wife over the head with a Bible club. This doesn't speak primarily of a chain of command; this is a line of responsibility. That's a much better term. To have headship is to have responsibility. That means if a wife is to submit to her husband, she is to submit to her husband for loving leadership. And God gives the model. What is the model? Verse 23 says, "as also Christ is head of the church."

- How does Christ lead the church?
- What implications does this have for how husbands are to lead their wives?

PRACTICE THIS What responsibilities has God given you to lovingly serve those around you? Take action in obedient love toward another today.

18

PRAY OVER THIS

Therefore, just as the church is subject to Christ, so let
the wives be to their own husbands in everything.
EPHESIANS 5:24

PONDER THIS The tendency today is to stress the equality of men and women by minimizing the unique significance of maleness and femaleness. The consequence is division and destruction. Why? People are throwing away their God-given identities. Oneness and equality are not the same. God is for oneness; God is not for sameness. God made us different that He might make us one. God, "made them male and female" (Mark 10:6). And for one to recognize the headship of the other does not mean the inferiority of the one.

If you work for a boss, you'd better be submissive, or you'll be looking for another job. That doesn't mean you're inferior to your boss. If you're on a team, you have to be submissive to the coach. That doesn't mean you're inferior to the coach. If you're a student, you'd better be submissive to your professor, or you're not going to learn and get the grades. That doesn't mean you're inferior to your professor. If you are a citizen, you'd better be submissive to the policeman. That doesn't mean you're inferior to the policeman; it simply means that in all of creation and society God has put order.

- What other examples can you think of in which differences and submission do not equal inferiority?
- Through His relationship with the Church, how does Jesus model the value husbands are to place on their wives?

PRACTICE THIS Write out the examples you thought of that display differences and submission but not inferiority. How do these better help you understand what Paul meant in this text?

PRAY OVER THIS

If I then, your Lord and Teacher, have washed your
feet, you also ought to wash one another's feet.

JOHN 13:14

PONDER THIS Jesus is the head of the Church, and yet we find in John 13 that Jesus washed His disciples' feet. And He said in John 13:13, "You call Me Teacher and Lord, and you say well, for so I am." Jesus never said He was not Master; Jesus never said He was not Lord, but listen to what He said next: "If I then, your Lord and Teacher, have washed your feet, you also ought to wash one another's feet." Husband, I want to suggest that you find ways to wash your wife's feet. That's the way you show your headship in the home. It is servant leadership. Jesus said, "I am the Lord and Master, but a husband is to love his wife as Christ loved the Church." A leader serves. Your wife is not there to serve you; you're there to serve her.

- What are some other ways Jesus served the Church?
- How does this model challenge the world's view of leadership?

PRACTICE THIS Write out the ways you can think of that Jesus served the Church. Consider how you might serve and love others by following the example of Jesus.

20

PRAY OVER THIS

Brethren, if a man is overtaken in any trespass, you who
are spiritual restore such a one in a spirit of gentleness,
considering yourself lest you also be tempted.

GALATIANS 6:1

PONDER THIS Some years ago, I read that each morning in Africa, a gazelle
wakes up and says to himself, "If I cannot outrun the fastest lion on these plains,
I will be devoured." And somewhere that same morning a lion wakes up and
that lion says, "If I cannot outrun the slowest gazelle, I will starve." So, both the
gazelle and the lion wake up running.

Every morning, you and I need to wake up running because we are
running from sin and Satan is running for us. And sometimes we're overtaken.
Sometimes we stumble and fall. When you get saved, that doesn't mean you
won't sin anymore. Sometimes we're overtaken in a fault. Do you know the
difference between my life before I was saved and after I was saved? Before
I got saved, I was running to sin, now I'm running from sin. In today's verse,
Paul was talking about brothers. He said, "Brethren, if a man is overtaken in any
trespass"—that is, run down by Satan, trapped and snared by a fault—then we
are to restore him.

- How have you experienced the reality of running from sin and
  being run after by Satan?
- What are some ways we actively "run" in this sense?

PRACTICE THIS Write out a list of ways to run from sin and Satan. Put one or
more of these into practice today.

21

PRAY OVER THIS

But the fruit of the Spirit is love, joy, peace, longsuffering,
kindness, goodness, faithfulness, gentleness, self-
control. Against such there is no law.

GALATIANS 5:22-23

PONDER THIS When you're setting a broken bone, what do you need? Gentleness. You need tender loving care. You can't restore somebody if you're harsh and overbearing. You've got to be gentle. Do you know what I've noticed about dads whose children love them most? They're gentle. All children want a strong dad, a dad they can look up to. But they also want a dad that's gentle. You can restore your children with gentleness rather than lashing out at them, screaming at them, and criticizing them. Try some tenderness with your children. If you've got backslidden children, they need tenderness. Your neighbor needs tenderness. "Restore such a one in the spirit of meekness" (Galatians 6:1, KJV). Do it gently.

- How has God been gentle with you when you needed restoration?
- How have you experienced the blessing of gentleness from a Christian brother or sister?

PRACTICE THIS Who do you know who needs encouragement or restoration? Take action to bless that person with gentleness today.

PRAY OVER THIS

Though He slay me, yet will I trust Him. Even so,
I will defend my own ways before Him.

JOB 13:15

PONDER THIS There are a lot of people who have a wrong theology of suffering today. They get on television and give this message: "If you get right with God, you're going to be healthy, and you're going to be wealthy. It's cash, comfort, and Cadillacs—you'll have it all. Oh, by the way, just send me a little money, and you can have it all." There's a lot of that going on. Have you noticed that? The idea is that the only reason you suffer is that you've done wrong. That you can get everything right and believe in God and have anything you want. There's just one thing wrong with that philosophy—it's not true. Some of God's choicest of saints have suffered, most of all God's own Son, Jesus.

- When have you heard the idea that if you do everything right, God will save you from suffering?
- What is tempting about this way of thinking? What is wrong with it?

PRACTICE THIS Make a list of biblical examples of righteous people who suffered.

23

PRAY OVER THIS

And he said: "Naked I came from my mother's womb, and
naked shall I return there. The LORD gave, and the LORD
has taken away; blessed be the name of the LORD."

JOB 1:21

PONDER THIS You can have faith and calamity at the same time. Faith does not mean you are always going to escape. Faith is not receiving from God what you want; faith is accepting from God what He gives. Now the question is this: can you trust God when you are submerged in suffering? Perhaps you're so sick and shut in that you can't even get out of the house, and the only way that you can worship is through television or the computer. Can you say with Job today, "Though he slay me, yet will I trust Him" (Job 13:15)? If you can, you will shut the devil's mouth.

The devil thinks, "Let those Christians have a little trouble, let them have some persecution, let them have some bankruptcy. Let one of their children die, let them have some greedy maladies that consume their bodies. Let them have those kinds of troubles, and let people blame them for doing wrong when they haven't done anything in the world wrong. They'll curse God." But Job said, "I'm not going to curse Him; I'm going to praise Him." Job said, "The LORD gave, and the LORD has taken away; Blessed be the name of the LORD."

- When have you faced suffering and your faith grew?
- How are we encouraged to hold onto the Lord in times of suffering?

PRACTICE THIS Journal about a time when your faith grew during suffering. Consider who you might tell about this time in your life.

24

PRAY OVER THIS

Now when evening came, His disciples went down to the sea,
got into the boat, and went over the sea toward Capernaum.
And it was already dark, and Jesus had not come to them.

JOHN 6:16-17

PONDER THIS It is a shallow theology that says if we're in the will of God, we're always going to sail smoothly on the sea of life. We'll have no sickness, no sorrow, no disappointment, and know no separation. There'll be no death in our families. There'll be no problems. This is the gospel of cash, Cadillacs, and tranquility, often known as the prosperity gospel. Friend, there's a Greek word for that and it's *baloney*.

We are going to have difficulty. And the first thing you can say when difficulty comes is that God's providence is over it all. We are governed by His providence. God's wonderful plan is in effect, no matter what. In today's passage, Jesus constrained the disciples to go into a storm. They were in this storm because of the providence of God.

- What storms are you currently facing?
- How might you trust God's providence regardless of your circumstances?

PRACTICE THIS List out truths about God that you can trust even as you face the storms of life.

25

PRAY OVER THIS

All my close friends abhor me, and those
whom I love have turned against me.
JOB 19:19

PONDER THIS Can you trust God when others forsake you? Maybe you're going through that right now. Has your husband forsaken you? Have your children abandoned you? Has a trusted friend or a business associate turned on you? The devil says, "Yes, let that happen to them. God, they'll curse You to Your face." But that wasn't true for Job.

Perhaps you're a preacher and your church has turned on you. Perhaps the pulpit committee that called you to the church now wants you to leave, and the reason is you're just preaching the Gospel. Don't think that if you preach the Gospel the world's going to love you. The same world that hated Jesus is going to hate you. You can get in trouble for preaching the Gospel. Sometimes your closest associates, the people you take counsel with, even in the house of God, will turn against you. You'd better trust God when friends forsake you.

- When was a time you felt forsaken by friends?
- How is God your ever-present friend, even in the darkest moments?

PRACTICE THIS Write a list of ways God is a faithful friend and worthy of trust in every season.

26

PRAY OVER THIS

You will keep him in perfect peace, whose mind is
stayed on You, because he trusts in You.

ISAIAH 26:3

PONDER THIS What is darkness? Darkness is merely the absence of light. The only way there can be darkness is for the light to be withdrawn. Who is the light? God is the light. But sometimes God may just back off and leave His servant in darkness. If you read biographies of great Christians, almost all of them will talk about something they call the dark night of the soul. They're serving God, they're loving God, and then things come, perplexities they can't understand.

There's going to come a time when all your theology will go upside down. There will be a time when you won't understand where God is and you're going to be in such darkness you won't see your hand in front of your face. What do you do then? Isaiah says stay upon your God; trust Him.

- Have you experienced a "dark night of the soul"? What was this like? How did God work and move in your life during and around this time?
- Why is it important to stay with God in these times?

PRACTICE THIS Do you know anyone who is facing a dark night of the soul currently? Pray for that person and reach out to encourage that person today.

27

PRAY OVER THIS

Therefore He is also able to save to the uttermost
those who come to God through Him, since He
always lives to make intercession for them.
HEBREWS 7:25

PONDER THIS You want a blessed thought? You are on Jesus' prayer list. There's nothing much more comforting than for somebody to tell me he is praying for me. How immeasurably more comforting is it to know Jesus prays for us?

There are almost eight billion people on Earth. Some people have never been prayed for one time. If you're on anybody's prayer list, you're blessed. I can tell you for sure that you're on Jesus' prayer list. The Lord Jesus knows you by name and He calls you by name. Did you come to God by Jesus? Then you're on His prayer list. And what is He doing? The finished work of Jesus is Calvary. The unfinished work of Jesus is His prayer ministry.

- How does it encourage you to know Jesus is interceding for you before the Father?
- How does this free you in your own prayers?

PRACTICE THIS Spend time today in prayer, thanking God that Jesus continually intercedes for you even when you don't know how to pray.

PONDER THIS The Greek word for "wiles" is *methodeia*. It's the word we get "methodical" and "methods" from. Satan is methodical. In warfare, he is strategic. He may even step back two steps to go forward three steps. He may let you think you're getting away with your sin. He may even seem to bless you and help you along your way. But don't be fooled. He has made a plan to sabotage your life and your home; the dynamite is in place, the fuse is laid, the match is struck, and Satan is working on you. He is wily, and he is subtle. Apart from the leadership of the Holy Spirit of God, Satan would deceive even the children of God.

- When have you experienced the strategy of Satan working in your life?
- How have you sought to stand guard against these methods of the devil?

PRACTICE THIS Make a list of ways you've seen the schemes of the devil in your life. Write out a few times you relied on God and were enabled to stand firm. Note also any times you relied on another source of strength, or did little to resist, and were deceived by Satan.

29

PRAY OVER THIS

Stand therefore, having girded your waist with truth,
having put on the breastplate of righteousness.
EPHESIANS 6:14

PONDER THIS It is integrity that holds everything else together. Truth and integrity are synonymous. You're to believe the truth, know the truth, love the truth, tell the truth, live the truth, and preach the truth. If you don't, your life is going to come apart. You cannot get into the battle against Satan unless you have the belt of truth. Satan is a liar, and he will come against you with lies. Jesus is the truth. Satan's attack is an untruth. His attack on you is to bring a lack of integrity into your life.

Are you wearing at this moment the belt of truth? Or are you living a lie? If you are not wearing truth, if you do not have integrity in your life—in the big things and in the small things—you are going to lose the battle. It is truth that holds everything together; without truth, everything falls apart.

- How have you seen the reality that everything in your life is held together by truth?
- What is the connection between today's verse and Jesus saying He is the truth in John 14:6?

PRACTICE THIS Identify anywhere you may be living falsely and take steps toward the truth today.

PRAY OVER THIS

For where your treasure is, there your heart will be also.

MATTHEW 6:21

PONDER THIS If you want financial freedom and the windows of Heaven to open, you must return to God. It is not your money that God wants. It is *you* that God wants. God needs nothing. In Psalm 50:12, God says, "If I were hungry, I would not tell you; for the world is Mine, and all its fullness." God loves you. It is not what you have that God wants. God wants you. God says, "Return to Me... and I will return to you" (Zechariah 1:3b). If you give your money without giving yourself, remember the adage, "The gift without the giver is bare." If you think God is trying to somehow get more money out of you, you are so wrong. In today's verse, Jesus said, "where your treasure is, there your heart will be also." God calls you to give your money because it reveals the truth about your heart.

- What connection have you noticed between your own heart and how you spend your money?
- Is there anything God is calling you to change regarding how you spend and/or give your money?

PRACTICE THIS Make steps today toward any financial changes God is calling you to make.

Faith is the link that binds our nothingness to His Almightiness.

ADRIAN ROGERS

PRAY OVER THIS

Keep your heart with all diligence, for out of it spring the issues of life.

PROVERBS 4:23

PONDER THIS If you study the great saints of God, you find out they failed at their point of strength, not weakness. What was Simon Peter's greatest strength? His courage. In Luke 22:33, he said, "Lord, I am ready to go with You, both to prison and to death." He was the one who pulled out a sword and went after the man in the garden of Gethsemane. (See John 18:10.) Peter had physical courage and strength. You wouldn't want to get in a fistfight with Peter. He was a big and tough fisherman. And yet where did he fail? At the point of his courage. Those who identified him as one of Jesus' disciples prompted him to curse and deny the Lord Jesus Christ. (See Matthew 26:74-75.) We must be careful that it is not our own strength we rely on and boast in. Proverbs 4:23 reminds us we must guard our hearts with diligence. If we don't, we'll trust in the place where we will certainly fail.

- Where are you most tempted to rely on your own strength?
- When have you failed because you trusted in your own strength over God's strength?

PRACTICE THIS Write out a list of your personal strengths. Take time to reflect on this list and thank God for the ways He has gifted you, then ask Him to help you guard your heart against trusting in yourself over Him.

2

PRAY OVER THIS

And having shod your feet with the
preparation of the gospel of peace.
EPHESIANS 6:15

PONDER THIS Do you have peace right now? Or are you churning on the inside? If you don't have peace right now, I'll tell you why. It's not because of circumstances. Peace in the Bible is not the subtraction of problems from life. Peace is the addition of power to meet those problems. The Bible says, "Great peace have those who love Your law, and nothing causes them to stumble" (Psalm 119:165). The only way you can live that way is to put on the shoes of peace. Jesus made peace with the blood of His cross, and if you don't have this, you're going to slip and fall in the battle. So many people fall, not because of a lack of integrity or a lack of purity, but because of a lack of tranquility. Something will happen, some sickness, some disappointment, some financial reverse, some wayward child, and they lose their peace. You put on the shoes of peace so you can have a firm place to stand. If you don't, you may slip and you may fall.

- How can you practically "put on the shoes of peace"?
- How has God's peace helped you stand firm in past spiritual battles?

PRACTICE THIS Write out what God is showing you about the truth of your peace in Jesus. Meditate on this throughout the day, seeking to memorize what you've written.

3

PRAY OVER THIS

Praying always with all prayer and supplication
in the Spirit, being watchful to this end with all
perseverance and supplication for all the saints.
EPHESIANS 6:18

PONDER THIS I was in Colorado where I have a friend who helps lead America in the Strategic Space Command. They keep the satellites high above the Earth in synchronous orbit: spy satellites, military satellites, and the space command. I went into a very small room there for a briefing. They asked, "What part of the world do you want to see?" I asked to see Libya. On a big screen, Libya comes up, and we can see the streets and the houses in Libya. You could see the lights that were twinkling at that very moment in all of Libya. They said, "If a missile is fired from here, we'll know it the minute it's fired." Sitting in Colorado, they're watching Libya. It's an amazing thing.

In the same way, we have a Commander who lives above us. And He knows what is going on; He knows what the enemy is doing. Therefore, we must stay in contact with our Space Command, "Praying always with all prayer and supplication in the Spirit."

- How does prayer keep us connected with God who is aware of and in control of everything?
- What practices can you put in place to stay in touch with "space command"?

PRACTICE THIS Write a list of ways you can stay connected with God in prayer each day and week. Put some of these practices into place this week.

4

PRAY OVER THIS

For if we would judge ourselves, we would not be judged.
But when we are judged, we are chastened by the Lord,
that we may not be condemned with the world.

1 CORINTHIANS 11:31-32

PONDER THIS What should you do if there's sin in your life? It may be the sin of coldness. It may be what you'd consider a very small sin. No matter what it is, deal with it immediately. In today's text, we are reminded God is not trying to get even with you. God just wants you to be corrected. When parents punish children, they're not trying to get even with them; they're trying to correct them. There are some children that all you have to do is look at them, and their little hearts will melt. And when a child shows change and no longer shows disobedience, you don't say, "I'm going to punish that child anyway." No. What you want is a change of behavior. Likewise, Paul reminded us, "If we would judge ourselves, we would not be judged." God is not trying to get even with you. God wants to lovingly correct you.

- How does God's correction display His love in our lives?
- When have you experienced the loving correction of God?

PRACTICE THIS Pray and ask God where He wants to correct you now. Respond appropriately.

5

PRAY OVER THIS

But Peter said, "Man, I do not know what you are saying!"
Immediately, while he was still speaking, the rooster crowed.
And the Lord turned and looked at Peter. Then Peter
remembered the word of the Lord, how He had said to him,
"Before the rooster crows, you will deny Me three times."
LUKE 22:60-61

PONDER THIS In today's passage, we should note the precision of the rooster's crow. It is nothing less than a miracle. Two things I want you to try. One, I want you to make a rooster crow. Number two, see if you can keep one from crowing. What our Lord did was keep every rooster in Jerusalem from crowing at all until that exact moment. Immediately after Peter had denied the Lord, the rooster crowed, and the Bible says Peter remembered the word of the Lord. When Peter remembered the word of the Lord, Peter had to remember: God is still in control. Do you know what Peter's problem was, why Peter was filled with fear, and why he denied the Lord? Things had gotten out of hand. His Lord and Master had been betrayed. He had been falsely accused. He was arrested. He had been carried away. He was bound, mocked, and forsaken. Everything was coming apart. Where was God? When the rooster crowed, Peter was reminded that our Lord was still in complete control. Nothing had gotten out of His hand.

- When was a time you recognized God's control in your life?
- How does this give you comfort when things are hard?

PRACTICE THIS Make a list of some hard situations you are facing right now. Make a corresponding list of how confidence in God's control can impact those situations.

6

PONDER THIS Peter was surprised at his failure. Nobody was more surprised than Peter. Peter was not a hypocrite, and he meant it when he said, "Lord, I will go with you to prison and to death." (See Luke 22:33.) Many times, I have done things, I have had thoughts and words erupt out of me, and I have literally been surprised at myself. I would say, "Where did that come from?" Peter did not realize what was in him. But he learned that, despite it all, Jesus, who is in complete control, had never stopped loving him.

There is nothing you can do that will make Him love you more than He loves you. And nothing you can do will stop Him from loving you. You may believe you have to earn His love. No, you don't. The Bible says, "God demonstrates His own love toward us, in that while we were still sinners, Christ died for us" (Romans 5:8). This is the sovereign grace of God. When you fail, don't ever let the devil say, "He is finished with you. He doesn't love you anymore. He has written you off." He has not. He loves you. This Christ of sovereignty is the Christ of sympathy. Thank God for that.

- What tempts you to believe you can make God love you more or less?
- How are you encouraged to know that's not true? How are you challenged?

PRACTICE THIS Journal today about how you would live differently if you truly believed God would never love you more or less than He does now in Jesus.

7

PRAY OVER THIS

Beloved, while I was very diligent to write to you concerning
our common salvation, I found it necessary to write to
you exhorting you to contend earnestly for the faith
which was once for all delivered to the saints.

JUDE 1:3

PONDER THIS Did you know that you can be certain and still be wrong? I was in New Orleans once when I was in seminary. I think I'd been preaching at the rescue mission. I was going back home I thought, but I got confused. I thought I was headed in one direction away from the river, but I kept on ending up at the river. I just knew I was going in the right direction. I turned around again, and the compass in my mind was all confused. Have you ever lost a sense of direction? I was so certain I was going in the right direction, but I kept ending up at the river. Do you know what I did? I read and followed every sign and I got straight home. In life sometimes you will be dead certain you are right, and you are dead wrong. That's the reason we have the Bible and the reason we have the faith that is not only complete but also correct.

- When was a time you were certain about something but turned out to be wrong?
- How are these types of experiences helpful in pointing us back to Christ?

PRACTICE THIS Make a list of several things you are certain about *and* know to be true from the Bible.

PRAY OVER THIS

Jude, a bondservant of Jesus Christ, and brother of
James, to those who are called, sanctified by God
the Father, and preserved in Jesus Christ.

JUDE 1:1

PONDER THIS What reason do we have for security? We have been called according to God's sovereign purpose. The word *sovereign* means "the decree of a king, a ruler against whom there is no rising up." God has a purpose that is seen in that God called you. The word *called* here does not mean call like, I call Paul, and I say, "Hi Paul, come over here." No, the word *called* means "an official summons." You see, your salvation did not begin with you. It began with God. If it began with you, you might lose it, but since it began with God, you can never lose it. The Bible says God is able to finish what He began, and He called you. Had he not called us, none of us would have been here. We must remember that we love Him because He first loved us.

- How does it encourage you to remember that God has called you?
- How does that give you the confidence to pursue the will of God each day?

PRACTICE THIS Make a list of things you know God has called you to do. Pick one of these to do right now.

PRAY OVER THIS

Jude, a bondservant of Jesus Christ, and brother of
James, to those who are called, sanctified by God
the Father, and preserved in Jesus Christ.

JUDE 1:1

PONDER THIS In this verse, many translations use the word *sanctified*. But some Bible scholars tell us that's not the best translation. Rather than sanctified, we might use *beloved*. Sanctified is good, but beloved is better in this particular instance because it tells something of the nature of God's special people. What's the difference? As an example, I love the members of my church, but Joyce is my beloved and there's a difference. She is my love; she is special. Who is the beloved of God? The Lord Jesus. He is God's beloved Son in whom He is well pleased. (See Matthew 3:17.) It is by Jesus that we are accepted, therefore God sees us as He sees Jesus, and God's name for His own dear children is beloved. The word *beloved* is a perfect participle. What does that mean? It means there's a finished action in the past that has a result in the present. It is something that cannot be changed; it is fixed. Because of what was done in the past, we are and will forever be God's beloved.

- How does it encourage you to be reminded that you are the beloved of God?
- How does that change the way you think about how God sees you?

PRACTICE THIS Make a list of what it means for God's people to be His beloved. What promises do you know from the Bible for God's beloved?

10

> ### PRAY OVER THIS
>
> And the glory which You gave Me I have given them, that they may be one just as We are one: I in them, and You in Me; that they may be made perfect in one, and that the world may know that You have sent Me, and have loved them as You have loved Me.
>
> **JOHN 17:22-23**

PONDER THIS How does God love you? He loves you *as* He loved Jesus. The same way. That's too much to take in, isn't it? That's the reason the Apostle John said, "Behold what manner of love the Father has bestowed on us" (1 John 3:1a). John was fishing for an adjective to describe that love, and he couldn't find one. He may have started to say what super love or what fantastic love or what colossal love or what spectacular love. He might have even thought of supercalifragilisticexpialidocious love. He didn't even know how to express it, so he just simply said, "Behold what manner of love." That phrase *manner of love* means love from another, a foreign kind of love, unearthly love, otherworldly love, or nonhuman love. Behold what manner of love that we should be called the children of God!

- How does it affect you to remember God loves His children in the same way He loves Jesus?
- How is this truly a foreign type of love from what people know?

PRACTICE THIS Take time today to share about the otherworldly love of God in Jesus.

PRAY OVER THIS

Beloved, while I was very diligent to write to you concerning
our common salvation, I found it necessary to write to
you exhorting you to contend earnestly for the faith
which was once for all delivered to the saints.

JUDE 1:3

PONDER THIS When I was a little boy, I liked to go to the movies on Saturday afternoons, and we would see *Tarzan*. Tarzan was the hero of every little boy when I was growing up. But there was one time that I was always concerned for Tarzan. Tarzan would be swimming in the river, but over on the shore would be a crocodile. The crocodile would blink his eyes a couple of times and then slide into the water. Tarzan would be swimming along and not know that the crocodile was there, and I would be so frightened because I can't think of anything worse than to be swimming with a crocodile. Somehow Tarzan would always out-swim the crocodile, but what happened in that movie is an illustration of what Jude wrote to warn the Church about. Jude gave a warning that there are certain people who have crept into the Church. (See verse 4.) He described somebody who could slip into the water without even making a ripple. This is very dangerous and sinister. So, Jude wrote this book to sound an alarm.

- What other warnings do you know in the Bible about people who are dangerous to the Church?
- Why do you need to stay alert, or sober, regarding these dangers?

PRACTICE THIS Read John 10 today. How did Jesus talk about others who might try to sneak into the Church?

12

PRAY OVER THIS

For certain men have crept in unnoticed, who long ago
were marked out for this condemnation, ungodly men,
who turn the grace of our God into lewdness and deny
the only Lord God and our Lord Jesus Christ.

JUDE 1:4

PONDER THIS Jude called those who had crept into the church ungodly. What does the word *ungodly* mean? It does not mean they did not mention God or even talk about Him. As a matter of fact, they spoke about God quite freely. He meant a person without reverential awe of God. The basic ingredient missing in the life of an apostate is a fear of God. They talked flippantly and carelessly and blasphemously about holy things. In verse 8, we see the same idea, "Likewise also these dreamers defile the flesh, reject authority, and speak evil of dignitaries." Their mouths and their tongues ran up and down through the land. There was no fear of God before their eyes, and they feared not to mock and speak of holy things. They took things upon their lips that ought to make us tremble. They lacked reverence.

- How does today's devotion give you a new way of thinking about the meaning of ungodliness?
- What are some ways you might tread close to ungodliness in your own life?

PRACTICE THIS Take time in prayer today to ask God to show you where you have been flippant with the things that belong to Him. Confess what you sense and ask Him to lead you in holiness.

PRAY OVER THIS

Likewise also these dreamers defile the flesh, reject
authority, and speak evil of dignitaries.

JUDE 1:8

PONDER THIS In today's verse, Jude called the apostates dreamers. He was talking about conjecture, imagination, something dreamed up. In the Book of Jude, verse 3, the Bible says we should "contend earnestly for the faith which was once for all delivered to the saints." Jude was talking about God's Word. There is a battle for the Bible. There is a fight for the faith. We should earnestly contend for the faith. This means we must refute the "dreams" or the imaginations of men because they are not something God has revealed. This is something people have dreamed up—their own subjective religion. They have their own existential ideas rather than the revealed Word of God.

- How has today's devotion reminded you of the importance of knowing and contending for the truth of the Bible?
- What are some ways we contend for the truth of the Bible? How does the Bible defend itself?

PRACTICE THIS Write out as many ways you can think of that the Bible defends itself. How does this give you further confidence in God's Word?

14

PRAY OVER THIS

Woe to them! For they have gone in the way of
Cain, have run greedily in the error of Balaam for
profit, and perished in the rebellion of Korah.

JUDE 1:11

PONDER THIS There are only two religions in the world—the true and the false. That's all. We like to divide religions up and say there's Confucianism, Buddhism, Islam, and all these other different kinds of religions. And then we take Christianity and subdivide it. We say there are Baptist, Methodist, Presbyterian, Episcopalian, Catholic, and so forth. But there are only two religions: the true and the false. One is the way of Cain and the other is the way of the cross. What is the way of Cain? The way of Cain is religion without the blood sacrifice and without the atonement. You may say, "Pastor, we don't have to worry about that. We hear about the blood very often." If so, thank God for a church that's based on the Book, the blood, and the blessed hope.

- How do you respond to the idea that there are only two religions?
- What are some ways you might be distracted from the truth of the Bible?

PRACTICE THIS Journal today about traits of the truth of Christ and traits of every other belief system. How do these contrast?

PRAY OVER THIS

Jesus said to him, "I am the way, the truth, and the life.
No one comes to the Father except through Me."

JOHN 14:6

PONDER THIS Years ago, I heard a story of a man who applied for a job as a riverboat pilot on the Mississippi. They said, "Can you run a riverboat?" He said, "Of course, I can." They asked, "Can you handle the business affairs and stay in command?" He said, "Of course, I can." They asked, "One other thing, do you know where all the sandbars are?" He said, "No, I don't." They asked, "Do you know where the sunken rocks are?" He said, "No, I don't." They asked, "Do you know where all the hidden logs are?" He said, "No, I don't." They asked, "Well, how do you ever expect to be a riverboat pilot?" He said, "I know where the channel is." Amen.

Friend, listen. You'd better know where the channel is. It's one thing to know about the logs and the sandbars, but it's another thing to know where the channel is. And you'd better know the Lord Jesus Christ as your personal Savior. The only way you can guarantee that you will not become an apostate and know you're saved and you're going to Heaven is to receive Christ as your personal Savior and Lord.

- How do the troubles of life tempt you to take your gaze off Christ?
- How does keeping our focus on Christ keep us steady no matter what troubles we face?

PRACTICE THIS What is one action you can take to keep your focus on Christ today? Take this step.

PONDER THIS Jude said the apostate rejects authority or despises dominion (v. 8, KJV). What did he mean by dominion? Who or what is dominion? Look in verse 25: "To God our Savior, who alone is wise, be glory and majesty, dominion and power, both now and forever. Amen." When apostates despise dominion, they despise the only wise God who alone has that dominion. An apostate literally hates God. Look in the last part of verse 4 in chapter 1: they "deny the only Lord God and our Lord Jesus Christ." As a reminder, these are not deniers of God outside the church. These are deniers of God inside the church. These are people who despise dominion and sit on church pews, teach in seminaries, and teach in Bible colleges. They are rebels at heart. They do not want anybody to box them in. Their battle cry is freedom. They don't want anybody to tell them what they must believe or how they must behave.

- How would you explain what it means to despise dominion?
- What are some ways you might be tempted to do this? How can you guard against it?

PRACTICE THIS Make a list of ways God exercises His dominion in the world. Make notes of ways you can submit to and praise His dominion in these areas.

Likewise also these dreamers defile the flesh, reject
authority, and speak evil of dignitaries.

JUDE 1:8

PONDER THIS The word *dignitaries* is the word we get *doxology* from. It literally means "glories, glorious things, and majesties." Jude was saying there is nothing too glorious or too holy that the apostate will not ridicule. Apostates receive the truth, refuse the truth, or repudiate the truth, and then they ridicule the truth. They have a way of speaking evil of glorious things. Most likely, Jude was writing about people there who were ridiculing and blaspheming the doctrine of the angels. (See Jude 1:9.) But you'll find this about the apostates, they have quick lips. They know how to ridicule holy things and are not ashamed to do so. There's nothing too sacred or too holy for them to revile and ridicule. And they don't do so from outside the church, they do it from inside the church.

- Why is it important that we have reverence for the holy things of God?
- How is it a slippery slope when we are not careful about this?

PRACTICE THIS Write down as many holy things of God you can think of that deserve our reverence and awe.

18

PRAY OVER THIS

These are spots in your love feasts, while they feast
with you without fear, serving only themselves.

JUDE 1:12A

PONDER THIS The Early Church would meet together for an agape feast, very much like churches do today. Don't think that's unspiritual for a church to come together for a fellowship dinner. The Early Church did it many, many times. They would get together for a great feast. They were having a wonderful time, and God's love boat was just sailing along. What wonderful fellowship, what love, and everything seemed to be so blessed. But then suddenly everything seems to come to a grinding halt and there is a horrible, rending sound, and the old ship of Zion is wounded in her side. What happened? Some devilish apostate had become a rock in the river of love to try to destroy the fellowship of God. I want to tell you, dear friend, that the devil hates the fellowship of God's Church. He hates the love we have. He hates the unity we have. And he will do, if he can, the worst thing that he could by putting a rock in the river of love so that our boat might run aground. How dangerous is apostasy? It causes division and can ruin the very fellowship of God's Church.

- What are some rocks in the river of Christian fellowship that threaten to wreck and divide today?
- How does unity in Jesus help us avoid these divisions?

PRACTICE THIS Is there anyone you have divided with over a secondary matter? Take steps toward reconciliation as you are able today.

19

PRAY OVER THIS

Raging waves of the sea, foaming up their own shame; wandering stars for whom is reserved the blackness of darkness forever.

PONDER THIS Jude described the actions of the apostate as belching out from the deep recesses, the murky caverns, of his heart, of his soul, in his shame. These people are like raging waves of the sea, deeply disturbed in the heart. They're not at peace and don't want you to be at peace either. That's the reason apostates are so dangerous, and the world is full of them. I have had seminarians and college buddies who became apostates. They studied for the ministry with me. They sat in the same classes with me. These men claimed to believe the truth. But they veered into apostasy. What they once believed, they rejected. And once they rejected, they ridiculed. I watched them, one after another, go down into debauchery of all kinds. There's something about apostasy, dear friend, that is different from most other sins. This is what Jude was saying. They are like raging waves of the sea. There's distress. There's a disquieting in the heart of apostates. And before long they will spew out the foam of their shame. Apostates are disturbed like wild waves.

- Contrast this description of the apostate person with those who are in Christ in Philippians 4:7.
- Why are those who reject God unable to truly be at peace?

PRACTICE THIS Write out a list of ways God gives you peace in Jesus.

20

PRAY OVER THIS

Now Enoch, the seventh from Adam, prophesied
about these men also, saying, "Behold, the Lord
comes with ten thousands of His saints."

JUDE 1:14

PONDER THIS The new birth is mentioned nine times in the Bible. Baptism is mentioned 20 times in the Bible. Repentance is mentioned about 70 times in the Bible. But more than 380 verses in the Bible speak clearly about the Second Coming of Jesus Christ. One verse out of every 25 points with an eager finger to the Second Coming of Jesus Christ. The Early Church was taken up in thinking about the Second Coming of Jesus Christ.

Alexander McClaren said those in the Early Church did not think primarily about death or about Heaven, but about the Second Coming of Jesus Christ. He said they were not looking for a cleft in the ground called a grave, they were looking for a cleft in the sky called glory. They were not looking for the undertaker, they were looking for the "upper-taker." And we ought to be looking for the Second Coming of our Lord and Savior Jesus Christ in the same way.

- How often do you think about the Second Coming of Christ?
- What might help you to think about Christ's return more?

PRACTICE THIS Spend some time researching various passages that refer to the Second Coming of Christ. Meditate on these truths throughout the day today.

PRAY OVER THIS

I tell you, in that night there will be two men in one bed: the one will be taken and the other will be left. Two women will be grinding together: the one will be taken and the other left. Two men will be in the field: the one will be taken and the other left.

LUKE 17:34-36

PONDER THIS In Luke 17:34-36, Jesus said, "I tell you, in that night there will be two [people] in one bed: the one will be taken and the other will be left. Two women will be grinding together: the one will be taken and the other left. Two men will be in the field: the one will be taken and the other left." Now that's interesting. Some are sleeping and some are working. In part of the world, it will be day, and part of the world will be dark when Jesus comes. One will be taken and the other left. What a marvelous thing it's going to be. And if Jesus were to come on a Sunday morning, many of us would look so sanctified. But not everybody is saved. One will be taken and the other left. Some are going to be swept up to glory and others would be left. Are you ready for that reality today?

- How can a person be ready for Jesus' return?
- How does regularly thinking about the return of Jesus give us the urgency to be ready?

PRACTICE THIS Take time in prayer today to ask God if you are ready for the return of Christ. Respond as He calls you.

PRAY OVER THIS

But you, beloved, remember the words which were spoken
before by the apostles of our Lord Jesus Christ.

JUDE 1:17

PONDER THIS When you see people defying God blatantly, you may just want to throw up your hands and wonder, "Is the Bible the Word of God after all?" Friend, apostasy proves the Bible is the Word of God. You need to understand that. It's precisely as God said it would be. God is not up in Heaven wringing His hands. And you don't need to be overwhelmed and bent out of joint like something has suddenly gone awry. Everything is on schedule. The Word of God stands.

That's what Jude was saying to these people: "Now, beloved, remember the words of the Apostles. It is exactly as they told you it would be." And it is so important that we remember this, that there are going to be these apostates in the last days.

- Where do you typically turn when you feel overwhelmed by the brokenness of the world?
- What promises of God can encourage you in these times?

PRACTICE THIS Make a list of promises of God that might encourage you when life is overwhelming. Keep this somewhere that you can review, and contemplate frequently.

PRAY OVER THIS

And God saw that the wickedness of man was great
in the earth, and that every imagination of the
thoughts of his heart was only evil continually.
GENESIS 6:5 (KJV)

PONDER THIS The word *imagination* is a very interesting word in this verse. John Phillips says the word *imagination* comes from a Hebrew root word that means "to make something or fashion something as a potter would fashion a vessel." Don't get the idea that in that day men were just having bad thoughts or that they were daydreaming. That's not what the word *imagination* means. It means they had carefully crafted, wicked, ungodly philosophies. God had given them His Word, but rather than clinging to the Word of God, they clung to these thoughts, these philosophies, and these theologies that they had fashioned. The days of Enoch were days of anarchy. They were days of apostasy. But they were primarily days of apathy.

- How might people craft ungodly thoughts today?
- How can we be careful that we craft godly thoughts instead?

PRACTICE THIS Write out an assessment of how you spend your time. Consider how the way you spend your time leads you to craft certain thoughts. What needs to change?

24

PRAY OVER THIS

The Lord is not slack concerning His promise, as some count slackness, but is longsuffering toward us, not willing that any should perish but that all should come to repentance.

2 PETER 3:9

PONDER THIS Why did Methuselah live so long? (See Genesis 5:27.) Methuselah represented the mercy of God. God knew that after Methuselah's death, the flood would come. The flood was due, and the judgment of God was smoldering. People deserved to be judged, but God kept pushing the judgment day back. God gave them another year. He gave them another month. He gave them another week. He gave them another day. He gave them another hour. But one day, Methuselah died, and one of these days our figurative Methuselah will die. And mercy will give way to judgment.

In Peter's time, there were people saying, "Where is the promise of His coming? For since the fathers fell asleep, all things continue as they were from the beginning of creation" (2 Peter 3:4). But Peter made it clear, "The Lord is not slack concerning His promise, as some count slackness, but is longsuffering toward us, not willing that any should perish but that all should come to repentance" (2 Peter 3:9).

- How does it change your perspective on the state of the world to remember that God is showing mercy by delaying the Second Coming of Jesus?
- How should this truth give us a sense of urgency?

PRACTICE THIS Take time today to share with someone about the mercy of God.

25

PRAY OVER THIS

Keep yourselves in the love of God, looking for the
mercy of our Lord Jesus Christ unto eternal life.

JUDE 1:21

PONDER THIS To "keep yourself in the love of God" doesn't mean God is not loving you. Consider the prodigal son. When he left the father's house to go to the far country and was down there in the hog pen, did the father still love him? Yes, the father still loved him. But he left the environment of the love of God. He did not enjoy the protection of the father's house, the provision of the father's house, and the feast of the father's house. The father was still loving him, but he did not keep himself in the love of his father. Likewise, we are called to stay in the Father's love.

In these last days, if you are going to survive the apostasy, the safe place is in the love of God. Keep yourselves in the love of God. We are to bask in the love of God. We are to keep ourselves in the love of God. We are not trying to keep God loving us any more than we are trying to keep the sun shining. But we are to stay in that environment. We are to stay in the love of God.

- What are some ways we "keep ourselves in the love of God"?
- What are some ways we go out from the love of God?

PRACTICE THIS Read the story of the prodigal son in Luke 15. Consider the reality that the father never stopped loving his son, but the son did remove himself from the father's love.

PRAY OVER THIS

But others save with fear, pulling them out of the fire,
hating even the garment defiled by the flesh.

JUDE 1:23

PONDER THIS Once I heard of a painting of a ship that was sinking. The ship had already gone down, the lifeboats were out on the water, and the people were in the water. One lifeboat had a man leaning over the railing of the boat extending his hand to one of the people in the water.

A man in the water was lifting his hand up. And their hands were about to meet. A little boy came in and he looked at that picture. Of course, the picture was meant to illustrate the rescue of the perishing and care for the dying. The little boy studied that picture for a while and then he asked, "Daddy, is that man trying to save those people, or is he just shaking hands with them?"

Every Christian must ask that question of themselves. Are we really endeavoring to bring people to Jesus Christ? Bringing people to Jesus Christ is the principal duty of every Christian. Jesus Christ did not come first as a great teacher or a great healer. The Bible tells us why He came in Luke 19:10, "For the Son of Man has come to seek and to save that which was lost."

- How are you joining the rescue mission of Jesus?
- How can you know if you are rescuing people or just shaking their hands?

PRACTICE THIS Make a list of people God has put on your heart that need to know Him. Spend time praying for them today and take any opportunity to connect with them this week.

PRAY OVER THIS

For the Son of Man has come to seek and to save that which was lost.

LUKE 19:10

PONDER THIS I heard of a tragic event. A father went to the hospital to pick up his newborn baby and wife. He left the automobile running with the keys in the car, and their three-year-old in the back seat. Then, someone came to steal the car; later, they found the car abandoned, but they couldn't find the boy, so people set out to find him. One man who joined the hunt thought, "Maybe the little boy just got out of the car and is somewhere in the vicinity of where the car was abandoned." He began to shine a flashlight up and down alleys. There was an old house with a swing and on the swing were some newspapers. He shined the light on the newspapers and saw some movement.

He cried out, "Billy! Billy!" Billy said, "Is that you, Daddy?" And this man praised the name of God. He said, "No, Billy, I'm not your daddy, but I'm here to take you to your daddy." Friend, that's the job of the church—to rescue the perishing, to seek them out, to find them, to bring them to Him. For this cause, Jesus came into the world.

- Who pointed you to God as your Father?
- What are some ways we point others in His direction?

PRACTICE THIS Take time today to point someone else toward God.

28

PRAY OVER THIS

Do not lay up for yourselves treasures on earth, where moth
and rust destroy and where thieves break in and steal; but lay
up for yourselves treasures in heaven, where neither moth nor
rust destroys and where thieves do not break in and steal.

MATTHEW 6:19-20

PONDER THIS Let's suppose you're on a luxurious cruise ship and everything is beautiful. You say, "This is the best vacation of my life." Then the captain says, "I have an announcement. We're going to continue the entertainment. The cooks are going to do an even better job. The crew is going all out to make you comfortable." Then he says, "But there has been one change in plans. We're not going to sail to any one port. Instead, we're going to go out in the middle of the ocean and sail around in circles until we run out of food, fuel, and water. When we do, we're going to empty the ship and sink it."

At that moment, no matter how much you're enjoying the cruise, it doesn't seem to be quite as good, does it? When you realize you're going around in a meaningless circle, it doesn't matter how beautiful the weather is. It is a hopeless, joyless matter. In the same way, the joy of this present life will not diminish the fact there is no hope for the future for those outside of Christ. We should seek to meet people's temporal needs as we are able, but first and foremost, we must point them to Christ. Apart from Him, there is no hope.

- How are you tempted to focus on current comforts and pleasures over the future reality of life eternal with God?
- Who do you know who needs to hear about the hope of Christ today?

PRACTICE THIS Take time to share with the person you identified about the hope of Jesus.

PRAY OVER THIS

Now to Him who is able to keep you from stumbling, and to present
you faultless before the presence of His glory with exceeding joy.

JUDE 1:24

PONDER THIS Jude began and ended this book by talking about the eternal
security of the believer. If he didn't do this, when you read what's in between,
you may start thinking that Jude was talking about people who had lost their
salvation. An apostate is not somebody who has lost his or her salvation. An
apostate is someone who has received the truth, rejected the truth, ridicules
the truth, and literally tries to replace the truth. But this person has never
been saved. He or she is like Judas, who was never born again. But people who
are truly born again, true children of God, can never again be lost souls—not
because they hold onto God, but because God holds onto them.

- How does it encourage you to remember that it is God who keeps
  you faithful and not your own effort?
- How does this reality provide more motivation for faithfulness to
  God?

PRACTICE THIS Write out a list of specific ways God has held onto you and
refused to let you go throughout your life.

30

PRAY OVER THIS

I in them, and You in Me; that they may be made perfect
in one, and that the world may know that You have sent
Me, and have loved them as You have loved Me.

JOHN 17:23

PONDER THIS How much does God love you? God loves you as much as He loves His Son, Jesus Christ. That's hard for me to take in. When the Apostle John was speaking about this love he said, "Behold what manner of love the Father has bestowed on us, that we should be called children of God" (1 John 3:1a)! Do you know why John said, "What manner of love"? It seems like he was grasping for an adjective suitable to use. What colossal love, what stupendous love, what...I just can't even think of a word. He just finally had to say, "What manner of love the Father has bestowed on us, that we should be called children of God." God loves you dear friend, and you are secure in God's sovereign love.

- How hard is it for you to believe God loves you as a father loves a child?
- What makes this difficult? What helps you believe this?

PRACTICE THIS Make a list of various passages that describe the love of God for His people, starting with the two verses in today's devotion.

PRAY OVER THIS

Moreover whom He predestined, these He also
called; whom He called, these He also justified; and
whom He justified, these He also glorified.

ROMANS 8:30

PONDER THIS There is an eternal, golden chain of redemption that cannot be broken. God predestined you, then God called you, then God justified you, and then God glorified you. You see, salvation is not your work, it is God's work, and that's the reason the Apostle Paul said he was "confident of this very thing, that He who has begun a good work in you will complete it until the day of Jesus Christ" (Philippians 1:6). This should cause us to say amen. What has been decreed by Heaven cannot be annulled by Hell. What has been settled in eternity cannot be undone in time. We were in the heart and mind of God before He spun this world into space. And we are the ones He has called.

- How would you live differently today if you really believed you were this secure in God's hand?
- What usually keeps you from believing this?

PRACTICE THIS Read Romans 8:31-38 for further reflection on God's matchless love for His people.

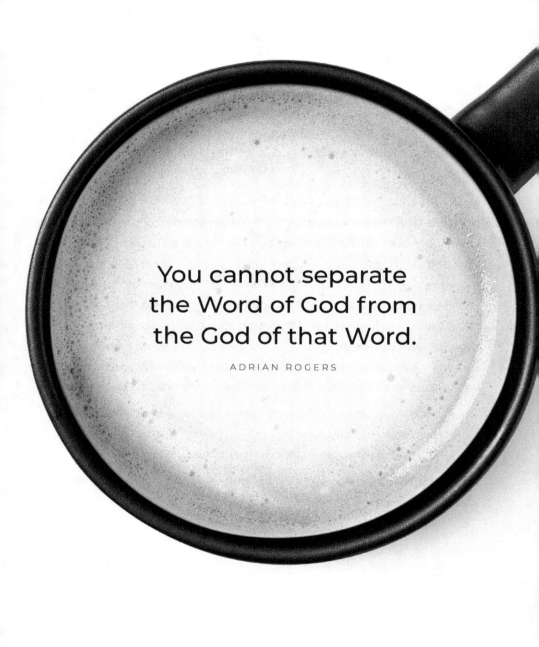

You cannot separate
the Word of God from
the God of that Word.

ADRIAN ROGERS

PRAY OVER THIS

Peter was therefore kept in prison, but constant prayer
was offered to God for him by the church.

ACTS 12:5

PONDER THIS What were the disciples going to do? How were they going to get Peter out of prison? Were they going to organize a mob and storm the prison? Not a chance. Were they going to put some petitions up? Were they going to say, "We are influential citizens in this city, and we demand that you release Simon Peter"? They had no influence. Were they going to take a collection to get a lot of money to go in and bribe Herod? They didn't have any money. What they had, they had distributed to feed the poor and to take care of those who were in distress at that time.

I'll tell you what they were going to do. They were going to pray. The intellectuals would sneer and say, "Look at these silly people down on their knees in prayer." I'll tell you one person who didn't sneer: the devil. It has well been said that Satan trembles when he sees the weakest saint upon his knees. There is an animal named the gnu, and when he's attacked, he drops to his knees. Oh, that the Church could learn the same thing. Every other door was closed, but there was one that was open, and it went straight up. They could pray.

- How quickly do you turn to prayer in times of crisis?
- What other "solutions" do you typically turn to before prayer?

PRACTICE THIS Set aside time today to pray about the most pressing issues in your life.

2

PRAY OVER THIS

Now faith is the substance of things hoped
for, the evidence of things not seen.
HEBREWS 11:1

PONDER THIS The word *hope* does not mean "a fond desire." It means a glorious assurance based on the Word of God. We use the word *hope* today to mean something similar to the word *wish*. We hope something will happen, but we also don't want to get our hopes too high so that we won't be overly disappointed. We would like for something to happen, but it isn't sure. That isn't what the word *hope* means in the Bible. The Second Coming of Jesus is called "the blessed hope." (See Titus 2:13.) How do we know that Jesus is coming again? We have God's promise. The Lord Jesus said, "If I go…I will come again" (John 14:3). He said, "I will!" Therefore, we have this hope like an anchor. You don't put an anchor in a cloud bank. The Bible calls hope the "anchor of the soul" (Hebrews 6:19)! An anchor holds firm and can be trusted in every season. This is the hope we have in Jesus.

- How much trust do you put in the promises of the Bible?
- How has today's devotion changed the way you think about hope?

PRACTICE THIS Write out a list of things you are hoping for. Make a corresponding list of promises from the Bible that you can have certain hope in.

PRAY OVER THIS

So then faith comes by hearing, and hearing by the word of God.
ROMANS 10:17

PONDER THIS If you've studied church history, you've likely heard the name Dwight L. Moody. He was not a literate man. He was basically uneducated. But his biographer said that he took two continents and shook them for God. Moody felt that he needed faith. And he kept praying for faith, but faith didn't seem to come. And then he read Romans 10:17: "So then faith comes by hearing, and hearing by the word of God." At that, Moody stopped praying for faith and began to saturate himself in the Bible. And there was the faith. Faith is the by-product of hearing from God. You can't have faith if you're merely guessing at the will of God. You can't have faith if you're just following a hunch. But when you say, "God said it, I believe it," there's the faith.

- How does today's verse change the way you think about faith?
- Where do you feel like you need faith right now?

PRACTICE THIS Write out several promises of God that you can place faith in.

4

> **PRAY OVER THIS**
>
> God sets the solitary in families; He brings out those who are
> bound into prosperity; But the rebellious dwell in a dry land.
>
> **PSALM 68:6**

PONDER THIS The most powerful and influential people on Earth do not occupy the houses of elected office, run industry, or handle the business of Wall Street. The most powerful and influential people on Earth are parents of faith. Amram and Jochebed's claim to fame is that they raised a child whose name was Moses, who literally changed the world. I cannot overestimate the importance of family. We've been told that it takes a village to raise a child. That's backward. It takes a family to raise a child, and families change the village. It begins with parents. Family is the primary classroom. The Bible says in Psalm 68:6 that God sets the solitary in families. It's no wonder the devil has unleashed all the artillery of Hell against the family.

- What are some things you learned about faith from your family?
- How are you seeking to encourage others in the faith in your family?

PRACTICE THIS If there are ways your family members encouraged you in the faith, reach out and share that with them today.

5

PRAY OVER THIS

Train up a child in the way he should go, and
when he is old he will not depart from it.
PROVERBS 22:6

PONDER THIS Are you training your children? The entry for the word *train* in the dictionary says this: to prepare for a contest, to instruct by exercise, to drill, to form to a proper shape, to discipline for use. You don't learn how to play basketball by reading a book. You are trained. You are coached. Likewise, you have to train and coach your children. You have to pray. You have to teach. You have to plead. You have to show by example. Do you have your children in a Bible-believing church? Do you have them in Sunday School under a Christian teacher? Are you training in the home by precept and by example? We're to train. If you teach a child and that's all you do, you'll teach him or her one thing, but somebody else can come along and teach them something else. But when you train, they get something through the pores of their skin into their very psyche. There's a difference between teaching and training.

- What are some ways you were trained by your parents or that you seek to train your children now?
- What are some ways we must continue to train ourselves as adults?

PRACTICE THIS Write out a list of disciplines you want to develop in your life and the lives of your children, then make a plan for how you will begin developing those disciplines.

PRAY OVER THIS

But that no one is justified by the law in the sight of
God is evident, for "the just shall live by faith."
GALATIANS 3:11

PONDER THIS Martin Luther, who led the Protestant Reformation, had a dramatic experience. In 1517, he was saved. He saw the Word of God, he understood it—that salvation is a gift that you receive by faith—and he received Christ. He was born again, even though he had been a priest. One day not long after, he had a bout with the devil, and the devil said to him, "Oh, you say you're a Christian. Do you feel your sin is forgiven?" Luther said, "No, I know my sin is forgiven because the Bible says so." Luther didn't rely on his feelings but on the unchanging Word of God. Likewise, you had better get out of the realm of emotion and get your faith in the unbreakable promises of God and the unshakeable power of God.

- Do you rely more on your feelings or on the Word of God to determine your standing with Him?
- How does the Word of God encourage you when you have doubts about your relationship with Him?

PRACTICE THIS Take time today to identify several passages that can serve as encouragement when your emotions lead you away from God.

PRAY OVER THIS

O Death, where is your sting? O Hades, where is your victory?
1 CORINTHIANS 15:55

PONDER THIS I have no fear of death. You may say, "You're lying." I am not; God is my witness. I don't look forward to the act of dying, but I have no fear of death, none.

There was a time when death laid his bony hands on the Lord Jesus Christ, drug Him into a dungeon, and put Him on a cold slab. Jesus was bound with the chains of death. One day passed. Two days passed. Three days passed. And death, that old monarch of terrors, laughed his hoarse laugh and clapped his bony hands saying, "I have Him." But on the third day, Jesus broke those chains and rose. A look of fear came over the face of death himself. Jesus reached up, pulled death from his throne, and threw him to the dungeon floor. The crown rolled off death's head. Jesus reached in and pulled the sting out of death, put his heel on the neck of death, put the crown on His head, and walked out of that tomb risen, living, and victorious as Savior. Because He lives, we live with Him. We no longer have to fear death. We have a Savior. Faith relies on the unbreakable promises of God. Faith recognizes the unshakeable power of God. And faith rests in the unmistakable peace of God.

- Do you have a fear of death?
- How does Jesus speak to that fear? If you have not trusted Him for salvation, how is He speaking to you today?

PRACTICE THIS Read 1 Corinthians 15 to be reminded how Jesus has defeated death.

8

> **PRAY OVER THIS**
>
> Now the blood shall be a sign for you on the houses where you
> are. And when I see the blood, I will pass over you; and the plague
> shall not be on you to destroy you when I strike the land of Egypt.
>
> **EXODUS 12:13**

PONDER THIS In the Passover, God was going to use a lamb to deliver His people. His people were in the land of Egypt. In the Bible, Egypt stands for bondage. It stands for the world, the flesh, and the devil. Pharaoh is a type, a picture, and an illustration of the devil. Now Pharaoh had a crown, and on his crown was a serpent. Look at some of those ancient Egyptian pictures and you'll see a serpent coiled up there on his crown. That's the symbol of Egypt.

On one side, you have the serpent. On the other, you have the lamb. But it's the lamb who was going to defeat the serpent. That's what Passover was all about. God was going to bring His people from the land of bondage, from the land of wickedness, from the land of sin, and from the land of cruelty. He was going to deliver them, and He would do it with a Passover lamb.

- The image of the lamb defeating the serpent illustrates the "upside-down" nature of God's kingdom. What other biblical examples can you think of that illustrate this?
- How has God brought you from the land of bondage through Jesus, the Lamb of God?

PRACTICE THIS Spend time in prayer today, thanking God for Jesus, the Lamb who saves God's people from bondage.

This month shall be your beginning of months; it
shall be the first month of the year to you.
EXODUS 12:2

PONDER THIS I performed a wedding for a young man, and he was frightened to death. After they said, "I do," he said, "Pastor, is it all over?" I said, "No, son, it's just beginning." When you give your heart to Jesus and you feed on the Lamb, you do it with your loins girded, your shoes on your feet, and your staff in your hand. (See Exodus 12:11.) You are getting ready to serve the Lord. And you become a new creature. Exodus 12:2 says: "This month shall be your beginning of months; it shall be the first month of the year to you." When you give your heart to Jesus, it's a brand-new day. You're all tomorrows; you're no yesterdays. It's the first day of the rest of your life when you get saved and feed upon the Lamb.

- How has Jesus given you a new start?
- How has it changed your life to view your future with Jesus as a "brand-new day"?

PRACTICE THIS Where do you need a fresh start? Journal about the things you need to leave behind to follow Jesus fully.

PRAY OVER THIS

By faith the walls of Jericho fell down after
they were encircled for seven days.
HEBREWS 11:30

PONDER THIS Many people are problem conscious. All they see is the problem. They see Jericho. Many of us need to take our eyes off Jericho and put them on Jesus. Here is the way of faith. Don't dwell on your problems, dwell on your Lord. Be looking to Jesus, the author and finisher of your faith. Catch a vision of Him. Worship Him. Bow before Him and you'll find your faith growing. Learn to glance at your problems and to gaze at your Lord. Keep your eyes on Him. Don't go around being negative or with a problem complex. Go around with your eyes, your hopes, and your affections fastened upon the Lord Jesus Christ. Set your affections on the things above. Put your eyes upon the Lord and your faith will begin to grow.

- Are you more prone to focus on your problems or on your Lord?
- What habits can you develop to focus more on Jesus than on your problems?

PRACTICE THIS Take action today. Begin practicing some of the habits you identified to help you focus more on Jesus than on your problems.

PRAY OVER THIS

Now Joshua the son of Nun sent out two men from
Acacia Grove to spy secretly, saying, "Go, view the land,
especially Jericho." So they went, and came to the house
of a harlot named Rahab, and lodged there.

JOSHUA 2:1

PONDER THIS Joshua told the men, "Go view the land," and they came to a particular house. Here's the question I have for you: Was that by mere chance? Was that a coincidence? Was it happenstance? No, it was the will of God and not mere chance that brought these men to the house of Rahab; it was the providence of God.

Let me tell you how the providence of God works. God works on both sides of the equation. God will find a person whose heart is tender, a person who wants to know Him, a person under conviction, a person seeking Him. And God will take a witness, a messenger, a soul-winner, and work in that person's heart as well. And then God gets the two together. We call that divine providence. The Bible is full of those kinds of stories.

- Think of a time during which you experienced the providence of God?
- How might God be prompting you now to be used by Him in the life of another?

PRACTICE THIS Ask God how He is calling you to act for Him today and then obey what He reveals to you.

12

PRAY OVER THIS

By faith the harlot Rahab did not perish with those who did
not believe, when she had received the spies with peace.

HEBREWS 11:31

PONDER THIS The whole Bible is about a blood sacrifice. You cut this blessed book anywhere, and it will bleed. The blood of Jesus seems to stain every page. You can begin with Abel's lamb, go right on through to Noah's sacrifice to Abraham's ram on Mount Moriah, then to all the smoking sacrifices on every Jewish altar till finally, you come to Calvary where the Lord Jesus Christ hung in agony and blood. All of it is saying, "When I see the blood, I will pass over you" (Exodus 12:13). The Bible says in Hebrews 11:31 that Rahab was delivered from destruction. This was because of the scarlet cord that hung in her window, representing the sacrifice of blood (Joshua 2:18). She did not perish. This reminds us of John 3:16: "For God so loved the world, that he gave his only begotten Son, that whosoever believeth in him should not perish." And if you've trusted in the blood of Jesus, neither will you.

- How does it build your faith to see the way the Bible points over and over again to the sacrifice of Jesus?
- Who do you need to tell about the sacrifice of Jesus?

PRACTICE THIS Share with someone today about the sacrifice of Jesus.

PRAY OVER THIS

And as they were eating, Jesus took bread, blessed and broke it,
and gave it to the disciples and said, "Take, eat; this is My body."

MATTHEW 26:26

PONDER THIS As Jewish families observed Passover through the centuries, they developed a tradition. They would take a bag called a Matzah Tash with three sections in it—top, middle, and bottom. In the middle section would be a piece of bread. At Passover, the father would reach into the middle section, pull out the piece of bread, break it, and give it to all of those around. It's still done in Seder suppers today. At the Last Supper, Jesus reached in and took that middle piece of unleavened bread. And Jesus said, "This is my body." He took that middle piece, broke it, and distributed it. When Jesus blessed that bread, not only was He showing His death by breaking the bread, but He was also showing His resurrection.

Do you know what is said when the bread is taken out at Passover? Here it is: "Blessed art thou, O Lord, our God, King of the universe, who bringeth forth bread from the earth." Jesus was prophesying His resurrection. He was the bread that would be broken and come from the earth. "This is my body." From the ground, it would be raised.

- How does it build your faith to see the connection to Jesus in ancient practices such as the Passover meal?
- How does it impact your daily life to regularly reflect on the resurrection?

PRACTICE THIS Reflect on Matthew 26:26-29, contemplating the truth of Jesus' body broken for you and His blood poured out for you.

PRAY OVER THIS

You shall eat nothing leavened; in all your
dwellings you shall eat unleavened bread.
EXODUS 12:20

PONDER THIS During the Jewish Passover meal, they have a little game. The father will take some crumbs of leavened bread, along with some cookies or cake, and put it on the mantle, on the bookshelf, or under the couch. Then, the little kids will burst into the room to try to find a crumb of leaven in the house. And they say, "Papa, papa, there's some leavened bread."

Their father comes in with a feather and a wooden spoon, gets it, carries it to the fire, and throws it in. Why? Because there's to be no leaven in the house when you take the Passover. What is God saying to us? Leaven is symbolic of sin. When we come to the Lord's Table, how do we come? With clean hearts—no unconfessed or unrepented sin—because we are celebrating the Lord's Passover. We're celebrating what the spotless, sinless Son of God did for us. When we come to the Lord's Table, we're not coming to mourn a corpse; we're coming to hail a conqueror.

- What does it look like to come to the Lord's Supper with a clean heart?
- Where is God calling you to confess any sin before Him today?

PRACTICE THIS Set aside time to prayerfully confess any sin in your life today.

PRAY OVER THIS

Gideon said to Him, "O my lord, if the LORD is with us, why then has all this happened to us? And where are all His miracles which our fathers told us about, saying, 'Did not the LORD bring us up from Egypt?' But now the LORD has forsaken us and delivered us into the hands of the Midianites."

JUDGES 6:13

PONDER THIS Some of us feel like Gideon—like the Lord has stopped working and there is no hope for the world. But there's not one shred of Scripture that says we cannot have a mighty revival in the day and age in which we live. Most of us don't believe that. You talk about revival, and all people do is give a sympathetic smile. They're simply waiting for Jesus Christ to get here. I'm here to tell you there has never been a greater day, a greater age, to live and to preach the glorious Gospel of Jesus Christ. And God wants you, sir; you, madam. God wants you to be in the middle of it. God has a mighty plan for you. And we need to stop moaning, groaning, and complaining about living in the last days.

- How difficult is it for you to believe God could move in a mighty way in your life, community, and country today?
- How might you present these challenges to God in prayer?

PRACTICE THIS Read Judges 6-8 to see the challenges Gideon faced. Compare these challenges with the challenges we face today. Consider how God might move today like He did in the time of Gideon.

PRAY OVER THIS

And Barak said to her, "If you will go with me, then I will
go; but if you will not go with me, I will not go!"

JUDGES 4:8

PONDER THIS What was the object of Barak's faith? The object of his faith was the Lord God of Israel. Now sometimes people say, "Just believe. Have faith." Believe what? Have faith in whom? Believe God. Have faith in God. That's what it's all about.

Just having faith is positive thinking. And positive thinking is not faith in God; it is faith in yourself. What is the origin of faith? The Word of God. The object of faith? The God of the Word. And the operation of faith is obeying the Word of God and the God of the Word. Barak said, "I will go." Faith is not mere mental intellectual assent; it is obedience. Faith is belief with legs on it. Our English word *believe* comes from an old English word *by-live*. What we believe we live by; the rest is just religious talk. Show your faith by your conduct.

- How does the way we live tell others what we truly believe or don't believe?
- Where does your life not align with your stated beliefs?

PRACTICE THIS Write out a list of things you believe. Write a corresponding list of how you show your beliefs with your life. Consider areas where your actions do not align with your stated beliefs. Determine what needs to change and change it!

PRAY OVER THIS

What then shall we say to these things? If God
is for us, who can be against us?

ROMANS 8:31

PONDER THIS When you love God, God is on your side, and you're programmed for victory. It may not seem like it to your naked eye. But if you wait, you'll learn what Priscilla Leonard meant when she wrote:

> On the far reef the breakers recoil in shattered foam, yet still the sea behind them urges its forces home; its chant of triumph surges through all the thunderous din—the wave may break in failure, but the tide is sure to win!...
>
> O mighty sea, thy message in changing spray is cast; within God's plan of progress, it matters not at last, how wide the shores the evil, how strong the reefs of sin—the wave may be defeated but the tide is sure to win.
>
> —Priscilla Leonard, "Wave and Tide," The Religious Herald 94, no. 3, (January 20, 1921).

God's purposes will prevail. Satan can't win. The stars in their courses are against the man who's against God. The stars line up for the man who loves God. And if you go against God, you're going to have a collision with the stars.

- How does it encourage you to remember that God's victory is certain?
- What tempts you to be distracted from this truth in daily life?

PRACTICE THIS Spend time today looking up God's certain promises about His victory in the Bible. Commit one or two of these to memory.

PRAY OVER THIS

These things I have spoken to you, that in Me you may
have peace. In the world you will have tribulation; but
be of good cheer, I have overcome the world.

JOHN 16:33

PONDER THIS God has not promised we will not know difficulty, but He has promised we will know ultimate victory. That's the reason one of my favorite books in the Bible, if not my favorite, is Romans, and one of my favorite chapters in Romans is chapter 8. Romans 8:35-37 asks a question: "Who shall separate us from the love of Christ? Shall tribulation, or distress, or persecution, or famine, or nakedness, or peril, or sword? As it is written: 'For Your sake, we are killed all day long; we are accounted as sheep for the slaughter.' Yet in all these things we are more than conquerors through Him who loved us." Paul didn't say you're not going to experience these things. Don't get the idea that somehow these things only happen to those who don't love the Lord. No, these are things that happen to the victorious. You see, God has promised never to leave us and never to forsake us, but He has not promised that we will never have difficulty.

- How have you experienced the reality that following Jesus does bring difficulty in this life?
- How does the promise of God's presence help you to persevere in difficulty?

PRACTICE THIS Journal about the difficulties you are currently facing, and the ways God is bringing comfort with His presence.

PRAY OVER THIS

But if not, let it be known to you, O king, that we do not serve your
gods, nor will we worship the gold image which you have set up.

DANIEL 3:18

PONDER THIS Shadrach, Meshach, and Abednego said in essence, "Our God is able, and we believe He will. But if He doesn't, it's not because He's not able, and we're not going to bow before your filthy image." (See Daniel 3:16-18.) Notice they had a settled faith. They didn't say, "Well, let's huddle about it." Their minds were already made up. They had a sure faith: "Our God is able." But they also had a steadfast faith to say, "Even if He doesn't, even if we're turned to bacon in that furnace, we're not going to worship your idol."

Are you ready to quit just because God doesn't do the thing you ask Him to do? You'd better have an "if not" clause in your faith. It doesn't mean your faith is weak. It means that it is stronger than ever. "God, I know You're able. But if You don't do it, Lord, I'm going to serve You anyway. I'm not going to make bargains with You." Sometimes we don't understand why God does things. A mature faith bows to the sovereign purposes of God.

- Where do you need to trust God, even "if not"?
- How hard is it for you to truly trust God if He doesn't answer as you desire?

PRACTICE THIS Take time in prayer today to submit an area of difficulty before God. Ask Him to build your faith and help you trust Him, even "if not."

20

PONDER THIS Years ago in New Jersey, there was a man who advertised that he was going to play a concert on an extremely valuable violin. People came from all over to hear him play. He tucked that instrument under his chin and began to play. You could hear the laughter of children as he played. You could hear the songs of the birds in the trees as he played. You could hear babies cry as he played. People were amazed at the music that came from that violin. When he had finished the concert, he took that violin and broke it on his knee. "Ah!" They were aghast. "Why has he done that?" Then he opened his case and brought out the expensive violin. He said, "The violin that I've been playing on is a fiddle I bought for a few dollars. It is not so much the violin that makes the music as it is the man who draws the bow." To the world, you may be just a cheap fiddle, but God is the one who can make music out of your life. God uses common people! God can use you.

- When have you been deterred because you felt dismissed or discarded by the world?
- How has God used you in unlikely situations? How are you hoping He will do it again?

PRACTICE THIS Make a list of ways God has used the "foolish things" of the world "to shame the wise" throughout the Bible and history.

21

PRAY OVER THIS

For God has not given us a spirit of fear, but of
power and of love and of a sound mind.

2 TIMOTHY 1:7

PONDER THIS Are you a fearful person? You may say, "Pastor Rogers, there are some things you need to be afraid of." I'm not talking about normal fears, like being afraid of a rattlesnake or getting in an airplane when the weather gets rough, and your heart rate goes up. Those are normal fears. Those are self-protecting instincts God has put into us.

But the Bible speaks of a spirit of fear. What is the spirit of fear? It's like a fog. It stays; it lingers in the air. It's not like a passing thunderstorm and then the sun comes back out. If you're a child of God filled with the Holy Spirit, God has given you the Spirit of power. Jesus said, "But you shall receive power when the Holy Spirit has come upon you" (Acts 1:8a). I'd rather die than be sentenced to preach without the power and the anointing of the Holy Ghost. God has given us the spirit of power and of love.

- What are some places you see a "spirit of fear" in the world?
- How has the Gospel given us courage in the face of a "spirit of fear"?

PRACTICE THIS Take time in prayer today, asking God to reveal to you anywhere you have a spirit of fear. Thank Him for His promise of power, love, and a sound mind. Ask Him to empower you to walk in that promise today.

PRAY OVER THIS

I press toward the goal for the prize of the
upward call of God in Christ Jesus.
PHILIPPIANS 3:14

PONDER THIS God has a race for you to run, and it doesn't end until you draw your last breath. There's no way for you to retire. There's no way for you to quit. There's no way for you to move aside. You're not running to make it to Heaven; no, salvation is what puts you in the race. You have to be saved even to get to the starting block. You have to be born again to qualify for this race. No man can run in the Olympic Games unless he is a citizen of the country for which he runs. You have to be a citizen of Heaven to get in this race. No exceptions. The Apostle Paul, late in life, said this in Philippians 3:14: "I press toward the goal for the prize of the upward call of God in Christ Jesus." That is, I'm running for the tape, and I'm pressing with every inch and every ounce of me. And then, in Acts 20:24, he said he wanted to "finish [his] race with joy." Paul said, "I'm not going to stop running until the race is over." Neither should we.

- What are the practical ways we "run the race" God has set before us?
- Why is it crucial that we rely on His strength to run?

PRACTICE THIS Identify one thing you need to do today to keep running. Obey God in that area today.

23

PRAY OVER THIS

Therefore we also, since we are surrounded by so great
a cloud of witnesses, let us lay aside every weight,
and the sin which so easily ensnares us, and let us run
with endurance the race that is set before us.

HEBREWS 12:1

PONDER THIS One of these days we're going to cross the finish line. In fifty years, many of us will not be alive; even after twenty-five years a great number will be gone; and even next year, by God's mercies, some will have already gone on. We will have come to the end of the line. We don't know when that's going to be.

One of these days, I'm going to breathe my last breath, but I'm not going to stop running—God helping me—until I do. I don't want to stroll over the finish line. I want to hit the finish line with a blaze of energy and power, going for the Lord Jesus Christ. You may say, "Well, you'll be an old coot." It makes no difference. "Even though our outward man is perishing, yet the inward man is being renewed day by day" (2 Corinthians 4:16b). That's the reason you ought to be an athlete—no matter what your physical condition or your economic condition. You are in a race, and that race is not over until you bow your head like the Lord Jesus and say, "It is finished. It is done." Don't give up before you get there.

- How do passages like this one help give perspective to everyday life?
- Where are you tempted to stop running the race God has given you?

PRACTICE THIS Take time in prayer today to renew your commitment to running the race God has set before you. Ask Him to empower you with the strength to endure to the end.

24

PRAY OVER THIS

Beloved, I now write to you this second epistle (in both of
which I stir up your pure minds by way of reminder).

2 PETER 3:1

PONDER THIS Many today are talking about what the world's coming to. Perhaps we ought to change the question and ask, "Who's coming to the world?" His name is the Lord Jesus. Many have a feeling that we're coming to the climax of an age, and this generation may be the last generation. We may be that generation that will be caught up to meet the Lord in the air. And Peter said to stir yourselves up. We get all excited about various achievements of men, whether in sports, business, or otherwise. When we witness one of these achievements, we stop and say, "That's something." We get excited about these accomplishments. Folks, I want to tell you something better than any achievement by people—Jesus is coming. We need to get excited about the things that really matter.

- What are some things you get excited about on a regular basis?
- How excited does it make you to remember that Jesus has promised to return? What would grow your excitement over this truth?

PRACTICE THIS Spend time today looking up and reading various Scriptures on the Second Coming. Ask the Lord to stoke the fires of your heart with excitement over this promised return.

25

PRAY OVER THIS

And saying, "Where is the promise of His coming?
For since the fathers fell asleep, all things continue
as they were from the beginning of creation."

2 PETER 3:4

PONDER THIS How do I know Jesus is coming again? Because I believe the Bible. The Bible has shown itself to be the Word of God, and repeatedly the Bible mentions the Second Coming of Jesus. Now the new birth is important, but a new birth is mentioned only nine times in the Bible. Baptism is important, but it's only mentioned 20 times in the Bible. Repentance is wonderfully important—it is only mentioned 70 times in the New Testament. But the Second Coming of Jesus Christ is mentioned 380 times in the New Testament alone. In our passage, Peter said that some will ask, "Where is the promise of his coming?" It's all over the Bible. He has promised, and He cannot lie. If you take the whole Bible, one out of every twenty-five verses speak of the Second Coming of Jesus Christ. Jesus has said He will return, and He won't break that promise.

- How often would you say you think about the return of Jesus compared with the amount of space the Bible gives to this truth?
- What could you do to remember this truth more frequently?

PRACTICE THIS Look up some of the passages that refer to Jesus' return. Work to memorize one or two of these as a way of regularly reminding yourself.

Then He said to Thomas, "Reach your finger here, and
look at My hands; and reach your hand here, and put it
into My side. Do not be unbelieving, but believing."

JOHN 20:27

PONDER THIS I've spoken to some Jewish people who say, "I don't believe in
God anymore." I ask why. They say, "Because of the Holocaust. I cannot believe
in a God who would allow such suffering." I've seen people when a loved one
has cancer or some other diseases say, "I don't want to have anything to do with
God. I don't believe in God. I can't understand this matter of suffering."

Here's the way the mind begins to think: "If God is a God of love, and He
loves me so much, but He doesn't do anything to relieve this suffering, then He
must not have any power." Or "If He has the power, but He doesn't do it, maybe
He has no love." Or maybe: "He doesn't have any love or any power. Maybe there
is no God. If there is, why do people suffer?" There's a bigger question. Not why
does God allow humans to suffer, but why does God allow Himself to suffer?

Have you ever thought about God as a God who suffers? Have you ever
thought about God as One who has pain? How did those scars come into the
hands of Jesus Christ? Those nail prints? That scar into His side? Because He
willingly suffered in our place. The question is not "Why is there suffering," but
"Why did God take our suffering?"

- What is most difficult for you about the reality of suffering?
- How are you comforted to remember that God has suffered in
  your place and on your behalf?

PRACTICE THIS Take time to worship God for paying the price for your sin and
suffering in your place.

PRAY OVER THIS

But, beloved, do not forget this one thing, that with the Lord one
day is as a thousand years, and a thousand years as one day.

2 PETER 3:8

PONDER THIS People who scoff at the Second Coming of Jesus are ignorant of what God has done and of what God is like. God is above and beyond time, and God doesn't wake up by an alarm clock. Second Peter 3:8 says, "But, beloved, do not forget this one thing, that with the Lord one day is as a thousand years, and a thousand years as one day."

As far as God is concerned, it's only been a few days since Jesus left this Earth. God hasn't forgotten. The reason Jesus is not yet come is that God has kept the door of mercy open. I believe God, in mercy, is waiting on our generation to come to Jesus, but one of these days, the Day of the Lord will come, and even now the raging waters of God's wrath are furiously pounding against the dam of His mercy. Jesus is going to come suddenly, like a thief in the night.

- How does it reframe your perspective to know the delay of Jesus' return is a sign of mercy and not neglect?
- How should this encourage us to share Jesus with others?

PRACTICE THIS Take time to thank God for His mercy. Pray and ask Him to point you to the people He wants you to share with today.

PRAY OVER THIS

Therefore, since all these things will be dissolved, what manner
of persons ought you to be in holy conduct and godliness?

2 PETER 3:11

PONDER THIS Once in Oklahoma City, there was a fire in an apartment. The flames were consuming that apartment, and there was a woman who'd been carried out by a fireman and was fighting to go back into the fire. She said, "My baby is in that apartment!" They had to hold her back because she surely would have perished. One fireman volunteered to go get her baby. He went up the ladder, through the window, into that smoke-filled room, and felt his way through. He found the baby crib, reached in and picked up that little bundle, held it close to him, and came back to the window, choking through the blinding smoke. The people gave a cheer as he handed the woman the bundle. But as she pulled the blanket back, she cried, "That's not my baby. That's my baby's doll!"

I wonder if we're going to come to the end of an age hugging the toys of this world when everything is going up in fire. My friend, the house, the car, and all these things—they're not that important. What is important? The souls of men! I want to get as many to come with me as I can. Even so, come, Lord Jesus.

- How can you be sure you are valuing the right things as you wait for the return of Jesus?
- How do we show others that they are more important than the "stuff" of the world?

PRACTICE THIS Have a conversation today to let another person know how much God values him or her.

PRAY OVER THIS

Jesus said to him, "Thomas, because you have seen Me, you have believed. Blessed are those who have not seen and yet have believed."

JOHN 20:29

PONDER THIS Suppose you've saved all your life for a vacation. The time for your trip has finally come, and you're in Hawaii in the finest hotel. You and your spouse are celebrating without a care in the world. The weather is perfect. The food is sumptuous. You're having a wonderful time. Let's suppose you've left your children home in the care of someone else, and one of your children is in an automobile accident while you're in Hawaii. Would you want somebody to get on the phone and call you and mess up your vacation? Or would you say, "Don't bother me. We're having a wonderful time. Yes, I understand my child has been hurt, but I don't want to know about it." Every parent knows the answer, right? "Yes, I want to know. Forget the vacation."

That's why Jesus left Heaven. He could have said, "I don't want to know. I just don't care." But He's a God of love. He loved us so much He stepped out of glory. He loved us so much He walked the dusty shores and the streets of Nazareth and the sandy beach of Galilee. He loved us so much He carried the cross to Golgotha and died in agony and blood. Those scars Thomas saw there in His hands say that He's a saving God. He has paid for our sins with His own blood.

- How do the actions and work of Jesus show you how much God loves you?
- How does imagining the scenario of loving earthly parents help you see God's love for you?

PRACTICE THIS Take time to read John 18-20 to see how Jesus' love for you caused Him to act.

30

PRAY OVER THIS

And when John had heard in prison about the works of
Christ, he sent two of his disciples and said to Him, "Are
You the Coming One, or do we look for another?"

MATTHEW 11:2-3

PONDER THIS At the beginning of Matthew 11, John was in prison and sent messengers to ask if Jesus was the promised One of God. Jesus knew John's heart and did not mistake the moment for the man. Jesus knew John had an honest doubt—John asked an honest question, and he got an honest answer. And look at the tribute Jesus paid to John in verse 11, "Assuredly, I say to you, among those born of women there has not risen one greater than John the Baptist, but he who is least in the kingdom of heaven is greater than he." And John the Baptist continued to serve the Lord up to the point of giving his head for the Gospel of Jesus Christ.

Do you know what real faith is? Real faith is not receiving from God what you want; real faith is accepting from God what He gives. Learn that and you won't get offended at God. If things don't work out like you think they should—if you're serving God but you end up in a dungeon—just remember that God is God. He is good, and He is in control.

- How does today's devotion remind you that you can bring your honest questions before Jesus?
- What question do you need to bring before Him today?

PRACTICE THIS Take time today to journal and write out questions you want to ask God.

PRAY OVER THIS

These things I have spoken to you, that you
should not be made to stumble.

JOHN 16:1

PONDER THIS What causes people to develop a grudge against God? Some possibilities are persecution, disappointment, rebuke, resentment at being rebuked, and envy at how somebody else is being blessed. The Lord Jesus knows we all have this tendency to resent God. In John 16:1-4, Jesus said, "These things I have spoken to you, that you should not be made to stumble. They will put you out of the synagogues; yes, the time is coming that whoever kills you will think that he offers God service. And these things they will do to you because they have not known the Father nor Me. But these things I have told you, that when the time comes, you may remember that I told you of them."

Jesus was saying, "I'm going to Heaven. I'm leaving you here. Don't get offended." If you've got a grudge against God, tell God about it. If you've got honest questions, bring them to God. Don't come to the Lord with false expectations. You say, "Pastor, I thought it was wonderful to serve Jesus." It is. If I had a thousand lives, I'd give every one of them to Jesus Christ. I'm not disappointed in Jesus, but I don't want to carry a grudge because of any false expectations.

- What are examples of false expectations a person might have of God?
- What are some specific false expectations you may have of God?

PRACTICE THIS Take time today to confess any false expectations you have of God. Ask Him to help you release these so that you won't hold a grudge against Him.

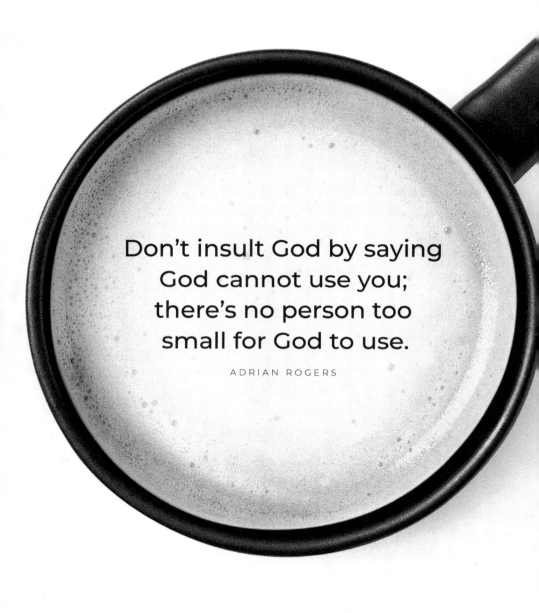

Don't insult God by saying
God cannot use you;
there's no person too
small for God to use.

ADRIAN ROGERS

1

PRAY OVER THIS

He who is not with Me is against Me, and he who
does not gather with Me scatters abroad.
MATTHEW 12:30

PONDER THIS I was witnessing on the streets of Pensacola, Florida, one time, and I saw two girls I'd never seen before. I said, "May I have a moment of your time?" They said, "Yes." And I explained the Gospel of Jesus Christ to these two young ladies. They both seemed to be under conviction, so I asked one young lady, "Would you like to pray and ask Jesus Christ to come into your heart and be your Lord and Savior today?" She said, "Yes I would," and I prayed with her, and she gave her heart to Jesus. And then I asked the other young lady, "Would you like to receive Christ as your personal Savior and Lord?" She said, "I'm not ready to do that right now." I said, "Well, now is the accepted time. There'll never be a better time, and why don't you give your heart to Jesus?" She said, "I just don't want to make a decision right now." I said, "Well, listen, if you don't accept Christ, you're rejecting Christ." "Oh," she said, "I would never reject Christ." She didn't understand that to refuse Christ is to reject Christ. Not to accept Him is to deny Him. And today, you'll either say, yes or no to Jesus Christ. Do you understand that?

- What does it mean that if you are not with Jesus, you are against Him?
- How does every person have a decision to make regarding Jesus?

PRACTICE THIS Have a conversation with another person regarding the decision everyone has to make with Jesus.

2

PRAY OVER THIS

When she saw that she was determined to go
with her, she stopped speaking to her.

RUTH 1:18

PONDER THIS Have you ever gone out to dinner at night, and you and your spouse get in the car and say, "Well, let's go out to a restaurant"? "Where do you want to go?" "I don't know, where do you want to go?" And you begin to talk this way while you're driving the car, and you turn this way and that way and all around town.

Last night I was invited to some friends' house for dinner; it was a wonderful meal. When Joyce and I got in the car, we didn't have to drive all over town. No, we didn't have to decide at every corner we came to, because we knew where we were going. When you make a big choice, a lot of little choices are automatically made. In the same way, when you are set on following Jesus, you don't have to weigh every decision along the way. You go in the direction He has called you. Ruth was determined to go with Naomi. A few big decisions take care of a lot of little decisions.

- How have you experienced the reality that the big decisions of your life take care of the little decisions?
- Where might some of your "little" decisions be out of line with your commitment to follow Jesus?

PRACTICE THIS Make a list of little decisions you face today. Consider the way your big decision to follow Christ should impact these.

PRAY OVER THIS

Now it came to pass, in the days when the judges
ruled, that there was a famine in the land.

RUTH 1:1A

PONDER THIS Why did Elimelech leave Bethlehem? He was afraid he couldn't survive. He left the house of bread with the wrong motive, the wrong method, and the wrong master. And what does he do over there? He dies. What happens to his boys that he was so concerned about? They die. (See Ruth 1:1-5.)

There's an old story about a rich merchant of Baghdad who had a servant. And the servant came to him and said, "Master, I want you to give me one of your best horses. I must flee." The merchant said to his servant, "Why do you need to flee?" The servant replied, "I was in the marketplace today and a sinister figure jostled me. I turned and I looked in his face and I was staring in the face of Death. Master, give me a horse, I must flee to Samara." The loving master said, "Take my best horse and flee if you will." Then the rich merchant went to the marketplace, and there he saw Death. He said, "Death, why did you startle my servant when you saw him?" Death said, "I didn't mean to startle your servant; it was your servant that startled me. I didn't expect to see him here. I have an appointment with him tonight in Samara." Elimelech sought life on his own terms, but all he found was death. We must be careful not to do the same.

- What are some ways we might seek our own solutions to the problems we face in life?
- What would it look like to give those over to God instead?

PRACTICE THIS Write out the problems you are facing today; seek to give those to God in prayer.

PRAY OVER THIS

Then they lifted up their voices and wept again; and Orpah
kissed her mother-in-law, but Ruth clung to her.

RUTH 1:14

PONDER THIS When Ruth made the decision to stay with Naomi, not only
was her life changed, but my life was changed. Did you know that Ruth, this
pagan girl, became an ancestor of the Lord Jesus Christ? She married into
the royal line and, according to the flesh, she became a part of the house of
David. Before this decision, she had so much against her. She had a cursed
life. The Bible teaches that there was a curse upon her. Deuteronomy 23:3 says,
"An Ammonite or Moabite shall not enter the assembly of the LORD; even to
the tenth generation none of his descendants shall enter the assembly of the
LORD forever." The Law said, "Keep her out! She's not worthy." She had a cursed
life. But what the law could not do, grace did for this woman. And what the
law could not do for me, grace has done. The Bible tells us in Ephesians 2:12,
"you were without Christ, being aliens from the commonwealth of Israel and
strangers from the covenants of promise, having no hope and without God in
the world." But thank God, the grace of God has brought us in.

- How does it encourage you to remember that you were previously
  without hope before God, but the work of Christ has changed
  everything for you?
- How does this encourage you about others who also need to know
  Jesus?

PRACTICE THIS Tell someone today about the hope you have because of Jesus.

PRAY OVER THIS

There was a relative of Naomi's husband, a man of great
wealth, of the family of Elimelech. His name was Boaz.

RUTH 2:1

PONDER THIS Consider how Boaz was a picture of Christ. Number one: he was from Bethlehem, as was the Lord Jesus. Number two: he was a near kinsman to Ruth, as Jesus is a near kinsman to us. He acted as a near kinsman to redeem us. That's why Jesus stepped out of the ivory palaces and came into this world of woe and was born of a virgin's womb. He took flesh and blood to be made like His brethren. Further, to redeem, you had to be wealthy enough. You had to have no obligations against you, you could not be bankrupt yourself. Boaz was a wealthy man, and all the riches of Heaven reside in the Lord Jesus Christ.

Not only did you have to be a near kinsman, and not only did you have to be wealthy enough to redeem, but you had to be willing to redeem. And the Lord Jesus, thank God, was willing to redeem, just as Boaz was willing to redeem. Boaz came to the fields where Ruth was, just as Jesus came to where I am. Boaz redeemed Ruth, but he also pointed to Jesus who is the Redeemer for the whole world.

- How does it help you grow in worship of Jesus to see examples like Boaz that pointed to His coming?
- How are we called to move toward others as Boaz moved toward Ruth and Jesus moved toward us?

PRACTICE THIS Go to someone today who you know needs to hear the Good News of redemption.

PRAY OVER THIS

So Ruth the Moabitess said to Naomi, "Please let me go to
the field, and glean heads of grain after him in whose sight I
may find favor." And she said to her, "Go, my daughter."

RUTH 2:2

PONDER THIS Ruth and Naomi were penniless, and by this time Naomi, who had turned to bitterness, couldn't go into the fields. She was too old for that. So, Ruth said, "Well, I'm going into the fields. Maybe I can find some grace here."

But I want you to see the hand of God in all of this. Number one, when did they get back to the land? Just in time for the barley harvest. This was not by accident. Then she went into the fields to glean, and whose field did she go into? There were no signs there that said this field belongs to this family or that family, and no fences of demarcation. She simply went into a field, and it was the field of Boaz, her near kinsman. You can see the hidden hand of God.

Then when she's there in the field of Boaz, who happens to come to the field at just that moment? Boaz himself. Boaz sees Ruth out there, and he says, "Who is that?" Ruth had gone through so much. She was broken and bankrupt, she was bruised and beaten, she was cursed and crushed. Did God do all of that out of cruelty? No, as you see the bigger picture, you see that God had a sovereign plan in it all.

- When was a time God used difficult circumstances in your life for greater good?
- How does this change your perspective on difficult situations as you look toward the future?

PRACTICE THIS Journal about a time God used hard circumstances in your life for good.

PRAY OVER THIS

Therefore wash yourself and anoint yourself, put on your best
garment and go down to the threshing floor; but do not make
yourself known to the man until he has finished eating and drinking.

RUTH 3:3

PONDER THIS Christianity is not a code, it is not a cause, it is not a creed, it is
not conduct, it is not church; it's Christ. The mark of a Christian is a love for the
Lord Jesus Christ. And the true desire of every child of God is to know Jesus
Christ intimately. We want more than redemption; we want a relationship. We
want more than the gifts; we want the Giver. We want Jesus Christ to be real
to us.

You can know about somebody without knowing somebody. I want to know
Jesus, not merely know about Him, don't you? I want Jesus to be more real to
me than any person I see face to face. The Apostle Paul said in Philippians 3:10a,
"That I may know Him." In today's passage, Naomi instructed Ruth on how to
know Boaz, and Ruth followed her direction. God has told us how to know His
Son, Jesus, through His Word. Will we follow?

- How would you describe what it means to know Jesus? What do
  you base this on?
- How might you seek to know Jesus more today?

PRACTICE THIS Commit today to read God's Word faithfully so that you may
know Him better.

8

PRAY OVER THIS

Then it shall be, when he lies down, that you shall notice the
place where he lies; and you shall go in, uncover his feet,
and lie down; and he will tell you what you should do.

RUTH 3:4

PONDER THIS We should be careful not to misinterpret Ruth's actions here. There was nothing improper, dirty, or impure. She was placing herself at Boaz's feet under his protection. In Ruth 3:9 she requested that Boaz take her under his wing. She was saying, "I place myself under your protection; I am fully committed to you!"

Question: Can you have an intimate relationship with the Lord Jesus Christ if you're not fully committed to Him? The answer is no. Is Christ Lord? I must ask myself every one of these questions. Have I placed myself at the feet of my Redeemer? The most sacred place on Earth is not in the pew, not at the altar, not behind the pulpit, not some temple somewhere. The most sacred place on Earth is at the feet of Jesus when you are fully committed to Him.

- What does it mean to place yourself at the feet of Jesus?
- How do you need to further commit yourself to Him today?

PRACTICE THIS Take time in prayer today to posture yourself at the feet of Jesus. Consider changing your physical posture to display this act of humility by kneeling if you are able.

9

PRAY OVER THIS

And the close relative said, "I cannot redeem it for myself,
lest I ruin my own inheritance. You redeem my right of
redemption for yourself, for I cannot redeem it."

RUTH 4:6

PONDER THIS Who was this nearer kinsman? If Boaz pictured the Lord Jesus Christ, who is the nearer kinsman who cannot redeem? He pictured Adam. Everyone is either in Adam or in Christ. Who is my real close relative? Adam. We're all related to Adam, and in Adam, all die. He is the near relative to us all.

I was preaching in a revival one time. A woman came up afterward and said, "You're a Rogers, aren't you?" I said, "Yes ma'am." She said, "Well, I have been doing some work on our genealogy." She stood up real tall. She said, "Because I'm a Rogers." And she said, "You will be happy to know that the Rogers came over on the Mayflower." I said, "Well that's wonderful." But then I said, "I traced it back further than that." Boy, did she get excited, and I said, "I traced it all the way back, and you need to know that we came from a crooked farmer and a drunken sailor. The farmer was Adam, and the sailor was Noah. That's how far back we go." Thanks be to God—our story didn't end there. Adam was our near relative, but Jesus has acted as our Redeemer.

- How have we all experienced the reality that Adam is our "near relative"?
- How did Jesus act as our Redeemer?

PRACTICE THIS Make a list today comparing the work of Adam and the work of Jesus. Prayerfully reflect in worship over the work of Christ your Redeemer.

Then Boaz said to his servant who was in charge of
the reapers, "Whose young woman is this?"
RUTH 2:5

PONDER THIS Samuel Rutherford, a man who knew suffering, has been quoted as saying, "Praise God for the hammer, the file, and the furnace." Has it seemed like you're a nail, and some hammer is coming out of nowhere, beating on you? Does it seem like you are a piece of metal, and there is some file that is gnawing and scraping and reducing you? Does it seem like you have been flung into a furnace and are being consumed? Remember that God holds the nail and the hammer. God holds the metal and the file. It is God who has allowed you to be in the furnace and watches over the furnace.

Ruth surely wondered, "Why this hammer? Why this file? Why this furnace of fire?" But if you back out and look at the bigger picture, you see that it was saving grace, it was sovereign grace, and it was God moving everything so that Ruth showed up just at the right time in the barley field when Boaz was there because God had a plan.

- When have you experienced suffering that felt like a hammer, file, or furnace?
- How does it encourage you to remember that God has a plan, even in difficult times?

PRACTICE THIS Journal today about a time during which you were able to see God's plan in very difficult circumstances.

PRAY OVER THIS

Let your eyes be on the field which they reap, and go
after them. Have I not commanded the young men not
to touch you? And when you are thirsty, go to the vessels
and drink from what the young men have drawn.

RUTH 2:9

PONDER THIS Ruth is out in the fields, and Boaz says, "Are you thirsty? Help yourself to the things I've got for my workers there. Ruth, go ahead, glean the fields among the sheaves. Fellows, leave some on the ground for her. When it's dinnertime and all the workers are eating, she doesn't have to go off there in the corner of the field. Invite her to the table and let her eat until she is satisfied."

Did you know she's soon going to own that field? She's gleaning in the field right now, but she is going to marry the owner of that field. All that he has will be hers. Think about it. Right now we're getting the first fruits, and thank God for those hands full of purpose. He gives me some day by day. He says, "Sit down and eat and be satisfied."

But bless the Lord, the meek will inherit the Earth. We're going to be united to the Lord Jesus Christ, our heavenly Boaz. Look around. Do you think God made all this for those that belong to the world? He made it for His people. One day it will be ours because we will be united with Him.

- How does it change your perspective to remember God has promised His people will one day inherit the Earth?
- How does it motivate you to join God's work as coheirs with Christ?

PRACTICE THIS Take a walk today for the purpose of observing God's creation. Be reminded that God has promised His people will one day inherit the Earth as coheirs with Christ.

12

PRAY OVER THIS

And I thought to inform you, saying, "Buy it back in the presence
of the inhabitants and the elders of my people. If you will
redeem it, redeem it; but if you will not redeem it, then tell
me, that I may know; for there is no one but you to redeem
it, and I am next after you." And he said, "I will redeem it."

RUTH 4:4

PONDER THIS I did a study on the word *redeem*. It means "to buy or to take out
of the marketplace, that is, to take off the slave block." When our Lord redeemed
us, He not only bought us, but He also took us out of the marketplace. We're no
longer for sale. That speaks of our eternal security. And then to redeem means
to set free. That's what happened to Ruth and that's what happened to Adrian.
I have been bought, I've been taken off the marketplace, and I have been set
free in the Lord Jesus Christ. That's redemption. That's the wonderful doctrine
of redemption we read over and over again. Even better, it's not just Ruth, and
it's not just me—it's all who have trusted in the Lord Jesus. If you've put your
faith in Him, it's you too.

- Have you been redeemed by Jesus?
- How is He calling you to respond further to Him today?

PRACTICE THIS Share with another person the way you've been redeemed by
Jesus.

PRAY OVER THIS

For I testify to everyone who hears the words of the prophecy
of this book: If anyone adds to these things, God will add
to him the plagues that are written in this book.
REVELATION 22:18

PONDER THIS There is a war over the Word. There are those who despise God's Word. They are against all it stands for. There are those who deny it saying they don't believe in it. There are those who distort it; they twist it to their own destruction. There are those who dissect it; they treat the Bible more like a math book than a love story. They're ever learning, but they're never able to come to the knowledge of the truth. There are others who disregard it. They say it's not relevant.

But I suppose the greatest enemy of the Word of God is found in churches. These are those who say they believe the Bible. They give lip service to the fact that the Bible is the inspired, inerrant, infallible, authentic Word of God. But they don't study it. They don't know it. They don't live by it. They don't stand on it. You've got to be able to say, "I know that I know that the Bible is the Word of God." Especially in these days, when everything that is not nailed down is coming loose. The devil is pulling nails as fast as he can. But there's really nothing he will be able to disturb you on if you can stand on this Book. God has given you the Word.

- How confident would you say you are in the Bible as the Word of God?
- What things present obstacles to your belief in the Bible?

PRACTICE THIS Spend time reflecting on, and seeking to memorize, 2 Timothy 3:16-17 as a way of meditating on the truth that the Bible is God's infallible Word.

14

PRAY OVER THIS

Where were you when I laid the foundations of the earth? Tell Me,
if you have understanding. Who determined its measurements?
Surely you know! Or who stretched the line upon it? To what were
its foundations fastened? Or who laid its cornerstone, When the
morning stars sang together, and all the sons of God shouted for joy?

JOB 38:4-7

PONDER THIS I believe the Bible is the Word of God because of its scientific accuracy. The skeptic, the atheist, or the unbeliever will say, "Well, of course, the Bible has scientific errors in it." But before you say that, make certain that you know two things. Number one, you must know science. And number two, you must know the Bible. Many consider the Bible an old-fashioned book. They claim it's not a book of science, it's a book of religion. That is true. It is not a scientific textbook. It is not written to teach us science. It is written to teach us God. It has well been said, "The Bible was not given to tell us how the heavens go, but how to go to Heaven." But the God of creation and the God of salvation are the same God. Science doesn't take God by surprise. And you don't have to check your brains at the door to believe the Bible is the Word of God.

- When have you heard a version of the argument that the Bible is not scientifically accurate?
- Can you name examples in which the Bible states truths about science?

PRACTICE THIS Read Job 38-39. Ask God to give you a humble spirit as you approach Him, the Creator of all things.

15

PRAY OVER THIS

These things I have written to you who believe in the name of the
Son of God, that you may know that you have eternal life, and that
you may continue to believe in the name of the Son of God.

1 JOHN 5:13

PONDER THIS The assurance of your salvation is extremely important. We're not talking about denominational preference. We're not talking about little idiosyncrasies of doctrine. We're not talking about political opinions. We're not talking about matters that only count in this world. We're talking about eternal life. We're talking about your soul. When God made you, God breathed into your nostrils the breath of life, and you became a living soul. You could no more cease to exist than God Himself could cease to exist. Your soul will go on endless, timeless, dateless, and measureless—either in Heaven or in Hell. How important it is, therefore, that you absolutely know you're saved.

- What are the ways we can know that we have been saved by Christ? (Read all of 1 John 5 for more on this.)
- How is God calling you to respond to Him today? Are there further steps you need to take?

PRACTICE THIS Journal the steps you feel God is calling you to take today in response to Him. Take action to obey.

16

PRAY OVER THIS

He who has the Son has life; he who does not
have the Son of God does not have life.

1 JOHN 5:12

PONDER THIS I've heard it said that if you cannot name the time and the place you were saved, you're not saved. Have you ever heard that? There's just one thing wrong with that—it's not in the Bible. The Bible never tells you to look back to past experiences for proof of your salvation. It does not say, "He who believed has eternal life." It says, "He who believes."

It doesn't matter what you've done in the past. If you're not believing on Jesus today, you're not saved. And if you are believing on Jesus today, you did believe on Jesus in the past. It's impossible to presently believe on Him without having believed on Him in the past. Indeed, there was a time. Indeed, there was a place. But, if you're not believing on Jesus now, whatever you call the past time and the place, there's something wrong with it. The big question is: are you believing Jesus now? If you have the time and the place, wonderful. But if you don't, that doesn't mean you're not saved. If you're trusting Jesus right now, you are saved.

- Are you more prone to rely on past or present evidence as assurance of your salvation?
- What evidence is there in your life right now that you are trusting Jesus?

PRACTICE THIS Write out the current fruit in your life that displays your trust in Jesus. Be honest with yourself. If the fruit is not there, respond to God, seeking salvation in Him today.

PRAY OVER THIS

...and if anyone takes away from the words of the book of this
prophecy, God shall take away his part from the Book of Life, from
the holy city, and from the things which are written in this book.

REVELATION 22:19

PONDER THIS Suppose we decided we were going to build a monument to the fifty states. And we decided to build it out of the native stone of the fifty states. We would get coral from my state of Florida. We would get granite from Georgia. We would get marble from another state. We'd collect gray stone, brown stone, red stone, and all kinds of stone. We would have these stones cut in the quarry in different shapes. Then let's suppose they're all shipped to our nation's capital, and the workers begin to uncrate them. As they go, they find that all the stones fit together. Not one stone too many, not one stone too few. No stone needs to be built up. No stone needs to be shaved down. They all interlock. They all fit together. And when they're finished there is a beautiful, symmetrical monument.

Now, would you say that happened by chance? Of course not. It would be absolutely, totally impossible. The only answer to that would be there was a master architect who designed the whole thing and sent the specifications to the quarry. How do you explain the unity of the Bible apart from divine inspiration? That's one of the reasons we believe the Bible is the Word of God.

- What examples can you think of that show how the Bible is unified?
- How do these examples encourage your faith in the truth of the Bible?

PRACTICE THIS Write out as many examples as you can think of that show how the Bible is unified in its message.

18

PRAY OVER THIS

Heaven and earth will pass away, but my
words will by no means pass away.

MATTHEW 24:35

PONDER THIS The Bible is not the book of the month. It is the book of the ages. No book has ever faced as much opposition as the Bible. Men have laughed at it, scorned it, ridiculed it, made laws against it, and burned it. There was a time in Scottish history when it was a crime punishable by death to own a Bible. Many a time a man has preached a funeral for the Bible, declaring it dead. Ironically, the corpse has outlived the pallbearers. People die, but the Bible has survived, and it is applicable. It is always up to date. A man of God, a woman of God, a child of God can open this book and know more today about what's going on in the world than everyone in the Pentagon and the White House put together. The Word of God is timeless, and it is true.

- How have you seen the wisdom of the Bible surpass that of man?
- What are some examples of ancient accounts in the Bible that apply to our lives today?

PRACTICE THIS Journal today about the ways the Bible applies to your life specifically in timeless ways.

PRAY OVER THIS

And I give them eternal life, and they shall never perish;
neither shall anyone snatch them out of My hand.

JOHN 10:28

PONDER THIS In 1937, the Golden Gate Bridge was built. I can remember very vividly the first time I saw that monumental structure as they began to build. At that time, it was the world's longest suspension bridge. But as they worked, they built it high above those swirling, perilous waters. Many of the workers were afraid that they might fall—and it seemed like the very fear of falling caused them to fall. At first, they failed to build a safety net when they were building the bridge and 23 fell from the first section of the bridge.

On the next section of the bridge, they spent $100,000 to build a safety net. Back in that time, that was a monumental sum, but they felt it was worth it. After they built the safety net, only 10 fell. But all 10 that fell were caught and were safe; lives were not lost. With the safety net there, the work went 25 percent faster. The people could concentrate on their work because they knew that beneath them was a safety net. So it is with the child of God! When we know our future is secure, we can concentrate on God's work in the present.

- How does it change your perspective to be reminded that nothing can take you from God's hand?
- How would you live differently today if you really believed you were totally secure in Christ?

PRACTICE THIS Take one action today based on your security in Christ. This doesn't mean living recklessly, it means living with bold faith.

20

For by one offering He has perfected forever
those who are being sanctified.

HEBREWS 10:14

PONDER THIS I want to give you a challenge. Find anywhere in the Bible where anybody was ever saved twice. You can't do it. Do you know why? It's impossible to be saved twice. Nowhere in the Bible will you ever find someone who was saved twice. Some people believe you can get saved and lose your salvation. They believe you must be born again and again and again and again. They believe you keep on getting saved. But as today's verse reminds us: by one offering He has perfected forever those who are being sanctified. Did you know for you to be saved twice Jesus would have to die twice? When you were saved, you received a ticket marked *good for one salvation*. You are perfected forever. Jesus is never going back to that cross. He's never going to die again. By one offering we're perfected forever.

- What kinds of things cause you to question the validity of your salvation?
- What might give you further assurance of your salvation? What might indicate that you've never been saved?

PRACTICE THIS Spend time looking up passages that speak of the once-for-all assurance of salvation. If you have doubts about your salvation, ask God to reveal the truth to you based on His Word.

PRAY OVER THIS

For it would have been better for them not to have known
the way of righteousness, than having known it, to turn
from the holy commandment delivered to them.

2 PETER 2:21

PONDER THIS Those who live by truth get more and more freedom. Those who do not live by truth but live by lies experience more and more bondage. Reformation without transformation leads to greater degradation and final condemnation. It's better for you not to have known the way of truth than to reform your life without meeting the Lord Jesus Christ. The classic example of that is Judas. Judas heard the truth. Judas reformed his life. Judas was a disciple of the Lord Jesus for a time. He escaped the pollution of the world for a while, but his latter end was worse than his first. Jesus said it would have been better for him if he had never been born. Sinful desires do not disappear by reformation. They only hibernate and wake up stronger. That's what Peter was saying. It would be better for them not to have known the way of truth then, after they've heard the holy commandment, to turn from it. Salvation, on the other hand, gives you a new nature.

- How can you know the difference between freedom and temporary reformation in your life?
- What are some other Bible passages that speak to this?

PRACTICE THIS Prayerfully examine your life today, assessing if you are living according to freedom from God or reformation in your own strength.

22

PRAY OVER THIS

Then many false prophets will rise up and deceive many.
And because lawlessness will abound, the love of many will
grow cold. But he who endures to the end shall be saved.

MATTHEW 24:11-13

PONDER THIS Someone might put today's verse before you and say, "Don't you see it? For you to be saved, you have to endure to the end." It's amazing how people get things 180 degrees out of focus. God teaches here that for you to endure to the end, you have to be saved. That's all He's saying. Do you want to know who's saved? Those who endure are the ones who are saved. They're not saved because they endure—they endure because they are saved.

- What about knowing Jesus motivates you to endure as a Christian?
- What tempts you to give up? How is the motivation of Christ better?

PRACTICE THIS Journal today about the things that tempt you to give up following Jesus. Pray over these things, thanking God for His secure salvation. Ask Him to give you renewed motivation for endurance in the finished work of Jesus.

23

PRAY OVER THIS

Against You, You only, have I sinned, And done this evil in Your sight.

PSALM 51:4A

PONDER THIS If all you're afraid of is the punishment for your sin, you may not be saved. If you're a child of God, when you sin, you don't weep primarily because you're going to get punished. You weep primarily because you have disgraced your God. Our sin causes us to say, "Against You and You only have I sinned and done this evil in Your sight. Oh God, I'm so ashamed. My sin is against You. Not only did I break your law, God, I broke your heart." That's the difference between a slave and a son. A slave, when he disobeys, fears the whip. He fears his master's lash. But a son, when he disobeys—if he's a loving son— fears his father's displeasure. He is brokenhearted that he has broken the heart of God.

- Does your sin bother you in the way that was described above? Why or why not?
- How might God be calling you to respond to Him based on how you typically respond to sin?

PRACTICE THIS Have a conversation with someone close to you to share the way you typically respond when you recognize sin in your life. Reflect on this in light of today's devotional thought.

24

PRAY OVER THIS

"But there are some of you who do not believe." For
Jesus knew from the beginning who they were who
did not believe, and who would betray Him.

JOHN 6:64

PONDER THIS Do you think Judas' betrayal took Jesus by surprise? Do you think He said, "What a revolting development this is! Oh no, how could I have chosen Judas? Wow, look, here's a man I was trusting, and now he's betrayed me!" Oh no, friend. Jesus chose Judas with His eyes wide open. Jesus knew Judas never believed in Him. John 6:70-71 says, "Jesus answered them, 'Did I not choose you, the twelve, and one of you is a devil?' He spoke of Judas Iscariot, the son of Simon, for it was he who would betray Him, being one of the twelve."

Peter endured. Judas didn't. Why did Peter, who denied Jesus, endure to the end, and why did Judas not endure? Very simple. Peter had faith; Judas didn't have any. Jesus knew from the beginning who they were that did not believe. Judas never believed. Simon Peter did. And those who endure to the end, those are they who are saved.

- Today we have discussed the way Peter and Judas were different. How were they similar? What might have led people to believe Judas would be the one to endure at the time?
- How does the difference between Peter and Judas help you further understand the distinguishing mark of those who endure to the end in following Jesus?

PRACTICE THIS Write out a list comparing Peter and Judas. List how they were the same and the defining mark that made them different.

25

PRAY OVER THIS

For it is impossible for those who were once enlightened, and have tasted the heavenly gift, and have become partakers of the Holy Spirit...to renew them again to repentance, since they crucify again for themselves the Son of God, and put Him to an open shame.

HEBREWS 6:4-6

PONDER THIS How should we understand today's verse? Think of it this way. You go to the supermarket and back in the dairy section is a table out with squares of cheese. You go and taste it. If you're a cheese hound you might say, "Hey, that is terrific cheese. I want two pounds of it." So, they wrap it up and you go to checkout. You're watching as that cheese goes over the scanner. Then you see a price come up and you say, "Oh wait, what's that?" "It's the cheese." You say, "You've got to be kidding. You expect me to pay that much money for that cheese?" "Well, that's a rare, imported cheese. I thought you wanted it?" So, you say, "Well I thought I did too, but I didn't know what it cost. Put it back."

In this scenario, you're an individual who has tasted the cheese. You've sniffed it. You know what it is. You've rolled it around on your tongue. You are aware of exactly what you are doing, but you say, "I will not pay that price," and you walk out. You refuse with your eyes wide open, and that's your privilege. The Bible is telling us here that those who do the same with the truth of the Gospel are in great danger.

- How has your life been changed by "tasting" the Word of God?
- What are ways you are tempted to neglect or reject the Word of God?

PRACTICE THIS Read Psalm 34:8. Memorize this as a reminder of the worth of following God.

26

> **PRAY OVER THIS**
>
> Yet in all these things we are more than
> conquerors through Him who loved us.
>
> **ROMANS 8:37**

PONDER THIS I used to play football. My team would work and practice and hit and do all these things to take a bag full of zipped-up air across a pasture and over a white line on that field. It actually sounds kind of dumb when you think about it. But when you finally get that piece of pigskin over that white line, they call it a touchdown, and everybody goes bananas. That's the goal, but there's a group of fellows on the other side that says, "You're not going to do that." That's what the game's all about.

But let's say I have figured out a secret to victory. We need to come out on the field at about 2:00 a.m. when the other team is not there. And then we can take that ball and shove it over that white line as many times as we want. Right? Well yes, theoretically. We could do that, but why don't people do that? Because that's no victory. If there's no opposition, there's no victory. God has not called you to a life of ease, but He has called you to a life of victory through our Lord Jesus Christ. Thanks be unto God who causes us always to triumph in the Lord Jesus Christ.

- How does today's illustration help you understand what it means to have victory in Jesus?
- Who or what is the opposition you face each day as a follower of Jesus?

PRACTICE THIS Journal about the opposition you are currently facing in your walk with Jesus. Pray over these thoughts and thank God for the promised victory in Jesus.

PRAY OVER THIS

No temptation has overtaken you except such as is common to man; but God is faithful, who will not allow you to be tempted beyond what you are able, but with the temptation will also make the way of escape, that you may be able to bear it.

1 CORINTHIANS 10:13

PONDER THIS What does the devil war against primarily? You may say the devil tries to get you to commit adultery. Not primarily. The devil tries to get you drunk. No, not primarily. The devil tries to get you on an ego trip. Not primarily.

Primarily, the devil wars against your spirit. What is your spirit? What is the difference between your spirit and your soul? Your soul is the sense of self-consciousness. Your spirit is the sense of God-consciousness. You know God through your spirit. Plants have a body, but they don't have a soul. Animals have a body and a soul. That means they have self-consciousness, but no animal has a spirit. Only man has a spirit.

That's what makes man more than an animal. Man can know God. And the Bible says, "God is Spirit, and they who worship Him must worship Him in spirit and in truth" (John 4:24). God's Spirit bears witness with our spirits that we are children of God. (See Romans 8:16.) The spirit in man is the vehicle of communication, worship, praise, and spiritual knowledge. What does the devil want to do? The devil wants to cut you off from God. He does this primarily by attacking your spirit.

- Think about the temptations listed at the beginning. How are these all symptoms of the devil attacking your spirit?
- How does the condition of your spirit guide the way you think and act?

PRACTICE THIS Have a conversation with another person today about the importance of a person's spirit.

28

PRAY OVER THIS

God is Spirit, and those who worship Him
must worship in spirit and truth.

JOHN 4:24

PONDER THIS Have you ever thought about what the Bible commands you to do? How are you going to do what the Bible commands? You don't have the strength to do it. For example, Ephesians 5:19-20 says, "speaking to one another in psalms and hymns and spiritual songs, singing and making melody in your heart to the Lord, giving thanks always for all things to God the Father in the name of our Lord Jesus Christ." But the reality is, none of us will live like this in our own strength. In our worship lives, we need to be filled with the Holy Spirit. Why? Because God is Spirit and they who worship Him must worship Him in spirit and in truth.

Have you ever been in a worship service where people are trying to worship God in the flesh? It's just some kind of a circus, and it's a program. How tedious and how tasteless that is. But you've also been in worship services where those who are leading the worship are filled with God's blessed Holy Spirit, and the people are singing praises to God, and they're worshiping God in spirit and in truth. The only way you can truly worship God is to worship Him in the power of His Spirit.

- How would you describe the difference between worshiping God in the power of the Holy Spirit and in your own power?
- Reflect on different experiences you've had with both of these.

PRACTICE THIS Take a walk outside today, asking God to fill you with His Spirit and to lead you to worship Him as you observe creation all around you.

PRAY OVER THIS

Bondservants, be obedient to those who are your masters
according to the flesh, with fear and trembling, in sincerity of
heart, as to Christ; not with eyeservice, as men-pleasers, but as
bondservants of Christ, doing the will of God from the heart,
with goodwill doing service, as to the Lord, and not to men.

EPHESIANS 6:5-7

PONDER THIS I want to let you in on a secret. If we would begin to live on Monday as these verses describe, people would start believing what we preach on Sunday. What better place could there be to witness for Jesus Christ than on the job? Your job is your temple of devotion; it is your lamp stand for witness. The boss would say, "I don't understand these Christians. They're here on time. They work with smiles on their faces. They're very careful. They're honest. They don't steal a thing. I can trust them with the entire business. They seem to be devoted to the business as if they own it." When a man goes to hire new workers, he ought to think, "Those are the kind of people I want."

But it's not in human nature to do that. Human nature is to get by with as little as you can and get as much as you can. How are we going to live as these verses describe? You don't have what it takes. That's not your nature. By nature, you are selfish, but by being Spirit-filled you can live this way.

- How does your relationship with the Lord change the way you work each day?
- How does this change your perspective on daily routine tasks?

PRACTICE THIS What tasks are in front of you today? Consider how it would look to do these tasks to the Lord and take action to follow through.

30

PRAY OVER THIS

It is good for me that I have been afflicted,

that I may learn Your statutes.

PSALM 119:71

PONDER THIS In today's Scripture, David said, "It is good for me that I have been afflicted." Have you ever said that? Oh, God thank You for this sickness. Thank You for this suffering. Thank You for this adversity. Thank You for this problem. Thank You for this heartache. Thank You for this thing I'm going through. It takes a lot of faith to say it is good for me that I have been afflicted. And David said, "It is good for me that I have been afflicted, that I might learn Your statutes." Did you know that affliction is sometimes the best teacher? We never see as clearly as when we see through eyes that have been washed through tears. When we get on our backs, it's then that we begin to look up into the face of God. A sick bed can often teach more than a sermon.

- How have you experienced the reality of learning faithfulness to God through suffering?
- Who do you know who is suffering today?

PRACTICE THIS Take action today in a specific way to encourage someone who is suffering.

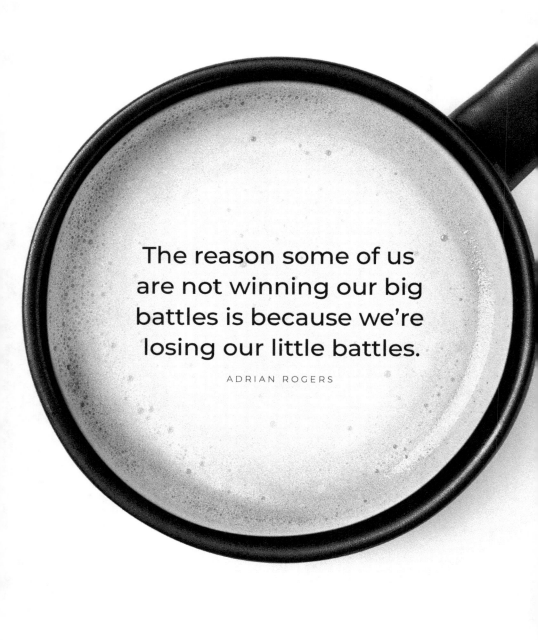

The reason some of us
are not winning our big
battles is because we're
losing our little battles.

ADRIAN ROGERS

PRAY OVER THIS

For we do not wrestle against flesh and blood, but against principalities, against powers, against the rulers of the darkness of this age, against spiritual hosts of wickedness in the heavenly places.

EPHESIANS 6:12

PONDER THIS Is there anybody who would deny that these are evil days? We're up against the organized, mobilized, and demonized forces of Hell—and those forces come at us in every way. Sometimes it's a direct attack. Sometimes it is very subtle. There is a war, but there also has never been a greater day, a greater age, and a greater opportunity to preach the Gospel of Jesus. There is more hunger for the Gospel now than ever before. There is more openness to the Gospel than ever before. You say, "Pastor Rogers, I thought you said things were getting bad?" They are. As the night grows darker, the saints grow brighter. The hungers are also more intense. There are people who are looking, waiting, and wondering, "Can we find a way? Is there an answer?" And there is an answer. The answer is Christ. But we need a generation of Spirit-filled people.

- How does awareness of our spiritual battle better prepare us to fight it?
- Who do you know who is struggling and looking for answers today?

PRACTICE THIS Initiate a connection or conversation with the person who came to mind who might be struggling with answers today. Take opportunities to share the hope of Jesus.

2

PRAY OVER THIS

Or do you not know that your body is the temple of the Holy Spirit
who is in you, whom you have from God, and you are not your own?

1 CORINTHIANS 6:19

PONDER THIS How are we to be filled with the Holy Spirit? This is a command and everything that God requires of us He also teaches us how to do. Do not think of the Holy Spirit as a substance. The Holy Spirit is a person. Don't refer to the Holy Spirit as "it." Refer to the Holy Spirit as Him. Jesus said, "He will teach you all things" (John 14:26). You wouldn't say of a person, "It wore a maroon tie." You'd say, "He did." Don't depersonalize the Holy Spirit. Don't think of being filled with the Spirit as if you are a vessel and the Holy Spirit is a liquid, or as if you are a battery and the Holy Spirit an electrical charge. No, the Spirit is a Person, and you are a temple.

- How does it change your perspective of the Holy Spirit to remember that He is a Person, not a thing?
- What is the connection between Bible study, prayer, and being filled with the Spirit?

PRACTICE THIS Make a list of qualities of the Holy Spirit that you have learned from Scripture. Research these as needed but seek to remember that He is a person, and you are His temple.

3

PRAY OVER THIS

And we know that all things work together for good to those who
love God, to those who are the called according to His purpose.

ROMANS 8:28

PONDER THIS Martin Luther led the Protestant Reformation and was a man of great faith. But he, like some of us, was given to fits of despondency and depression. He got his eyes on the circumstances rather than on God. There in his room, he was brooding in a state of melancholy. He wouldn't come out. His wife, Katharina, tried to coax him out of the room, but he wouldn't move.

So, one day she put on a black dress, a black hat, a black veil over her face, and black gloves and came into that room. She was dressed for a funeral. He looked at her and asked, "Who has died?" She said, "Martin, haven't you heard? God is dead." He said, "That's blasphemy!" She replied, "Yes. And it's blasphemy for you to be living like He's dead."

In response to this experience, Luther wrote the well-known hymn, "A Mighty Fortress." Some of the words include, "A mighty fortress is our God, a bulwark never failing; our helper He, amid the flood of mortal ills prevailing." The hymn goes on to say, "Did we in our own strength confide, our striving would be losing; were not the right Man on our side, the Man of God's own choosing." That man is Jesus. We know all things work together for good, and God is the cause of it.

- What kinds of things tempt you to take your focus off Jesus and put them on the world around you?
- How do you typically respond in these situations?

PRACTICE THIS Look up the hymn "A Mighty Fortress" today and listen to it two or three times, seeking to meditate on the truth of God's good purposes in our lives.

PRAY OVER THIS

Or do you not know that as many of us as were baptized
into Christ Jesus were baptized into His death? Therefore
we were buried with Him through baptism into death, that
just as Christ was raised from the dead by the glory of the
Father, even so we also should walk in newness of life.

ROMANS 6:3-4

PONDER THIS I visited our wonderful missionaries in Kenya, Jim and Peggy Hooten. Jim took me out in his Land Rover. We went on the hard road, then we got on the gravel road, then we got on no road. Then we kept going further and further out to the foot of Kilimanjaro, there in the Maasai country where those great tall magnificent Maasai warriors are. Jim Hooten had a tent out there. That was his church, and he was telling those warriors about the Lord Jesus. Then he said, "Come over here, I want to show you this." He had dug a pit in the ground that looked so much like the graves that I have stood beside so many times when I preach funerals. He'd lined that pit with plastic, and he had brought water on his Land Rover and filled the pit with water. He baptized the Maasai in that grave. It looked like a grave because indeed that's what the baptistery is—it is a liquid tomb.

- What connection is there between a grave and the practice of baptism?
- Why is it important to recognize the death that takes place in our baptism?

PRACTICE THIS Journal today about your experience of being baptized into the death of Jesus and how it has changed your life.

5

PRAY OVER THIS

What shall we say then? Shall we continue in sin
that grace may abound? Certainly not! How shall
we who died to sin live any longer in it?

ROMANS 6:1-2

PONDER THIS Baptism speaks about what God did for you when He saved you. When we get saved, we die to sin. That's the old way; being saved means dying to the old way. There was a teenage boy who lived in West Palm Beach. He gave his heart to Jesus Christ, and when he did, that teenage boy died. His name was Adrian Rogers. The old Adrian died. When did he die? He died not as a teenage boy, but he died 2,000 years ago when Jesus died on that cross because His death had my name on it. He took my sins, carried them to the cross, and was hung up there for me. He suffered, bled, and died in agony for me. He bore my sins in His body on the cross. He paid my sin debt in full. When He died, through faith, I died with Him.

- How have you experienced a death to your old way of living through Jesus?
- Why is this a requirement for every follower of Jesus?

PRACTICE THIS Make a list of things that you have died to or need to die to now from your old way of living. Ask God for the power through His Spirit to die to those old-way things that remain.

6

PRAY OVER THIS

A good man out of the good treasure of his heart brings forth good things, and an evil man out of the evil treasure brings forth evil things.

MATTHEW 12:35

PONDER THIS The problem with mankind is what we received at birth. We are born into the natural world. If you have an apple and see a wormhole in that apple, don't worry about the worm having come in through that hole. He didn't come in through that hole; he went out through that hole. The wormhole didn't let the worm in; it let the worm out. You say, "How did the worm get in the apple?" He was born in the blossom. The egg was laid in the blossom and that worm came out of the heart of that apple. Likewise, Jesus said all the sins that are in mankind come out of the heart.

- Why is it important that the root cause of our sin problem be addressed and not just the symptoms?
- How has Jesus addressed your sin at its root?

PRACTICE THIS Have a conversation today with another about the work of Jesus to remedy our sin.

PRAY OVER THIS

For though by this time you ought to be teachers, you need
someone to teach you again the first principles of the oracles
of God; and you have come to need milk and not solid food.
HEBREWS 5:12

PONDER THIS The author of Hebrews said in effect, "I'd like to give you a steak today, but I can't. If I gave it to you, you couldn't chew it. If you could chew it, you couldn't swallow it. If you could swallow it, you couldn't digest it. You're a little baby. So today I'm going to give you some formula. I'm going to give you some milk, but I can't give you meat because you're not able to digest it." There are those who ought to be teachers, but you need somebody to teach you again the first principles. There are those who have been members of the church for their whole lives, and they've never taught anybody anything. They just say, "Feed me." They want to come to church on Sunday, let the pastor give them a Bible, and burp them on the way out. God calls us to grow up into Christ so that we may pass on what we've received.

- What does it look like for God's people to still be on spiritual milk when they should be ready for more?
- Is God speaking to you about this in your own life? How do you need to respond?

PRACTICE THIS Make a list of mature traits of a follower of Christ. Make a corresponding list of the traits of an immature follower of Christ. Assess which of these most resembles your life.

8

> ### PRAY OVER THIS
>
> Then Philip said, "If you believe with all your heart, you may."
> And he answered and said, "I believe that Jesus Christ is the
> Son of God." So he commanded the chariot to stand still. And
> both Philip and the eunuch went down into the water, and
> he baptized him. Now when they came up out of the water,
> the Spirit of the Lord caught Philip away, so that the eunuch
> saw him no more; and he went on his way rejoicing.
>
> **ACTS 8:37-39**

PONDER THIS Why should you be baptized? Baptism proclaims your commitment to Jesus. The Bible says, "We were buried with Him" (Romans 6:4). Baptism says, "Jesus, I'm identifying myself with You openly and publicly." Someone may ask, "Does baptism make you a Christian?" No. But it does show you're a Christian.

I have a wedding ring I wear. Do you know what that ring means? It means I love Joyce. It says I belong to Joyce. It doesn't make me married, but it shows I'm married. And it shows I'm not ashamed to let everybody know I'm married. I belong to another person. I belong to my wife that I love with all my heart, and when you get baptized, you're saying, "I belong to Jesus." When Jesus was baptized, He identified Himself with us, and when we get baptized, we identify ourselves with the Lord Jesus Christ.

- What are some things that change when you make a commitment to someone?
- Have you ever had a difficult time proclaiming your commitment to Jesus? Why or why not?

PRACTICE THIS Write out a few ways you demonstrate the commitment you have made to Jesus.

PRAY OVER THIS

In Him you were also circumcised with the circumcision
made without hands, by putting off the body of the sins of
the flesh, by the circumcision of Christ, buried with Him in
baptism, in which you also were raised with Him through faith
in the working of God, who raised Him from the dead.
COLOSSIANS 2:11-12

PONDER THIS When you come out of the waters of baptism, you're saying, "I
have come out of the grave of that old life. I have risen to walk with the Lord
Jesus because I've been born again. I have a new life."

Baptism speaks of your past—you're buried. It speaks of your present—a
new life. And it also speaks of your future. One of these days they are going to
put each of us in the grave, but I want to tell you that the grave that could not
hold the Lord Jesus will not be able to hold you down. And we will be in the
likeness of His resurrection, and the God who raised up Jesus Christ from the
grave is the God who's going to raise up each of us. Therefore, we don't need
to fear death.

I want you to know, one of these days, we are all going to be caught up to
meet the Lord Jesus in the air. We'd be foolish to be afraid of death, in the same
way, a grubby, wormy caterpillar wouldn't be afraid of being a butterfly.

- How have you experienced the hope of the resurrection in daily
  life?
- How does the hope of your future in Christ change your
  perspective on death?

PRACTICE THIS Share with a friend your testimony in terms of the things that
you have buried, the new life you have, and the future of your hope beyond the
grave.

10

> ## PRAY OVER THIS
>
> I beseech you therefore, brethren, by the mercies of God, that you present your bodies a living sacrifice, holy, acceptable to God, which is your reasonable service. And do not be conformed to this world, but be transformed by the renewing of your mind, that you may prove what is that good and acceptable and perfect will of God.
>
> **ROMANS 12:1-2**

PONDER THIS There are two great questions: 1) "Who are You, Lord?" 2) "Lord, what do You want me to do?" I want you to ask yourself those today. I read about a young Navy officer who made his first trip on a destroyer. He had impeccable training, and he was assigned to take the destroyer out of the harbor. The deck was buzzing with action. He was barking commands, and everything was moving like a Swiss clock as that destroyer set sail. They were on their way in record time. Someone came to the officer and said, "You have a message from the captain." He read it, "Young man, you've done an excellent, speedy job. You've done it according to the book, but there is an unwritten rule you've overlooked. The next time you set sail, make certain the captain is on board."

No matter how wise your plans are and how capable you are before you set off on a journey, you'd better make certain the captain is on board—that you are in the will of God.

- Have you ever asked God, "Who are You, Lord?" and "What do You want me to do?" Why or why not?
- How might asking these questions change the way you live?

PRACTICE THIS Pray and ask God to reveal where you have not allowed Him to be the captain of your life. Share that with another follower of Christ, seeking to hold each other accountable in keeping Him as your captain.

11

PRAY OVER THIS

Then he fell to the ground, and heard a voice saying to him, "Saul,
Saul, why are you persecuting Me?" And he said, "Who are You,
Lord?" Then the Lord said, "I am Jesus, whom you are persecuting.
It is hard for you to kick against the goads." So he, trembling
and astonished, said, "Lord, what do You want me to do?"

ACTS 9:4-6A

PONDER THIS If you want to know the will of God, there must be willingness. And there must also be meekness. Saul said, "Lord what will you have me to do?" That is, "You are in control. I'm not in control." Do you know what meekness is? Meekness means you are teachable. Psalm 25:9a says, "The meek will He guide..." (KJV). Are you meek? If you're not willing and you're not meek, you won't know God's will.

Now, here's a third thing: Not only did Saul have willingness and meekness, but he also had openness. He sought the will of God. Have you been open to the will of God? Don't just simply say, "If God wants to show me, He can." Have you earnestly prayed and said, "Oh God, I want to know Your will"? Do you report for godly duty? Do you think it's up to God to put His hand on your shoulder and snatch you and turn you around? Or, after you've met the Lord Jesus, are you going to be like Paul and say, "What is it Lord that you really want me to do?"

- Where have you seen an example of meekness in someone close to you?
- Has God ever guided you to do something? What was that like?

PRACTICE THIS Talk to a close friend or family member and ask if that person has seen meekness in you. Ask that person to keep you accountable as you seek God's guidance.

12

All things are lawful for me, but all things are not helpful. All things are lawful for me, but I will not be brought under the power of any.
1 CORINTHIANS 6:12

PONDER THIS An expedition is a journey. You're going somewhere if you're on an expedition. In the KJV, this verse is translated as "all things are not expedient." The word *expedient* means, "something that brings you to your goal." Every Christian ought to have some God-given goals. Every one of us ought to have a holy ambition in our lives. I have goals for my life. I believe they have been given by God, hammered out on the anvil of prayer, and they've become goals for my life. Now, I can tell whether a thing is right or wrong for me by assessing if it will bring me to my appointed goal or hinder me. Is this activity an anchor that keeps me out of God's harbor, or is it something that propels me toward my God-given goal?

But if you don't have any God-given goals, then expediency makes no difference for you. God has laid His hand upon you. This was the great goal of the Apostle Paul. He said, "...that I may lay hold of that for which Christ Jesus has also laid hold of me" (Philippians 3:12b).

- What are your God-given ambitions and goals?
- What are some things that have hindered you from your spiritual goals?

PRACTICE THIS Make a list of some God-given goals that are on your heart today. Share them with a friend and find some practical steps to pursue these goals.

PRAY OVER THIS

If then you were raised with Christ, seek those things which
are above, where Christ is, sitting at the right hand of God. Set
your mind on things above, not on things on the earth.

COLOSSIANS 3:1-2

PONDER THIS There was a man who took his shirts into a dry cleaner and gave instructions on how he wanted the shirts cleaned. But after several visits, the dry cleaner never truly matched his formula. Frustrated, he said, "Look, I brought them in the first time, I told you how. I brought them in the second time and told you how, and now you're wasting my time."

Later, this same man went for visitation with his church, and he got a card with the name matching the name of the dry cleaner. He asked the card distributer, "Do they (the dry cleaners) know me?" He said, "Yes, they do know you." He asked, "What do they think about me?" The card distributer responded, "They think the most important thing to you is the way your shirts are done."

Do you know what I want people to think of when they think of me? The most important thing in my life is Jesus Christ. But that doesn't just happen on its own. That's a principle to guide my life.

- What are some things that are important to you? How is that evident in the way you live?
- What are some things you want to be remembered for? How do you need to live today in pursuit of that goal?

PRACTICE THIS Ask a friend to share honestly about things that come to mind when he or she thinks of you. Ask where you can grow in reflecting Christ as the most important thing in your life.

But the manifestation of the Spirit is given
to each one for the profit of all.

1 CORINTHIANS 12:7

PONDER THIS If you have a spiritual gift, it is not a means to an end. It is not for your personal use. It is not to make you feel good. It is not to prove something. These gifts are meant to put you to work for the Lord Jesus Christ. God has given you a gift to profit others.

One of my favorite stories is about a woman who'd taken a first-aid course, and later gave a testimonial to her class. She shared that in front of her house there was a horrible wreck—an old man driving a car had lost control, hit an oak tree, and was thrown out on the pavement. It was terrible. But she said, "I remembered my first aid. I remembered if I were to put my head between my knees I wouldn't faint." And she said, "I did; it was wonderful." That's the way some people think about gifts. They think a spiritual gift is supposed to be a particular blessing to them, but the Bible says here that the gift is a service to others. It is to profit the whole body. It is not for your enjoyment; it is for your employment.

- What changes when we remember that our spiritual gifts are to benefit the body and are not just for our own use?
- How have you used your spiritual gifts? Have they been used to benefit others in the body of Christ?

PRACTICE THIS Take action and serve someone around you today using the gifts God has given you.

15

PRAY OVER THIS

Be diligent to present yourself approved to God, a worker who
does not need to be ashamed, rightly dividing the word of truth.
2 TIMOTHY 2:15

PONDER THIS Imagine you pull your car in behind a man pushing an old car into a gas station. All four of his tires are flat. The headlights have been broken out. The battery is gone. All the fenders are dented and flopping. It has a gas tank but there's a hole rusted in the bottom. You are sitting behind him, waiting to get gas for yourself, and you are amazed when you see his attempt to fill the tank up. If you were watching, what would you think? You'd likely wonder, *What for?* We say "Oh, God, show me your will." God says, "Why? Why should I show you My will? You're not prepared to do My will. You don't really mean it when you say you want to know My will."

Are you yielded to God? Don't say, "I want to know the will of God," unless there is willingness. Unless there is meekness. Unless there is openness. All those things were there when the Apostle Paul prayed and said, "Lord, what do you want me to do?" (Acts 9:6).

- What would it look like to yield to God in your life today?
- How do you prepare yourself for receiving direction from God?

PRACTICE THIS Write out the steps you need to take to prepare yourself for God's will. Follow those steps.

PONDER THIS Do you know what wisdom is? Wisdom is seeing life from God's point of view. When you pray and you have the Spirit of God and the Word of God in you, you will begin to have wisdom. Knowledge comes by looking around, but wisdom comes by looking up. God will lead you and give you wisdom. When a person is walking in the Spirit, he can say, "I have the mind of Christ." He's not afraid to trust what the Spirit says. That is not natural; it is supernatural.

Wisdom is not a feeling like getting teary-eyed and warm around the heart. It is having a mind that is fixed on God, full of the Word of God, and led by the Spirit of God. The Bible says God will guide you with wisdom.

- How have you measured wisdom in the past?
- What does it look like to seek God's wisdom? How can you do that today?

PRACTICE THIS Share with someone the value of godly wisdom.

17

PRAY OVER THIS

Strengthened with all might, according to His glorious
power, for all patience and longsuffering with joy.
COLOSSIANS 1:11

PONDER THIS Romans 12:1 says, "I beseech you therefore, brethren, by the mercies of God, that you present your bodies a living sacrifice, holy, acceptable to God, which is your reasonable service." Paul was talking about service to the Lord, and he went on to say in verse 2, "And do not be conformed to this world, but be transformed by the renewing of your mind, that you may prove what is that good and acceptable and perfect will of God." Do you want to find the will of God for your service? Present yourself to God. Say, "Lord here I am." Your gift must have the power to operate, and God is the One who provides the power.

Suppose you got married and received a lot of gifts. You got a waffle iron. You got a toaster. You got a blender. You got a TV. Then, you moved into an apartment with no power. What good is the gift if you can't plug it in? You see, God gives you the gift when you get saved, but the gift begins to operate when you get the power to operate it. The power to operate that gift comes when you present yourself to the Lord Jesus Christ saying, "Here I am, Lord. I give myself to you."

- What would it look like to present yourself to God as this passage calls you to?
- Have you ever tried to use your spiritual gifts without the power of God? What was that like?

PRACTICE THIS Present yourself to Jesus today. Ask a friend in Christ how God changed his or her life when he or she approached Him this way.

PRAY OVER THIS

Trust in the LORD with all your heart, and lean
not on your own understanding; in all your ways
acknowledge Him, and He shall direct your paths.

PROVERBS 3:5-6

PONDER THIS There was a river that had frozen over, and there was a man who decided he would walk across the ice. He didn't see anyone else out there but decided to move forward. As he got farther out, he became more nervous. Out of caution, he decided to crawl and then squirm across the river. Growing more anxious still, he began to cry and then he heard a cracking sound. He thought he was a goner, but as the noise got closer, the ice didn't seem to be breaking. He looked up and saw a man with a team of horses with a wagon loaded with logs driving across that river. When he realized that was the noise he had heard, he brushed the ice off and strolled across the rest of the river with confidence.

What was the difference between these two men? One knew the ice and the other did not. Where does faith come from? It comes from a knowledge of God. Those who believe in God will not be ashamed. Do you want to have a strong faith? Don't try to make yourself believe. Get to know God.

- How has knowing someone well helped you trust him more?
- What are some things you are carrying because you've had a hard time trusting God to carry them for you?

PRACTICE THIS Take some extra time in the Word to learn more about God and His promises today.

19

PRAY OVER THIS

For the word of God is living and powerful, and sharper
than any two-edged sword, piercing even to the division
of soul and spirit, and of joints and marrow, and is a
discerner of the thoughts and intents of the heart.

HEBREWS 4:12

PONDER THIS Not only did we need to be saved in the past, but we also need to be saved in the present from the power of sin, and we will be saved in the future from the possibility of sin. But that day is not here yet. Only the truths found in the Word of God can save our souls. The Greek word for *soul* is *psyche*. That's what the soul is, the psyche—your mind, your emotions, and your will. When your mind, your emotions, and your will are guided by the Word of God, then you're living in the victory of Christ's salvation.

The thing that keeps me going is not primarily how I feel. It is what I know from the Word of God. I've been on the trail long enough to look back and analyze and consider, "What is it that keeps me? What is it that holds me?" It is the Word of God. His sanctifies us through His Word. His Word is truth.

- How has the Word of God changed your life?
- What is your rhythm for staying in the Word of God? How might this improve?

PRACTICE THIS Share with another person today the ways God's Word has impacted your life.

20

PONDER THIS I've had the joy of preaching overseas in different countries, including China. In my experience, the people there were wonderful and gracious. I learned from my guide that it is an honor for them to have you come under their roof. They know how to welcome you. They will say, you are welcome in our home, and serve you something. At that moment, you should receive what they give you to show that you accept their hospitality. The guide said when they serve you something—tea for example—never reach out and take it with one hand. That implies you're grasping. Take it with both hands to express that you are receiving it.

Likewise, you don't just reach out and take God's Word. We lift our hands to Him, and we welcome the Word, we receive the Word, and we take the Word by faith. It is by grace we let God's Word come into our hearts.

- Why is it important that we view God's Word as something we receive from Him and not something we gain on our own?
- What is your typical attitude when you come to the Word of God?

PRACTICE THIS Evaluate your attitude about God's Word. Write out a prayer that addresses any struggles you face when you come to the Word. Ask God to lead you in this area.

PRAY OVER THIS

Woe to you, scribes and Pharisees, hypocrites! For you pay
tithe of mint and anise and cummin, and have neglected the
weightier matters of the law: justice and mercy and faith. These
you ought to have done, without leaving the others undone.
MATTHEW 23:23

PONDER THIS The Pharisees had heads full of Scripture but hearts full of sin.
They had religion, but they didn't have reality. They had laws, but they didn't
have life. Oh, they were careful all right. They would dot every *i* and cross every *t*,
but they didn't understand Christ. They did not have the love of the Lord Jesus
Christ in their hearts. Legalism is not the answer.

I am a Bible-believing Christian. I believe all of the Bible. I believe it is
absolutely true. I believe all Scripture is given by the inspiration of God, but I
am not a legalist. I pray to God that He will save me and you from the loveless
leaven of legalism. Legalism is not what our world needs today. The Bible is a
wonderful sword, but it is a terrible club.

- How do you relate to the Pharisees? Where are you prone to
  legalism?
- What is dangerous about legalism? How does it cause us to miss
  Jesus?

PRACTICE THIS Discuss with a brother or sister in Christ what it looks like to
walk in step with Christ instead of walking in legalism.

22

PRAY OVER THIS

Therefore lay aside all filthiness and overflow of
wickedness, and receive with meekness the implanted
word, which is able to save your souls.

JAMES 1:21

PONDER THIS Do you know what the word *filthiness* is in the original Greek?
It means, "ear wax." God says if you want to hear, you've got to clean your ears.
You can't hear if your ears are stopped. God says sin in your life is like wax in your
ear. You need to get rid of it. The reason God's truth does not come to us is that
we've got spiritual wax in our ears. As a result, it is absolutely crucial that when
you study the Bible, you make a full confession of sin and ask God to search
your heart and see if there is some wickedness in you. Get your heart clean; get
your heart right with God.

If you're going to a garden, before you plant the seed, you weed the garden.
That's what it's all about—get your heart right. After we weed the garden,
then the seed will grow. After we get the wax out, then we can hear. Do you
understand that? Receive the Word. Welcome the Word with a repentant heart.

- What does it look like to lay aside all filthiness?
- When has sin stopped up your ears from understanding the Word
  of God clearly?

PRACTICE THIS Take time for intentional repentance during your time in the
Word today and find a way to add this to your regular Bible reading routine.

23

PRAY OVER THIS

But be doers of the word, and not hearers only, deceiving yourselves.

JAMES 1:22

PONDER THIS I heard of a famous actor who was in a crowded theater when a fire broke out in the wings of the theater prior to his performance. The manager came to the actor and asked him to tell the audience to calmly leave the theater in an orderly fashion.

This actor followed the instructions. He came forward and told everyone about the fire and asked everyone to leave calmly. They applauded. They thought it was part of the act. So, he came back a second time and shared the same message. But still, they did not understand. Then, realizing the gravity of the situation, he got down on his knees, and with tears he said, please for your safety, leave the theater. The audience was moved by his performance but never understood that the message was for them. This illustrates how many people hear the Word of God from the preacher. But God said consider yourself deceived if you read the Word and hear the Word but don't heed the Word. Be doers of the Word and not hearers only.

- What is the difference between being a hearer and a doer of the Word?
- How can you prioritize being a doer of the Word this week?

PRACTICE THIS Think of someone you know to be a doer of the Word. Tell that person you see God at work in his or her life, and ask for insight on how to apply the Word to everyday circumstances.

24

PRAY OVER THIS

You are the salt of the earth; but if the salt loses its flavor,
how shall it be seasoned? It is then good for nothing but
to be thrown out and trampled underfoot by men.

MATTHEW 5:13

PONDER THIS Salt speaks of the saving life of our Lord and Savior Jesus Christ. And what does salt do? Jesus said, "You are the salt of the earth." He was speaking to fishermen who preserved their fish with salt. For one thing, salt decontaminates. There's a purifying element to salt. It is the salty ocean that bathes the shores of this world, that keeps this Earth from decaying. If you took the salt out of the ocean, everything would turn to a stench.

We need the decontamination of the salty Gospel in our world today. We can try to point to many different things, but the problem in our world is bigger than one issue. It is saltless saints. That's where the problem is. The problem is in churches all around—salt that has lost its flavor in a world that is rotting. Jesus said, "You're to be the salt of the Earth." How will you respond?

- What are some ways you can live as the "salt of the Earth?"
- Who has shown you the hope and joy of the Gospel? How are those people like salt in your life?

PRACTICE THIS Think about one person you can share the joy of being a follower of Christ with today. Share the hope of God's cleansing Word.

25

PRAY OVER THIS

Among whom also we all once conducted ourselves in the lusts
of our flesh, fulfilling the desires of the flesh and of the mind,
and were by nature children of wrath, just as the others.

EPHESIANS 2:3

PONDER THIS I read about a missionary who went to the mission field. They showed her where the missionary residence was, and it was a nice little cottage, but the floor was filthy so she decided she would scrub the floor. And she scrubbed the floor, but she couldn't get the dirt up. She proceeded to put on more water and more suds.

She got down on her hands and knees and kept scrubbing, but it was still dirty. Over and over again she'd scrub but it was still dirty. Finally, somebody said, "Madam, I hate to tell you, but that is a dirt floor." She was scrubbing a dirt floor, and the more she scrubbed the more dirt came up. You can never take your sinful nature and clean it up because your sinful nature is like that dirt floor.

All people are sinful in their nature. You may think you have not done so many bad things, but God looks at your nature. This is why we all need Jesus.

- When have you tried to clean up your sin in your own strength?
- How does a right understanding of our nature help us understand the Gospel?

PRACTICE THIS List the ways you have seen God transform you from being a slave to sin to being free in Christ. Pray and ask Him to keep transforming you from the inside out.

PRAY OVER THIS

Therefore, whether you eat or drink, or whatever
you do, do all to the glory of God.
1 CORINTHIANS 10:31

PONDER THIS Why did God make you? To know Him, to love Him, and to serve Him. If you've not known Him, loved Him, and served Him, you've been walking on God's Earth, eating God's food, using God's sunshine, breathing God's air, and not returning to God that which is His—glory.

Man's basic problem is not that he's a sinner because of what he *has* done. Man's basic problem is what he has *not* done by failing to give God glory. Now, this may not seem as bad as other sins like murder or stealing, but sin isn't always as it appears on the surface. Consider if you had to choose between a mountain of garbage and a teaspoonful of tasteless but deadly poison. One of those looks worse than the other, but the lesser of the two is more dangerous. The great sin is the sin of unbelief. It is the crowning sin, and it is proof of man's wickedness.

- How have you been guilty of taking credit for yourself instead of giving glory to God?
- How does unbelief keep us from giving God glory?

PRACTICE THIS Praise God today for all that He is doing in your life. Share your testimony of God's faithfulness with someone you know struggles with unbelief.

PRAY OVER THIS

And be kind to one another, tenderhearted, forgiving
one another, even as God in Christ forgave you.

EPHESIANS 4:32

PONDER THIS Think of someone who has wronged you. If you are harboring a hurt in your heart, I want to give you a compelling reason why you ought to forgive that individual. We ought to forgive one another because God has so willingly forgiven us. We owed a debt we could never repay, and God, in the riches of His mercy, forgave us. If God has forgiven us, then we ought to forgive others.

I received a letter some time ago from a woman who was in the hospital in Memphis. She was from Rome, Georgia and she said, "I was away from home, and I needed surgery. Some young men from your church, who did not even know me, came to the hospital and donated blood on my behalf and left a note." The note said, "We gave our blood for you because Jesus gave His blood for us." Wasn't that beautiful? In forgiveness, God has not called us to do anything He has not already done for us. I want to extend forgiveness to you because Jesus forgave me.

- How have you been changed by someone's forgiveness?
- How has Christ's forgiveness changed the way you forgive other people?

PRACTICE THIS If possible and appropriate, speak to a person who has wronged you and make steps toward reconciliation.

28

> **PRAY OVER THIS**
>
> Brethren, if a man is overtaken in any trespass, you who
> are spiritual restore such a one in a spirit of gentleness,
> considering yourself lest you also be tempted.
>
> **GALATIANS 6:1**

PONDER THIS Growing up, one of the things I loved to do with my brother was collect coconuts to sell. We learned how to climb coconut trees like monkeys to reach the leaves. One day, I was up in a tall coconut tree. I had my left arm around a palm frond, and my right hand was disconnecting a coconut when that palm frond broke. I did not look closely enough to see that it was a dying frond. When it broke, I fell about thirty feet. I fell on the grass, but my left arm fell on the sidewalk. As you can imagine, it was a bad situation.

As I was lying there, having fallen because of my own carelessness, what did I need from my brother? I didn't need a lecture. I didn't need my brother to ignore me and walk away. I didn't need my brother to go around and say, "Did you hear about Adrian? He fell out of a coconut tree." I had that arm in a sling for a while, and it healed just a little crooked. But I can use it because I got what I needed—somebody to realize that I'd fallen. I needed somebody to come and help me. What do we do with broken brothers and sisters in Christ? We help restore them in the name of Jesus.

- How are you tempted to react when you hear about another person's struggle?
- How has someone cared for you when you felt like you had fallen far from God?

PRACTICE THIS Extend love and restoration to someone in your community who has been rejected.

29

PRAY OVER THIS

Now all things are of God, who has reconciled us to Himself
through Jesus Christ, and has given us the ministry of
reconciliation, that is, that God was in Christ reconciling the
world to Himself, not imputing their trespasses to them,
and has committed to us the word of reconciliation.

2 CORINTHIANS 5:18-19

PONDER THIS I had a brother in Christ that I loved very much and still do love very much. He wronged me, and there was anger that rose up in me that said, "I'm finished with him. I can't trust him. He's been dishonest." As I paused and reflected, I thought, now why should I do that? I love this man. He is a brother. I refuse to let his mistake ruin what has been a good relationship. I prayed about it, gave it to God, and went and restored the relationship.

You may ask, "What if the person who has wronged me is not a follower of Christ?" Well, he or she is still a potential brother or sister in Christ. If that person is not a follower of Jesus and if you have an unforgiving spirit toward him or her, what chance do you have to bring that person to Christ? Would you let a sense of revenge cut off an opportunity to bring a person to the Lord Jesus Christ? That person is more than a person who has hurt you; he or she is a person who needs you.

- Who have you been tempted to cut out of your life? Why?
- How is God calling you to take part in His ministry of reconciliation?

PRACTICE THIS Think about a person you have been tempted to give up on. Pray about it, and make the first step toward reconciliation as you are led.

PRAY OVER THIS

Confess your trespasses to one another, and pray for
one another, that you may be healed. The effective,
fervent prayer of a righteous man avails much.

JAMES 5:16

PONDER THIS Ms. Bertha Smith, a Christian missionary, and Dr. Charlie Culpepper, a seminary professor, were both a part of the Great Shantung Revival in China. Both said that, for a time, the missionaries on the field had been in conflict with one another over petty things. But it was not until they began to confess their faults one to another, pray one for another, ask for forgiveness, and reconcile, that a great and mighty revival was set loose. I believe a revival can take place like that today. In businesses, schools, churches, and communities. When people begin to believe in the Bible—the Word of God—and practice it, they are set free.

So, here is your question: Is there anybody that you're harboring hate toward or carrying a grudge over? Is there bitterness in your heart? In the name of Jesus, deal with it. If you don't, you have destroyed the bridge over which you yourself must travel.

- How has forgiveness brought healing in your life?
- Who are some people in your faith community you need to reconcile with?

PRACTICE THIS Confess your sin, and pray with another brother or sister in Christ.

PRAY OVER THIS

Then I will give them a heart to know Me, that I am the
LORD; and they shall be My people, and I will be their God,
for they shall return to Me with their whole heart.
JEREMIAH 24:7

PONDER THIS I read about a man who had a very fine dog. He'd trained the dog quite well, and the dog loved to play in the water. The dog was out in the lake, and the man wanted to go, so he called the dog, but the dog wouldn't come. He called him several times. He still wouldn't come. So, the man said, "I know what I'll do," and he got a stick, and threw it out in the water. When the dog saw it, he swam over, got the stick, came back, and laid it at his master's feet.

It may be that God has given you a burden because He can't get your attention. It may be that God has given you a burden so that you might come and lay it at your Master's feet, "casting all your care upon Him, for He cares for you" (1 Peter 5:7). If you are a broken brother, there's hope for you; a fallen sister, there's hope. And if you are a spiritual person, there's a responsibility for you. If your heart is aching and breaking, there's a Savior who loves you. Cast your burden upon the Lord. He'll sustain you when you need it most.

- When has a burden brought you back to remembering your need for God?
- Who do you need to share this hope with?

PRACTICE THIS Write down some of the difficulties you have struggled with and describe how God has worked in those situations.

Thankfulness comes
before praise.

ADRIAN ROGERS

1

PRAY OVER THIS

The LORD is my shepherd; I shall not want.

PSALM 23:1

PONDER THIS How many truly satisfied people do you know? People can have all of the things of this world and not be satisfied. John Muir, the great naturalist, was speaking to Mr. Harriman—a man of great wealth and influence. John Muir said to Mr. Harriman, "I am richer than you are." Mr. Harriman responded, "Well, how is that?" He said, "Because you don't have all you want, and I do. So, I am richer than you."

Ecclesiastes 5:10a says, "He who loves silver will not be satisfied with silver." But it's not just money that fails to truly satisfy. There's really nothing that can satisfy us apart from the Lord. "The LORD is my shepherd; I shall not want." That's the only way that anyone will ever have satisfaction. It is only when you can say that phrase wholeheartedly that you can also say, "I shall not want."

- Is there a time in your life that you were truly satisfied?
- How does living with the Lord as our Shepherd change our struggle with contentment?

PRACTICE THIS Make a list of different things in which you have tried to find satisfaction. Write down the outcome of pursuing those things. Pray and ask God to help you find satisfaction in Him.

2

PRAY OVER THIS

As the deer pants for the water brooks, so
pants my soul for You, O God.

PSALM 42:1

PONDER THIS So many people think the secret to satisfaction is having a God who can give you everything. That is not the secret to satisfaction. The secret of satisfaction is the Lord Himself. Jehovah is my Shepherd. Your needs will never be met until they're met in Him. Things will never satisfy you. So many people misunderstand Psalm 37:4, which says, "Delight yourself also in the LORD, And He shall give you the desires of your heart." Many think that means if I love Jesus, I can have a luxury car; but that isn't what it means. Delight yourself in the Lord, and He will give you the desire of your heart. What that means is when you delight in the Lord, the deepest needs of your heart will be met.

The desire of your heart is Jesus. That's what your heart yearns for whether you know it or not. That's what you were made for—for Him. The Bible says it is "in Him we live and move and have our being" (Acts 17:28a). You'll never be satisfied apart from Him. It's not what He gives me but that He gives me Himself.

- When have you felt your deep need for Jesus? What was that like?
- What would it look like to have Jesus as the desire of your heart? What things would change in your life immediately?

PRACTICE THIS Think about someone who has lived as an example of having Jesus as the desire of his or her heart. Ask that person to share his or her testimony with you.

PRAY OVER THIS

He will feed His flock like a shepherd; He will gather
the lambs with His arm, and carry them in His bosom,
and gently lead those who are with young.

ISAIAH 40:11

PONDER THIS We're the flock, the Lord's the Shepherd. He shall gather the lambs with His arms. He shall carry them in His bosom. He shall gently lead those that are with young. Isn't that great? Aren't you glad the Lord is so tender to us? Aren't you glad God gives us what we need and do not deserve? Has He ever carried you closely? He takes little baby Christians; those are the lambs. They don't know anything yet. They come down the aisle and give their hearts to Jesus. We are wrong to put them through a theological test. We are wrong to say, "Now, you can't do that; you must do this; and why did you fail?" Jesus doesn't do that. Do you know what Jesus does for the little lambs? He picks them up. He carries them closely. When I was a little lamb, thank God, He carried me. If He hadn't, I never would have made it. He didn't just say, "Get yourself together." He is a compassionate and caring Shepherd who carries us gently.

- When has another follower of Jesus led you gently in your faith?
- When have you allowed correctness to distract you from grace?

PRACTICE THIS Think about the last person you critiqued. Were you, like Jesus, tender and compassionate toward him or her? Pray and repent for those areas of your sin.

4

PRAY OVER THIS

You will show me the path of life; in Your presence is fullness
of joy; at Your right hand are pleasures forevermore.

PSALM 16:11

PONDER THIS Suppose you go to the doctor with a terrible headache, fever, pain, and swelling in your arm. It seems like an infection on the inside, but all the doctor does is give you strong medicine to kill the pain and reduce the fever. If he never deals with the infection, he's not a good doctor. I want him to kill the pain if he can, but he only really helps me if he gets at the infection, which is the real problem.

People who are trying to be happy primarily in this life are only treating the symptoms. If you'll seek after righteousness, you'll be dealing with the infection. Seek righteousness and then you'll be happy. What you need is to have the deepest need of your heart and your life met. It is to worship God. It is to drink of the Spirit. It is to feed on the Word of God. That's the deepest need of your heart, and it will only be met in Jesus.

- When have you chased after worldly happiness?
- In what ways have you experienced joy as you began to follow Jesus?

PRACTICE THIS Make a list of all the things you need or want to do in the next week. Write next to this list the quote from today's devotional "The deepest need of your heart will be met only in Jesus." Place this note in a place where you can see it regularly.

5

PRAY OVER THIS

I am the good shepherd. The good shepherd
gives His life for the sheep.

JOHN 10:11

PONDER THIS Jesus laid down His life for the sheep. He said, "No man takes My life from Me. No man can kill Me. I lay it down." (See John 10:18.) It wasn't the nails that held Him to the tree. The silver cords of love and the golden bonds of redemption held Jesus Christ to that cross.

We can conceive of sheep dying for the shepherd when he wants food. But whoever heard of a shepherd dying for sheep? Jesus said, "I am the Good Shepherd that lays down His life for the sheep." You say it's unthinkable that a shepherd would die for sheep. It's even more unthinkable that God would die for Man.

Jesus is the Good Shepherd who laid down His life for the sheep. When He laid down His life for the sheep, He dealt with the penalty of sin. "For the wages of sin is death" (Romans 6:23a). That's what Jesus Christ paid. Your sin will be pardoned in Christ or punished in Hell, but it will never be overlooked unless there's a Good Shepherd who has died for your sins.

- How do you feel when you consider that Jesus laid His life down for you?
- How does this message of Jesus' selfless sacrifice change how you interact with others?

PRACTICE THIS Share the Gospel with yourself today; write it out or tell yourself in the mirror what Jesus did on your behalf.

6

PONDER THIS What did God make a fish to do? Swim in the sea. What did God make a bird to do? Fly in the sky. If you take a fish out of the sea and put him in a tree, he'll be an unhappy fish. If you take a bird out of the sky and put him in the sea, he'll be an unhappy bird. Both are out of their elements.

What is the element you were created for? God Himself. Until you know Him, you will be like a fish in a tree or a bird in the sea. You'll be out of your element.

A little girl misquoted the twenty-third Psalm, but I believe she had it just right when she said, "The Lord is my Shepherd; I've got all I want." That is the secret of satisfaction. It is Jehovah Himself. "The LORD is my Shepherd; I shall not want" (Psalm 23:1). In Him, in the Shepherd, are the wellsprings of my heart's desire and purpose.

- Have you ever wrestled with the purpose of your life? What was that like?
- How does knowing that your purpose is Christ Himself change how you live daily?

PRACTICE THIS Encourage a friend today in his or her purpose for God's glory.

7

PRAY OVER THIS

He restores my soul; He leads me in the paths
of righteousness for His name's sake.
PSALM 23:3

PONDER THIS Do you know what's wrong with so many of us? We're always trying to get out of trouble rather than get into righteousness. If you don't go from restoration to righteousness, you're going to be right back to the same old problem. So many of us simply want to get right, but we don't get on the track of following God, and that's the reason we fall back to where we were. A person who has been restored ought to follow closer than ever. He who has been forgiven much, ought to love much. (See Luke 7:47.) We ought to be like that lamb with the broken leg that just nuzzles the shepherd and stays close to the shepherd so that He might lead it and guide it so that it will never go astray again.

When are we going to learn? How many times are we going to slip and fall before we learn to stay close to the Good Shepherd? Jesus said, "My sheep hear My voice, and I know them, and they follow Me" (John 10:27).

To follow the Shepherd, you've got to love the Shepherd, observe the Shepherd, and obey the Shepherd. Sheep don't have good eyesight. You have to stay close to the Shepherd. Only in Him can you be made righteous.

- When have you tried to get out of trouble more than you desired to be made right with God?
- What would it look like to stay close to the Shepherd in your life?

PRACTICE THIS Spend some time thinking about the things that keep you close to the Shepherd and those that distract you from Him.

8

PRAY OVER THIS

Not unto us, O LORD, not unto us, but to Your name give
glory, because of Your mercy, because of Your truth.

PSALM 115:1

PONDER THIS The name *Jehovah* is the most sacred, solemn name for God in
all of the Old Testament. And yet, it's not found one time in the New Testament.
Do you know why? Because Jesus is our Jehovah. Do you know what the name
Jesus means? It means "Jehovah saves." And if we are His sheep, and He is our
Shepherd, we don't want to disgrace that name.

A good name is to be chosen over great riches. When I would take my little
children to school, each morning I would say, "Daddy loves you. Remember
who you are, and remember whose you are." I believe the Lord would say to His
sheep, "Remember who you are. You are My sheep, the people of My pasture;
My name is linked to you. I want to lead you in the paths of righteousness for My
name's sake." We know a good name is important. How much more important
is the name of our God? There is in my heart a burning desire to give glory to
that name. Do you feel that way?

- How do you remind yourself each day who you are and whose you
  are?
- What would it look like to make it a priority to give glory to God's
  name every day?

PRACTICE THIS Create a new step in your daily routine to remind you who you
are and whose you are.

PRAY OVER THIS

Yea, though I walk through the valley of the shadow
of death, I will fear no evil; for You are with me;
your rod and Your staff, they comfort me.

PSALM 23:4

PONDER THIS There was a great preacher whose wife died when she was still a very young woman. She left behind a young daughter. The little girl didn't understand all the intricacies of life and death. But sometime after her mom had passed, the girl and her father were downtown doing some shopping. The little girl was in the car, and she looked over at the wall of a department store and saw the shadow of a truck. The shadow was even larger than the truck, because the sun was setting low in the west and it made a huge shadow on the department store wall. The little girl said, "Daddy, look at the big shadow of the truck." And he said, "Sweetheart if you had your choice, would you rather be hit by the shadow of the truck or by the truck?" She said, "Daddy, that's easy. I'd much rather be hit by the shadow of that truck than be hit by that truck." He said, "That's right, darling. It was only the shadow that hit Mama. The truck hit Jesus two thousand years ago at Calvary." The truck hit Jesus. Jesus has taken the sting out of sin and the dread out of the grave. Jesus has become our Victor. And there cannot be a shadow unless there's a light.

- How has knowing Jesus changed your perspective on death?
- Who do you know who needs to know this hope beyond the grave today?

PRACTICE THIS Make a list of people you know who do not know this hope for themselves. Begin praying for them today, that they would come to know hope in Jesus.

10

> **PRAY OVER THIS**
>
> You prepare a table before me in the presence of my
> enemies; You anoint my head with oil; My cup runs over.
>
> **PSALM 23:5**

PONDER THIS Who sets the table in your house? It likely depends on who's coming. If no one's coming, I may set the table, but I never can get it quite right.

But when we are expecting company, generally, Joyce will set the table. No longer do we have the placemats. We have the linen tablecloth. No longer do we have the glass. We get the crystal. No longer do we have ordinary dishes; the best China comes out, and there will be lit candles and fresh flowers on the table. Everything is just right, and the music will be playing softly in the background. We really love to set the table. Do you know why we set the table that way? To honor the person who's coming.

You see, here's what David was saying: "God has put on an apron. God, Jehovah, has prepared a table for me. For me! The Lord of glory has prepared a table for me. He loves me. He welcomes me. I'm special to Him."

- How does it feel to know God values your place at His table?
- Who is someone in your congregation who needs to be reminded that God has a place for him or her at His table?

PRACTICE THIS Encourage someone who may be feeling left out that God has a special place at His table for him or her.

11

PRAY OVER THIS

For our citizenship is in heaven, from which we also
eagerly wait for the Savior, the Lord Jesus Christ.
PHILIPPIANS 3:20

PONDER THIS Many people ask what Heaven is going to be like. Are we going to have beds? Are we going to sleep? Will we eat? How old will we be? What will we do? I don't know the answers to those questions, but that doesn't bother me.

First John 3:2 says, "It has not yet been revealed what we shall be, but we know that when He is revealed, we shall be like Him, for we shall see Him as He is." You don't have to know. Let me tell you what Heaven is going to be like. It's going to be the presence of all that is good and the absence of all that is evil.

Now, if that doesn't satisfy you, let me give you something else. Heaven is going to be all that the loving heart of God can conceive, and the omnipotent hand of God can prepare. That is what Heaven is going to be. It's a present place; it's a perfect place; and it's a purposeful place.

- What questions about Heaven have you wrestled with?
- What does it look like to hold to the certainty of Heaven without knowing exactly what it will be like?

PRACTICE THIS Cast on the Lord your fears and questions about death and Heaven. Ask Him to grow your trust in Him, believing His Word even if you don't have all the answers.

PRAY OVER THIS

Now to Him who is able to do exceedingly abundantly
above all that we ask or think, according to the power
that works in us, to Him be glory in the church by Christ
Jesus to all generations, forever and ever. Amen.

EPHESIANS 3:20-21

PONDER THIS I was thinking about all the feasts and the meals that our Lord prepared for His disciples. The Lord Jesus Christ fed the five thousand. He prepared a table of replenishment when there was the enemy of inadequacy. And you know, He has done that for me so many times. I feel so inadequate, and I run out of resources, but the Lord just prepares a table before me. I can't even explain how He meets my needs day by day.

And I'm not just talking about physical needs. I want to ask you a question. Is there any way you can explain the feeding of the five thousand? There's not any way except God. What is there about your life that cannot be explained apart from God?

If your neighbor can explain everything, and you're just like him, only you're religious, that won't convince him. But when he sees God supernaturally meeting your needs and preparing for you a table of replenishment in your greatest need, then you'll be believable. God will not only provide a table of replenishment but also a table of restoration.

- When have you seen God work in a way you could not explain?
- What are some areas in which you feel inadequate? How does God meet you in those times?

PRACTICE THIS Write out the ways God is providing for your needs right now. Praise Him and share with someone else how He is working in your life.

13

PRAY OVER THIS

So he said, "I will do this: I will pull down my barns and build
greater, and there I will store all my crops and my goods. And
I will say to my soul, 'Soul, you have many goods laid up for
many years; take your ease; eat, drink, and be merry.'" But God
said to him, "Fool! This night your soul will be required of you;
then whose will those things be which you have provided?"

LUKE 12:18-20

PONDER THIS The man in today's passage owned property that brought forth
so much that he said, "I have no room to stow my goods." So, he said, "I know
what I'll do. I'll pull down my barns and build bigger barns. I don't want it to run
over. I don't want it to bless anybody else. I want it all for me."

Our response as followers of Jesus should be the opposite—freely we have
received, so freely we give. Let the cup run over and be a blessing to somebody
else. What do we have in the Lord Jesus? We have fullness in Christ; He prepares
a table. We have freshness in Christ; He anoints our heads. We have freeness in
Christ; our cup runs over. Don't let the devil get you to think negatively about
God or hoard His abundance only for yourself. Jesus says to you, "I prepared a
table for you. Come and dine." This is for your sake and the sake of others.

- When have you been blessed by someone sharing God's goodness
  with you?
- What are some things you have because of your relationship with
  Jesus?

PRACTICE THIS Share a blessing God has given you with someone else.

14

PRAY OVER THIS

Do not fear, little flock, for it is your Father's good
pleasure to give you the kingdom.

LUKE 12:32

PONDER THIS Sheep are nomadic. They always wander. If they're not wandering, they're being led by the shepherd. Beside the still waters, in the green pastures, through the dark valley, over hill, and beyond—they're led. (See Psalm 23.) They don't settle down and stay in one place. God doesn't intend for us to settle down here because this world is not our home. We're just passing through. Hebrews 11:8 says, "By faith, Abraham obeyed when he was called to go out to the place which he would receive as an inheritance. And he went out, not knowing where he was going." He didn't have to know. By faith, he sojourned in the land of promise.

Hebrews 11:10 says, "For he waited for the city which has foundations, whose builder and maker is God." I feel the same way. One of these days I'm going to settle down. All of us are just pilgrims right now. Heaven, our true destination, is going to be a place of constancy: a place of constant joy, a place of constant service, and a place of constant praise.

- What are some things you long for in Heaven?
- What would it look like to treat Earth like a temporary home without neglecting the things God has called you to while you are here?

PRACTICE THIS Set up a daily reminder to keep sight of Heaven as your true destination. Consider an index card, a reminder on your phone, or a strategically placed sticky note.

15

For you did not receive the spirit of bondage again to fear, but you received the Spirit of adoption by whom we cry out, "Abba, Father."

ROMANS 8:15

PONDER THIS When I was a kid, my dad was a car salesman. I remember how my dad would carry his black leather folder with his paperwork inside. I never knew what those papers were all about, but I was fascinated by that thing. He'd put that folder in his hand and walk out of the house in the morning. I had no earthly idea where he went, what he did, or what he said. And when he would come back home, I would welcome him.

I didn't have to know what he did or how he did it to know him and love him or experience his love for me. He was my daddy. I don't understand today where God goes when He goes to work, how He flings out the stars, scoops out the oceans, heaps up the mountains, and runs His mighty Universe. There are a lot of things about God I don't know, and that doesn't bother me. You don't have to know all that your Father does for Him to be your Father.

- What are some questions you have for God? How do you trust Him with those questions?
- Do you ever feel like you need to have all the answers? Why or why not?

PRACTICE THIS Make a list of reasons God is great and worthy of trust despite the things you can't know or understand.

PRAY OVER THIS

God is Spirit, and those who worship Him
must worship in spirit and truth.

JOHN 4:24

PONDER THIS There is something significant about our coming together to worship. The significance of coming to church is not primarily that we bring ourselves to worship but that we bring our worship to church. We have been with the Lord all week long. When we come together—all of us full of God—we don't come here to get filled up; we're already full of God. We come to celebrate together.

What are you saying about your life when you come to church to worship? You're saying, "God is important to me," and you're saying, "God's people are important to me." That's why we do not forsake "the assembling of ourselves together" (Hebrews 10:25), but we exhort one another. We encourage each other with the sermon, songs, and every piece of our gathering.

This worship continues through the rest of your week. Every day is a holy day, and every ground is sacred ground. But we still assemble as brothers and sisters in Christ, bringing our worship to the Lord and encouraging one another.

- How are you "filling up" in your relationship with Christ during the week?
- What value have you seen in corporate worship?

PRACTICE THIS Encourage your pastor or other leaders in your church; thank them for how they serve others as they worship.

17

PRAY OVER THIS

And He said, "My Presence will go with you, and I will
give you rest." Then he said to Him, "If Your Presence
does not go with us, do not bring us up from here."

EXODUS 33:14-15

PONDER THIS It's frightening to have success, to have possessions, and to have protection but not to have the presence of the Lord. That would be like people getting married and living in separate bedrooms. Don't settle for seeming success without the Lord.

When you have the presence of God, you need nothing more, but you should settle for nothing less. There are many who would say, "I have salvation and eternal security. I may not be walking in joy or victory, but I honestly expect to go to Heaven." But if you would be honest with me, you might say, "God is not real in my life. I have His protection, His provision, and His promise, but I do not have the presence of God in my life."

Don't think that just because you have provision and protection you're right with God. Even a non-believer has certain provisions: food, air, clothes, and shelter. We can be so preoccupied with getting provision and protection, and with claiming God's promises, that we fail to value His presence.

- Do you desire God's presence in your life?
- Why is God's presence so valuable?

PRACTICE THIS Make it a point to acknowledge God's presence throughout your day.

18

PONDER THIS Did you know you can only grieve somebody who loves you? Let me illustrate, and you'll understand what I'm talking about. The neighbors' kids may frustrate you; your own children grieve you. What's the difference? Grieve is a love word. The Holy Spirit of God loves you, but you can so grieve Him when you disobey the commandments of God that the Holy Spirit just closes up. The Bible says in 1 Thessalonians 5:19, "Do not quench the Spirit." Do you know what the word *quench* means? It means "to pour cold water on a fire." The Holy Spirit is like a gentle dove, like a glowing ember. You can frighten away that dove, and you can pour water on that ember.

If you willfully, knowingly, and deliberately disobey God, you grieve the Spirit, you quench the Spirit. You may even wonder, "Am I saved?" I've met many people who doubt their salvation that I believe are truly saved, but they're living in direct disobedience to God, and as a result, they do not have the manifested presence of God.

- How does it make you feel that God grieves when you are apart from Him?
- How does it give you hope to have the Holy Spirit—the presence of God—in your life?

PRACTICE THIS Consider where you might be grieving the Spirit. Where do you need to make changes to stop this? Take action today.

PRAY OVER THIS

Now to Him who is able to do exceedingly abundantly
above all that we ask or think, according to the power
that works in us, to Him be glory in the church by Christ
Jesus to all generations, forever and ever. Amen.

EPHESIANS 3:20-21

PONDER THIS Is there something you love more, fear more, serve more, or trust more than Almighty God? If there is, no wonder God's presence is not real in your heart and in your life. You are holding onto an idol. You have divided devotion.

If the glory of God is gone in your life—if God is not real to you—ask this question: Is there anyone or anything that takes precedence over God in my life? You say, "Well I give God a place in my life." God doesn't want *a* place in your life. You say, "Well I give God prominence in my life." God despises prominence in your life. God demands preeminence in your life. He will take nothing less. God's throne is not a duplex. Is there anything that is a greater controlling factor in your life? Is there anything that gets more of your attention than Almighty God? If so, it should not come as a surprise to you that because of that golden calf in your life, God says, "I'm not going with you." Any direct disobedience, any divided devotion, will hinder your relationship with Him.

- What has been dividing your attention from God?
- What is the danger of having a heart that is divided, giving God only some of your attention?

PRACTICE THIS Take a day to fast and pray about what is dividing your attention from God.

PRAY OVER THIS

By this we know that we love the children of God, when
we love God and keep His commandments. For this
is the love of God, that we keep His commandments.
And His commandments are not burdensome.

1 JOHN 5:2-3

PONDER THIS A man came to talk with his pastor and said, "I don't know what's wrong with me. God isn't real to me anymore. I don't have the joy and presence of God like I used to." The wise pastor asked a direct question, "Is there any unconfessed sin in your life?" The man said, "I used to bring a tithe of my income to God. But I got the idea that perhaps God didn't need that as much as I needed it. I have ceased to be honest with God." The pastor said, "Do you know what you've done? You've begun to steal from God. Would you steal from the offering plate when it is passed?"

There will always be someone who will give you a reason or excuse to disobey God; it may even be a religious leader. They'll lead you into an unscriptural marriage, immorality, or some transgression of the commandments of God, and they'll say, "Times have changed, and things are different." But I remind you that Jesus says "He who has My commandments and keeps them, it is he who loves Me. And he who loves Me will be loved by My Father, and I will love him and manifest Myself to him" (John 14:21).

- What excuses have you made to God for your sin in the past?
- What would it look like to truly love God and keep His commands? What would change? What would stay the same?

PRACTICE THIS Create a list of the excuses you have made to God. Make another list of all the reasons to trust God and His commands.

PRAY OVER THIS

A son honors his father, and a servant his master. If then I am
the Father, where is My honor? And if I am a Master, where is My
reverence? Says the LORD of hosts to you priests who despise My
name. Yet you say, "In what way have we despised Your name?"

MALACHI 1:6

PONDER THIS Did you know you are a priest? First Peter 2:9a says, "But you are a chosen generation, a royal priesthood, a holy nation." We are priests. We're to offer to the Lord sacrifices day by day, and we're to do it with enthusiasm, not weariness. I'm as excited today about serving Jesus as I have ever been in my whole life. God knows I'm telling the truth. There is so much I love about serving the Lord Jesus Christ, and every day it gets sweeter.

I want you to keep the wonder in your worship. I want you to keep the fire in your faith. Jesus would rather have you cold than lukewarm. Why? At least a person who's against Christ has enough respect for Him to be against Him. But a person who is lukewarm says, "I believe. I'm just not excited about it." We come to church sometimes and yawn in the face of God. God says, "I'm a Father. Where is my honor?" That's the reason why Jesus taught us to pray, "Our Father in heaven, Hallowed be Your name" (Matthew 6:9). Let's remember the God we serve, as we seek to honor Him today.

- How have you lived out your role as one of God's priests?
- When do you struggle most with having enthusiasm as you serve God?

PRACTICE THIS Speak to another Christian who has joy in his or her walk with Jesus; ask that person for some words of wisdom and advice to keep faith growing.

22

PRAY OVER THIS

But whenever Moses went in before the LORD to speak with Him, he would take the veil off until he came out; and he would come out and speak to the children of Israel whatever he had been commanded. And whenever the children of Israel saw the face of Moses, that the skin of Moses' face shone, then Moses would put the veil on his face again, until he went in to speak with Him.

EXODUS 34:34-35

PONDER THIS Moses had an encounter with God. The life and presence of God was so real in Moses' life that his face literally shone. He had to wear a veil over his face when he went out in public. He took the veil off his face when he went in to speak face-to-face with the Lord. The people knew Moses had a message from God because of his shining face.

But the purpose of a veil is not only to hide beauty. Some wear a veil to hide shame. I'm wondering if there are some of you who are wearing veils, not to veil the glory, but maybe to hide the fact that the glory is not there. I wonder if there are not some deacons like that, some Sunday school teachers like that. Maybe for you, there was once a time when God was very real to you, and you still go through the motions, but inwardly you know you're hiding behind a veil.

- What are some struggles in your faith you have not shared with others?
- What makes it difficult for you to share your struggles with others?

PRACTICE THIS Speak honestly with a brother or sister in Christ about where you are struggling in your walk with Jesus.

PRAY OVER THIS

Then he said to Him, "If Your Presence does not go with us,
do not bring us up from here. For how then will it be known
that Your people and I have found grace in Your sight, except
You go with us? So we shall be separate, Your people and I,
from all the people who are upon the face of the earth."

EXODUS 33:15-16

PONDER THIS There must be a determination to have God in your life. Moses said, "If You don't go, I'm not going." I think many of us would have settled for what God said to Moses. Many of us would say, "Lord, You promised me eternal life. I've got it. You promised me Heaven. I've got Heaven. You promised me You would see me through and You are. Thank You, Lord." We might settle for that without the conscious presence of God, but I want to beg you not to do it.

Do you know what that's like? That's like a husband and wife who are married but separate. He says, "I'll pay your rent and your groceries. I'll cut the grass, but we're not going to live together." Do you want that kind of relationship with God? Do you want only what God will give? Or are you saying, "I am not satisfied with being separate? I want to know the Lord intimately." I pray this determination is true for all of us so that we'll say, "We want the conscious presence of God in our lives and in our church. We don't want to go one step more without Him."

- What would it look like to be determined in your faith this week?
- What are some areas that you want to grow in your faith?

PRACTICE THIS Write out the areas you want to grow in your faith and some steps to start growing in those areas.

PRAY OVER THIS

If I say, "My foot slips," Your mercy, O LORD, will hold me up. In the multitude of my anxieties within me, Your comforts delight my soul.

PSALM 94:18-19

PONDER THIS What is your greatest strength? Your intellect, your money, your personality? No, your greatest strength is God. When we sail through life without any difficulties, though, we tend not to depend on God. Joyce and I read from the Oswald Chambers devotional, *My Utmost for His Highest*, almost every morning. In the devotion, "Beware of the Least Likely Temptation" he said, "Unguarded strength is actually a double weakness because that is where the least likely temptations will be effective in sapping strength. The Bible characters stumbled over their strong points, never their weak ones." Difficulty and heartache cause us to depend on the Lord Jesus Christ.

Many times, by His grace, God allows us to have trouble that brings us to depend on Him. "Pride goes before destruction, and a haughty spirit before a fall" (Proverbs 16:18). If your trouble, your heartache, your tears, and your difficulty cause you to depend more on God, can't you thank Him for it? In those moments, we can say, "Lord, I have to thank You because this has caused me to depend on You."

- Where are you most likely to depend on yourself?
- When have you depended on God's presence in a time of struggle?

PRACTICE THIS Write out some of the events that have brought you to depend on God. Thank God for those things and ask Him to continually draw you closer to Him.

PRAY OVER THIS

But the hour is coming, and now is, when the true worshipers
will worship the Father in spirit and truth; for the Father
is seeking such to worship Him. God is Spirit, and those
who worship Him must worship in spirit and truth.

JOHN 4:23-24

PONDER THIS Have you ever heard a person say, "I went to church, but I didn't get anything out of it?" It's not about you. The question is, "Did God get anything out of it? Did you praise Him? Did you give Him glory?" What if somebody came to my birthday party and said, "Well, I didn't get anything out of it." It's not about you; it's about Him. We have come to worship Him and glorify Him. We're to worship God "in spirit and truth" (John 4:24).

In John 4, we read about the woman at the well and some may say, "I'm glad that wicked lady got saved. She sure needed it." In John 3, there was Nicodemus, a religious leader, who also needed to be saved. What's the lesson? There is no one so good they need not be saved and no one so bad they cannot be saved. Nicodemus was thirsty. The woman at the well was thirsty. If you're thirsty, what you're thirsting for is the Lord Jesus Christ, the Living Water. He will save you, and He'll keep you saved.

- Who do you relate with more: the woman at the well or the religious leader, Nicodemus? Why?
- When have you been focused on what you got out of worship instead of what you brought to God? What needs to change in your approach to worship?

PRACTICE THIS Read the Word and worship God for who He is instead of focusing on what you are getting out of it.

PRAY OVER THIS

Giving thanks always for all things to God the
Father in the name of our Lord Jesus Christ.
EPHESIANS 5:20

PONDER THIS Did you know that trouble in your life may give you a greater testimony? It may be through deep sorrow and pain that God gives you the greatest testimony. The Apostle Paul, who knew much sorrow, said this in 2 Corinthians 1:3-4, "Blessed be the God and Father of our Lord Jesus Christ, the Father of mercies and God of all comfort, who comforts us in all our tribulation, that we may be able to comfort those who are in any trouble, with the comfort with which we ourselves are comforted by God." This verse tells us God is the source of comfort, and it is God who comforts us in tribulation. If you didn't have tribulation, you wouldn't need comfort. It also says God takes that comfort He gives us and allows us to comfort others with that same comfort we have received from Him.

Joyce and I experienced the loss of a child, and I've seen mothers—not just once, but many times—come to Joyce and receive comfort when they themselves lost children. And I have seen Joyce—not in a theoretical way, but in a very real way—share the comfort that she has received from the Lord with others. We're able to comfort others with the same comfort we ourselves receive from God. Don't get the idea that if we just sail through life with no difficulties, it's going make us better witnesses. That's not so.

- What is a trial or difficulty through which you've received the Lord's comfort?
- When have you been comforted by someone else's testimony of going through a difficult time?

PRACTICE THIS Share your testimony about how God was with you through a difficult time with another person this week.

PRAY OVER THIS

But let patience have its perfect work, that you may
be perfect and complete, lacking nothing.
JAMES 1:4

PONDER THIS What is God's plan for you? God wants you to be mature. You may think God's plan for you is health and wealth. That's not it. You may think God's plan for you is service and usefulness. He does want that, but that's not God's plan for you. So then, what is God's plan for you? The Bible tells us in Romans 8:28-29, "And we know that all things work together for good to those who love God, to those who are the called according to His purpose. For whom He foreknew, He also predestined to be conformed to the image of His Son, that He might be the firstborn among many brethren."

The word *patience* in James 1:4 is not the ability to thread a needle or build a model airplane; James used a Greek word that means "endurance." You'll never learn anything if you don't learn patience. You won't learn the piano or grow in that skill. You're not going to learn Greek until you have enough patience to learn the verbs and you're not going to learn to be a true child of God in true maturity until you learn patience. The only way you can learn endurance or patience to move toward maturity is by having something to endure.

- What are some plans you thought God had for you that turned out differently than you expected?
- What value have you seen in endurance in your own life?

PRACTICE THIS Think about some of the difficult things that have happened in your life that have built endurance in your faith. Spend some time praising God for the different ways your relationship with Him has grown through these difficulties.

28

PONDER THIS When Jesus came to Earth the first time, He came to a tree—but when He comes again, He's coming to a throne. When He came the first time, He came to redeem—but when He comes again, He will come to reign. When He came the first time, He came as a Savior—but when He comes again, He is coming as the Sovereign.

I heard about an individual who was arrested for a crime and was guilty, but he thought perhaps he could find mercy in the court because the judge sitting on the bench had one time represented this man as a lawyer. The judge said to him, "I'm sorry to inform you of this, but I can show absolutely no partiality on your point. At that time, I was your lawyer to represent you, but now I am your judge to judge you." I want to tell you this: if you do not allow the Lord Jesus Christ to be your Savior, you will meet Him as your Judge, and the Lamb will become the Lion when He returns. You may have cursed Him behind His back, but no one will curse Him to His face.

- How have you prepared to face Jesus as sovereign and judge at His return?
- How do God's words in today's verse give you confidence in your faith in Him?

PRACTICE THIS Place a reminder that Jesus is returning as Sovereign somewhere you will see it every day.

PRAY OVER THIS

And when I saw Him, I fell at His feet as dead. But
He laid His right hand on me, saying to me, 'Do
not be afraid; I am the First and the Last.'

REVELATION 1:17

PONDER THIS Sometimes we come into church and pray nonchalantly saying, "Lord, show up here today. Reveal to us Your glory and Your majesty." Imagine if one day God answered that prayer and boom, the back door opened, and He came down that aisle in the same way John saw Him in Revelation. Imagine, His hair glistening, whiter than snow. His face with a Shekinah glory, brighter than the sun. His feet glowing as if in a furnace. He comes, and His voice is deafening. He's wearing regal robes, and He begins to walk down the aisle. What would you do? Would you ask Him your biggest question or give Him a hug? You'd fall on your face before Him, would you not? That's what John did.

When you truly see the Lord Jesus as He is, it will bring your full submission. The Apostle John fell before Him prostrate as an acknowledgment of His lordship. Have you surrendered everything to Jesus? When we truly see the glory of God, it will bring us to full submission, giving us reverence for Him and great assurance.

- What are some things you struggle with putting under the full submission of God?
- How does knowing who God is change the way we respond to Him?

PRACTICE THIS Take some time to silently reflect and focus on the glory of God.

30

PRAY OVER THIS

For it pleased the Father that in Him all the fullness
should dwell, and by Him to reconcile all things to Himself,
by Him, whether things on earth or things in heaven,
having made peace through the blood of His cross.

COLOSSIANS 1:19-20

PONDER THIS A college student asked his pastor, "Do you think there is life on other planets?" The pastor said, "No, I don't think so." He said, "Then why did God go to all the trouble to make all that stuff?" The pastor said, "What trouble? It was no trouble. He spoke and it was so. The only trouble that God ever had was bloody Calvary."

When Jesus died, He didn't just speak and say, "Be forgiven." No, by the blood of His cross He paid the sin debt and became both the just and the justifier of those who believe in Him. Your sin will be pardoned in Christ or punished in Hell, but it will never be overlooked. God is holy and knew for us to be reconciled with Him, there must be shedding of blood for the cost of our sin. There is a chasm of sin that separates man from God. But Jesus has reconciled us—He built the bridge that spans the chasm. Jesus is the One and only. He is the One who reveals the Father, He is the One who rules the universe, and He is the One who reconciles the lost. I am so glad that I can tell you He is my Savior and Lord, and I love Him with all my heart, and I want you to do the same.

- Do you take sin seriously? Why or why not? What evidence does your life give to support your answer?
- How has the work of Jesus changed your life?

PRACTICE THIS Share with someone today how Jesus has changed your life.

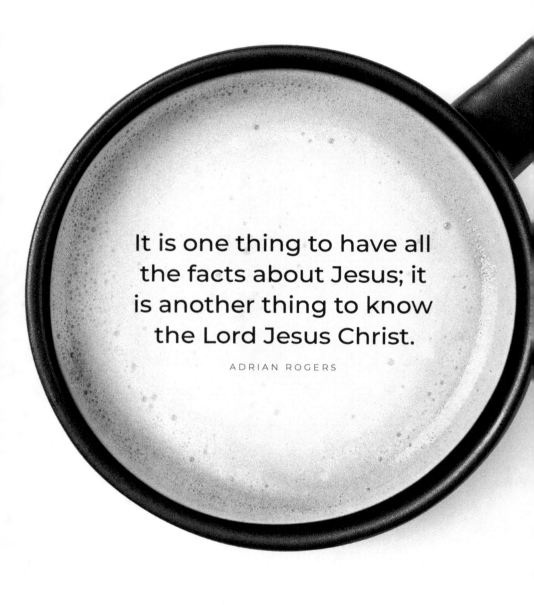

It is one thing to have all the facts about Jesus; it is another thing to know the Lord Jesus Christ.

ADRIAN ROGERS

PRAY OVER THIS

Jesus said to them, "Fill the waterpots with water." And they filled them up to the brim. And He said to them, "Draw some out now, and take it to the master of the feast." And they took it. When the master of the feast had tasted the water that was made wine, and did not know where it came from (but the servants who had drawn the water knew), the master of the feast called the bridegroom.

JOHN 2:7-9

PONDER THIS The first miracle of Jesus took place at a wedding, a happy occasion. Jesus attended both weddings and funerals. Jesus never broke up a feast, but He often broke up a funeral. Jesus lived a life of great joy. Jesus is not a cosmic killjoy, but He came that we might have abounding joy.

A little boy was setting the communion table at church, and he saw the cross on the table. He had just begun school learning addition and subtraction, and when he saw the cross on the communion table, he said, "Mother, what is that plus mark doing on that table up there?" That plus mark was a cross, but I remind you that the cross is a plus mark; it is not negative. Jesus has come so that we might have incredibly bright, beautiful, and joyful lives.

Jesus was present at the wedding in John 2 and turned what could have been a disaster into something delightful. Jesus has a way of turning the monotonous into the momentous. He is the Lord who cares about the things—even the little things—that concern you.

- How have you experienced joy in your relationship with Jesus?
- How has God cared for the small things in your life?

PRACTICE THIS Serve a friend today to remind him or her that God cares for the small things in his or her life.

PRAY OVER THIS

The thief does not come except to steal, and to kill,
and to destroy. I have come that they may have life,
and that they may have it more abundantly.

JOHN 10:10

PONDER THIS The life Jesus gives is abundant life. There was more than enough wine for the wedding in John 2. When Jesus fed the five thousand in John 6, there were twelve baskets full left over. When the prodigal son returned to the father's house in Luke 15, he remembered his father's house had bread to spare. When our Lord saves us, He does more than just deliver us from Hell, He gives us life abundant and free. He doesn't merely pardon our sin—the Bible says, "He will abundantly pardon" (Isaiah 55:7b).

If you have mistreated somebody and said, "Would you please forgive me?" and that person said, "That's all right, I forgive you," that is a pardon. But if he takes you into his arms and embraces you, that is abundant pardon. That's the kind of pardon we have in our Lord. He gives us not only abundant pardon but also abundant provision. Our Lord abundantly blesses us. Jesus said in John 10:10, "that they may have life...abundantly." And Ephesians 3:20-21 reminds us, "Now to Him who is able to do exceedingly abundantly above all that we ask or think, according to the power that works in us, to Him be glory in the church by Christ Jesus to all generations, forever and ever. Amen." Jesus took our stony hearts and our vessels of clay filled with meaningless ritual and religion and then gave Himself as the well of endless joy.

- What stirs in you when you consider the abundant pardon Jesus has given you?
- When have you experienced abundant joy from Jesus?

PRACTICE THIS Encourage someone you have seen exemplify joy from Jesus.

3

PRAY OVER THIS

But Simon answered and said to Him, "Master, we
have toiled all night and caught nothing; nevertheless
at Your word I will let down the net."

LUKE 5:5

PONDER THIS May I challenge you to make the words of Peter in this passage the motto of your life? "At Your word I will." You do not have to understand the command of God to obey that command. Don't parade it past the judgment bar of your reasoning to see if it makes sense or not. It may not make sense. Throwing the net out on the other side of the boat did not make sense; except it made sense to Jesus.

Jesus is in the transformation business. He transforms worthless water into sparkling wine. And He's still in the business of transforming people today—human beings like me, like you. Someone wisely said, "Nature forms us, sin deforms us, education informs us, penitentiaries reform us, but Jesus transforms us." He is a transformer, and He is changing us now.

I think about how He transformed Simon Peter, a blustering, big-mouth fisherman into the fiery apostle of Pentecost. I think about how He transformed the Apostle John, the Son of Thunder, into the apostle of love. I think about how He transformed Matthew, who was a tax collector, into the writer of the Gospel of Matthew. I think of how He transformed Mary, who was a demon-possessed harlot, into a herald of the resurrection. I think of how He transformed my own life. The miracle is in the transformation.

- Have you ever followed someone's advice, even if you didn't think it would work? What happened? Why did you decide to listen?
- What commands of God don't seem to make sense to you or are hard for you to trust?

PRACTICE THIS Write down the commands of Christ that seem hard to understand or follow.

4

> ### PRAY OVER THIS
>
> Oh, taste and see that the LORD is good;
> blessed is the man who trusts in Him!
> **PSALM 34:8**

PONDER THIS Years ago, I was walking through an alley behind a Sunday school. My family did not attend church. I heard them singing a song. They were singing "Every day with Jesus is sweeter than the day before." I was in my early teen years, but I said to myself, "That is not true; that is impossible. Nothing can keep getting sweeter." But since I have been saved, I know it is totally true.

I love the Lord Jesus Christ as much now as I ever have in my life, and yet, I'm looking forward to loving Him more tomorrow. You see, the devil gives the best first. That's the way it is with life. You start out in life as a child with the joy and wonder of childhood, and then there's the vision and the enthusiasm of youth and in manhood. But then about middle age, you get into the battle of life and the weariness of age, and things begin to deteriorate and run downhill *if* you don't know the Lord. Without Jesus, life gets worse and worse.

I'm telling you, when Jesus performed His first miracle, it was a manifestation of His glory, but I can hardly wait for Him to come again. Thank God that we have hope as we age—we can look forward to His coming.

- Have you ever gone into an experience questioning how it would turn out, only to be pleasantly surprised that things went well? What was it like?
- What leads you to have low expectations? How can you change your thinking knowing that Christ is with you and for you?

PRACTICE THIS Write out the parts of your walk with God where you feel His joy the most.

PRAY OVER THIS

So Jesus came again to Cana of Galilee where He had made the water wine. And there was a certain nobleman whose son was sick at Capernaum. When he heard that Jesus had come out of Judea into Galilee, he went to Him and implored Him to come down and heal his son, for he was at the point of death. Then Jesus said to him, "Unless you people see signs and wonders, you will by no means believe."

JOHN 4:46-48

PONDER THIS When this nobleman heard Jesus was coming to Galilee, he went up to Him. At that point in time, he had just heard about Jesus. That in itself is a wonderful thing. Everybody should hear about Jesus. But when it came down to it, all he had was hearsay. He had only listened to other people talk about miracles Jesus had performed.

But secondhand faith is not saving faith. You can't go to Heaven on your mother's faith, your pastor's faith, your neighbor's faith, or anybody else's faith. You can hear about Jesus and what Jesus has done for others, that is secondhand faith. In Matthew 16, Jesus asked His disciples, "Who do men say that I, the Son of Man, am?" They responded, "Some say John the Baptist, some Elijah, and others Jeremiah or one of the prophets." But then Jesus asked the pertinent question, "But who do you say that I am?"

This question is for you today. Do you know *about* Jesus, or do you *know* Him?

- Do you remember having a "secondhand" faith? What was that like? If you know Jesus, how did secondhand faith differ from the firsthand faith you have now?
- If you need firsthand faith, will you invest in a personal relationship with Jesus today?

PRACTICE THIS Write down your answer to Jesus' question: "But who do you say that I am?"

6

PRAY OVER THIS

That if you confess with your mouth the Lord Jesus and believe
in your heart that God has raised Him from the dead, you will
be saved. For with the heart one believes unto righteousness,
and with the mouth confession is made unto salvation.

ROMANS 10:9-10

PONDER THIS One time I was praying with a woman in the hospital, and I heard somebody down the hall call, "Come see me too." I went and there was a precious lady with pain on her face and despair in her heart. She had little time to live. She said, "I'm not ready to meet God. Can you help me?" I told her about Jesus. "If you'll trust Him, He'll save you." She asked for my help, so I asked her to pray with me, repeating my words, "Dear God, I know You love me and want to save me. Jesus, I believe God raised You from the dead. I open my heart, and I receive You now as my Lord and Savior. Amen."

When I opened my eyes, I expected to see peace on her face, but I saw a tortured look. She asked, "How can just saying that do any good?" I said, "You're right. It is more than words. It is believing and trusting in Jesus that saves. Now, let's pray it again and this time, put your faith in Jesus." We prayed again and she said, "Lord, I really trust You." I saw the peace of God come over that precious woman's face.

- When was a time you received encouragement that didn't feel sincere? What was that like?
- Have you ever read a promise in Scripture and agreed without absorbing the full meaning? Have you found the Word of God to penetrate more when you gave it your full attention?

PRACTICE THIS Ask a friend to speak to an area of your life where you may be saying the right words but not trusting God with a sincere heart.

PRAY OVER THIS

Now a certain man was there who had an infirmity thirty-eight years. When Jesus saw him lying there, and knew that he already had been in that condition a long time, He said to him, "Do you want to be made well?" The sick man answered Him, "Sir, I have no man to put me into the pool when the water is stirred up; but while I am coming, another steps down before me." Jesus said to him, "Rise, take up your bed and walk." And immediately the man was made well, took up his bed, and walked.

JOHN 5:5-9A

PONDER THIS In this passage, Jesus asked the paralytic a profound yet simple question: "Do you want to be made well?" That question is also one for you. Jesus is not merely in the healing business. He only healed one person in this passage. The Bible says there was a great multitude there. Had Jesus been only a great healer He would have healed them all. This miracle had a message: that we might believe Jesus is the Christ. (See John 20:31.) We need to go beyond miracles and on to Jesus.

In G. Campbell Morgan's article "Ability for Disability," he said, "Every miracle which Jesus wrought was a teaching…" Now, he didn't mean the miracles were not real, but there is a miraculous message in the miracles. Jesus healed this one man to get a message across to all of us who feel we need spiritual strength. Apart from Christ, we are spiritually paralyzed and without strength, but in Christ, we have power for living. Jesus is God's answer to man's spiritual disability.

- Who do you go to for help? Why that person?
- Who do you see struggling right now that you could ask Jesus to make whole?

PRACTICE THIS Ask God for help with something you know you can't do on your own.

8

PRAY OVER THIS

For when we were still without strength, in
due time Christ died for the ungodly.

ROMANS 5:6

PONDER THIS We are sinners by birth, sinners by nature, sinners by choice, and sinners by practice. The Bible says all have sinned and come short of the glory of God. (See Romans 3:23.) Sin is the primary source of our weakness. Many of us do not realize we are paralyzed. You may say, "I'm not weak. I lift weights. I'm very strong." I'm not talking about physical weakness. You may say, "I'm not weak. I have a PhD." I'm not talking about intellectual weakness. You may say, "I'm not weak. I have a million dollars in the bank." I'm not talking about financial weakness. I'm talking about spiritual weakness that has paralyzed you.

Do you know what our weakness is? We don't have the strength to be godly. We are without strength, so Christ died for the ungodly. God's plan for all of us is that we be godly. I don't care how hard you try to be godly; you don't have what it takes. You see, you may be strong to do as you want, but you're not strong to do as you ought. While we were yet without strength, Christ died for the ungodly. The primary source of our weakness is sin, and the paralyzing force of our sin is that we cannot be what God would have us be.

- Is it easier for you to see your strengths or weaknesses? Why?
- How have you experienced hope through Jesus in the middle of your spiritual weakness?

PRACTICE THIS Take some time and make a list of your weaknesses. Pray over those things, asking God to be the strength in your weakness.

PRAY OVER THIS

"Most assuredly, I say to you, you seek Me, not because you saw the signs, but because you ate of the loaves and were filled. Do not labor for the food which perishes, but for the food which endures to everlasting life, which the Son of Man will give you, because God the Father has set His seal on Him."

JOHN 6:26B-27

PONDER THIS On one of my Israel trips, I knew we were going to where Jesus fed the five thousand. To make it memorable, I asked my guide, "Would you get me some loaves of bread and some fish and put them in a paper sack and bring it with you? When we get to this spot, it'll just remind us of the miracle that Jesus performed right there." The trip required a boat to cross the Sea of Galilee. When we arrived, I brought out the fish and unwrapped the bread. It was so hot, and after a trip on rough water, one of the men looked at the loaves and fish and said, "If everybody feels like I do, you can feed five thousand with that."

I realized there comes a time in our lives when the things of this world do not satisfy us. We want something more. Why is that? Because there is a deeper hunger in our hearts.

- Think of a moment when you tried something for the first time. Why did you try it? What were you looking to get out of it?
- Have you ever "wasted" your free time doing an activity you thought would bring you joy but didn't? Why didn't it bring you joy?

PRACTICE THIS Make a list of things that make you feel satisfied. Thank God for how these little moments point to a deeper, greater reality in which we receive true satisfaction in Christ.

PRAY OVER THIS

Jesus said to him, "Rise, take up your bed and walk." And
immediately the man was made well, took up his bed, and walked.

JOHN 5:8-9A

PONDER THIS Ephesians 2:8-10 says, "For by grace you have been saved through faith, and that not of yourselves; it is the gift of God, not of works, lest anyone should boast. For we are His workmanship, created in Christ Jesus for good works, which God prepared beforehand that we should walk in them." Now, apply this verse to Jesus' words in today's verse, "Rise, take up your bed and walk." How was this man delivered? By grace. There was nothing he could do; he was paralyzed. The Bible says immediately he was made well. Salvation is by the sheer grace of God. Had you and I been standing there, we might have asked, "How can you tell a paralyzed man to get up? If he could get up, he would've gotten up a long time ago. That's impossible. And because it's impossible, it's unreasonable. And because it's impossible and unreasonable, it's unfair." But even in our dispute, the man would rise.

Let me tell you what Christianity is. Christianity is the impossible, the unreasonable, and Jesus Christ. Jesus does the impossible, and He does the unreasonable, but it's possible with Him. He says to a paralyzed man, "Rise." And that's what He says to every sinner. It is by grace, through faith.

- When have you tried to work for God's favor? What kind of obstacles did you face?
- How do you feel knowing God has done the impossible in your own life, bringing you from death to life in Him?

PRACTICE THIS Think of a friend who is struggling with hopelessness right now. Ask God to show you a way to encourage that person in the hope He has given you in the impossible moments of life.

11

PRAY OVER THIS

Now faith is the substance of things hoped for, the evidence of things not seen. For by it the elders obtained a good testimony. By faith we understand that the worlds were framed by the word of God, so that the things which are seen were not made of things which are visible.

HEBREWS 11:1-3

PONDER THIS Suppose you wanted to see the NBA playoffs, so you went to the ticket counter several days early and waited in a long line. But then a buddy comes up to you and says, "Hey Man! I've got two tickets, right down front. Best tickets available. I got them. Come on, let's go!" Would you get out of line? Yes, if you believed him.

You see, Jesus says, "It is by grace, but it's through faith. You just obey me. You just trust me." The paralytic man in John 5 put his faith into action. Faith is belief with legs on it. You are saved by grace through faith unto good works.

Was the man healed because he walked, or did he walk because he was healed? He walked because he was healed. You're not saved by doing good works, you're saved unto good works. It is by grace through faith unto good works. You live the Christian life not to be saved but because you're saved. Jesus did not say to this man, "Walk, take up your bed, and rise." He couldn't walk until he was up, and you cannot live the Christian life until after you receive the Christian life.

- How did your life change once you began following Jesus?
- What are some ways you put your faith into action?

PRACTICE THIS Share with a friend a testimony of a time you put your faith into action.

12

PRAY OVER THIS

For He satisfies the longing soul, and fills
the hungry soul with goodness.
PSALM 107:9

PONDER THIS You can have programs at church that will get people to come. You can get them there with fun, dinners, plays, and programs, but if you don't give them Jesus, then you have missed the whole thing. What you catch them with is what you have to keep them with. There are different platforms for preaching the Gospel, but there is no substitute for the Gospel. Christ came as the Bread of Life, so that people might be saved. They must be born again. Jesus is our spiritual bread.

Men are searching everywhere for satisfaction. They'll never find it until they find it in the Lord Jesus. What did God create you for? You may think, "God created me to serve Him." But if He only wanted someone to serve Him, He'd get somebody a lot better than you or I. He could get angels. God made you to love Him—to know Him and to love Him. God made a bird to fly in the sky and a fish to swim in the sea. God made you to know Him, to love Him, and to worship Him, and until you do, you'll be like a bird in the sea or a fish in the air; you'll be out of your element.

- Who do you know who lives a life that is satisfied in Jesus? How does that testimony shine through that person?
- If God has made you to know Him and to love Him, how can you make these things more of a priority in your life?

PRACTICE THIS Write out your normal routine. Now write another routine where knowing and loving God would be the top priority. Note what is similar and what is different.

PRAY OVER THIS

Then Jesus spoke to them again, saying, "I am the
light of the world. He who follows Me shall not
walk in darkness, but have the light of life."

JOHN 8:12

PONDER THIS If you visit Carlsbad Caverns, at one point the guide turns out all the lights and the darkness is so deep that you can almost slice it. Even if you have perfect vision, you can't see in that dark cave because there's no sight without light. There is no sight without light, but there can be light without sight. A man could be standing blind at high noon and still not see. Men need more than light to be saved.

In 2 Corinthians 4:3-4, Paul said, "But even if our gospel is veiled, it is veiled to those who are perishing, whose minds the god of this age has blinded, who do not believe, lest the light of the gospel of the glory of Christ, who is the image of God, should shine on them." Satan cannot put out the light. So, what does he do? He blinds the heart; he blinds the mind. Once you have the light, you must learn to see. That's the way people come to the Lord. God has to open their eyes. The Holy Spirit must give them spiritual insight, and then they begin to grow in knowledge.

- Where do you need spiritual insight from God?
- How have you pursued God's truth in your life?

PRACTICE THIS Make a list of situations in which you have been struggling with discernment on what to do. Ask God to give you spiritual insight in these situations.

14

PRAY OVER THIS

And His disciples asked Him, saying, "Rabbi, who sinned, this man or his parents, that he was born blind?" Jesus answered, "Neither this man nor his parents sinned, but that the works of God should be revealed in him. I must work the works of Him who sent Me while it is day; the night is coming when no one can work. As long as I am in the world, I am the light of the world."

JOHN 9:2-5

PONDER THIS I used to think as a young preacher that to get people saved you just had to tell them how to be saved—just turn on the light. But a person who is blind cannot see the light no matter how strong or how pure. I can preach the truth, but only the Holy Spirit can impart truth. That is the reason we must stay on our knees in prayer. That is the reason you must be a spirit-filled soul-winner. We are dependent on God to open blinded eyes.

We need to understand that nobody can be argued or educated into the kingdom of Heaven. I'm not against letting the light shine. You must let the light shine. You must preach. But remember there is another dimension. This man was face-to-face with the Light of the World, but he could not see. A Christian with a glowing testimony is worth a library full of arguments. We tell them the truth and trust God to work in their hearts.

- When have you seen God at work in someone else's life?
- Do you trust the Holy Spirit to give those around you vision? Why?

PRACTICE THIS Make a list of those you know who are not followers of Jesus or are distant from Him right now. Ask God to give them vision to see who He is.

PRAY OVER THIS

"For there is born to you this day in the city of David a Savior,
who is Christ the Lord. And this will be the sign to you: You will
find a Babe wrapped in swaddling cloths, lying in a manger."
And suddenly there was with the angel a multitude of the
heavenly host praising God and saying: "Glory to God in the
highest, and on earth peace, goodwill toward men!"

LUKE 2:11-14

PONDER THIS Why did Jesus Christ come the way He did? He laid aside all the glory and majesty and came as a baby. He was very ordinary and nondescript, yet there were people who believed in Him. You may think, "They believed in Him because of His miracles." No. Some of the people who believed because of the miracles left Him. Why did He come the way He did? He wanted us to have faith. Jesus laid aside all of the splendor, but He laid aside none of the character of God. The heart responds to Jesus when the heart is right, not because of proof. If you get your heart right with God, and you look at Him as revealed in the pages of Scripture, you're going to find your heart turning to Him.

Those who sought Jesus were looking for a dazzling, political Messiah. Israel rejected Him; the people were looking for a miracle worker. But He didn't come that way. That's the simple life of the King. It's one of the great fulfillments of Scripture. If you want to know Him, you do so by faith.

- What was most compelling to you when you first learned about Jesus?
- What are some areas in your life where God is growing your faith in Him?

PRACTICE THIS Share with another person about a time God blessed you in an unexpected way.

PRAY OVER THIS

When they heard the king, they departed; and behold, the star
which they had seen in the East went before them, till it came and
stood over where the young Child was. When they saw the star,
they rejoiced with exceedingly great joy. And when they had come
into the house, they saw the young Child with Mary His mother, and
fell down and worshiped Him. And when they had opened their
treasures, they presented gifts to Him: gold, frankincense, and myrrh.

MATTHEW 2:9-11

PONDER THIS The wisest thing you can do is to worship Jesus. That is the
bottom of all bottom lines. The wisest thing anybody could ever do is simply
worship Jesus. There are a lot of people who want the joys of Christmas without
the worship of Jesus. Impossible! You may have a giddy time, but you're never
going to know the joys until you learn to worship Jesus Christ.

The men in today's passage were so interested in worshiping the Lord
Jesus Christ that they did so despite great difficulty. They were going against
Herod's direction and they faced a long journey. There were no planes and no
hotels. They faced rugged terrain. They faced all of that to worship the Lord.

Does worship mean that much to you? The Bible says, "And you will seek
Me and find Me, when you search for Me with all your heart" (Jeremiah 29:13).
God have mercy upon our half-hearted worship. If He's worth anything, He's
worth everything. The word *worship* means "worth-ship." What is Jesus worth
to you?

- How does the worship of the wise men challenge you?
- How do you worship God in your everyday life? Where have you
  been guilty of worshiping comfort or convenience over Jesus?

PRACTICE THIS Take some dedicated time and worship God, praising Him for
who He is through word or song.

17

PRAY OVER THIS

Take My yoke upon you and learn from Me, for I am
gentle and lowly in heart, and you will find rest for your
souls. For My yoke is easy and My burden is light.

MATTHEW 11:29-30

PONDER THIS Have you noticed when we get caught doing something wrong, we often try to justify ourselves? Jesus was innocent, but He never spoke a word. Why was that? Because not only was He taking my sin; but He was also taking my shame.

When people stand before God as sinners—not saved—they'll stand there speechless. The Bible talks about a man who tried to come in without a wedding garment: the Bible said he was speechless. (See Matthew 22:11-12.) When you are outside of Christ and stand before God, every excuse will falter, every alibi will be gone, and you will have absolutely nothing to say!

Jesus could not have justified Himself without condemning me. Jesus did not say, "Pilate, I want you to know, I'm going to go ahead and let you crucify Me. I'm laying down My life, but I'm not guilty. I am dying as an innocent substitute. I'm just bearing these sins." Had He done that, He would've died in dignity, but He didn't die in dignity. He died in shame! He took my shame to the cross. I love Him for that. Because Jesus Christ took my shame, I made up my mind that I'm never going to be ashamed of Him. The Gospel of Christ is the power of God unto salvation. (See Romans 1:16.)

- What shame are you carrying that Jesus has already taken care of?
- Do you beat yourself up when you have done something wrong? Why or why not?

PRACTICE THIS Write out some things that would change in your life if you allowed Jesus to carry the load of shame you have on your shoulders.

> ### PRAY OVER THIS
>
> And they made His grave with the wicked—but with the rich
> at His death, because He had done no violence, nor was any
> deceit in His mouth. Yet it pleased the LORD to bruise Him;
> He has put Him to grief. When You make His soul an offering
> for sin, He shall see His seed, He shall prolong His days, and
> the pleasure of the LORD shall prosper in His hand.
>
> **ISAIAH 53:9-10**

PONDER THIS Jesus took your sufferings. He suffered because of sin. Nobody ever suffered as the Lord Jesus Christ did. There's no grief like His, none. Nobody's ever known the suffering He did. You say, "Well, other people have been crucified." No, you don't understand what happened there. He suffered the pain and separation from the Father He had been united with for all eternity. When Jesus died on the cross, the sins of the world were distilled upon Jesus, and the eternities were compressed upon Him. No one can ever describe how much He suffered.

Somehow, somewhere, sin must be paid for and Jesus, as my substitute, took my sin, my shame, my separation, my sorrows, and my sufferings, and Jesus paid it all. I want to tell you something: all to Him I owe. What a darling Savior. What a wonderful Savior that Isaiah spoke about seven hundred years before He was born.

- How does knowing about Jesus' suffering change your perspective on your own suffering?
- Who do you know who needs to know the hope that Jesus can take away sin, shame, suffering, and separation?

PRACTICE THIS Pray for someone you know who needs to know this good news about Jesus. Ask God to give you an opportunity to share His hope.

PRAY OVER THIS

And He will reign over the house of Jacob forever,
and of His kingdom there will be no end.
LUKE 1:33

PONDER THIS Jesus said in Mark 12:17, "Render to Caesar the things that are Caesar's, and to God the things that are God's." I'll guarantee you that when tax season comes around, you're going to pay your taxes. You render to Caesar the things that are Caesar's.

I want to ask you a question—have you rendered to Jesus the things that are His? Do you realize that He is King of kings and Lord of lords? Have you taken the crown from your head and put the crown upon His head? Do you say, "Lord Jesus, I surrender my gold to You. I pay tribute to You. I do homage to You. I bow my knee to You"? In every person's heart, there's a throne. When self is on that throne, Christ is on the cross; when Christ is on that throne, self is on the cross, and every person is in one of those two categories every day. Even the wise men fell and worshiped Jesus. These men were truly wise, not because of their accolades, but because they recognized His sovereign dominion.

- What would it look like to recognize Jesus as King of kings and Lord of lords in your life?
- What are some areas in your life in which you have a hard time giving authority to God?

PRACTICE THIS Ask a close friend in the faith to be your encouragement and accountability as you live to recognize Jesus as sovereign over all of your life.

20

PRAY OVER THIS

For unto us a Child is born, unto us a Son is given;
and the government will be upon His shoulder. And
His name will be called Wonderful, Counselor, Mighty
God, Everlasting Father, Prince of Peace.

ISAIAH 9:6

PONDER THIS Do you stand in awe of the Lord Jesus Christ? Or have you become oblivious to Him? Do you get excited when you think of Jesus? If you don't, you've lost the wonder. You have calluses on your soul. Jesus is wonderful. Wonderful in His birth. Wonderful in His life, in His death, in His resurrection, and in His second coming. His name is wonderful.

I heard of a man riding on a train looking out the window and he kept saying, "Wonderful, wonderful, wonderful." The man sitting next to him said, "Why do you think everything is wonderful?" He said, "I've been blind, but I've just had surgery, and I'm seeing beautiful things that I had long since forgotten. They are wonderful to me."

If Jesus is not wonderful to you, you need something done to your spiritual eyes so you can see just how wonderful He is. There is wonder in His name. There is also wisdom in His name because His name is Counselor. People come to me for counsel at times. I can't solve their problems, so when I counsel them, I try to lead them to the One who can solve their problems—the Lord Jesus Christ. I don't want them dependent upon me. I want them to know Jesus. There is wonder and there is wisdom in His name.

- Would you say you live in wonder of Jesus? Why or why not?
- What are some things that amaze you about Jesus?

PRACTICE THIS Think of someone you know who lives with wonder at Jesus. Ask that person to share a testimony with you about the day-after-day wonder of knowing Jesus.

PRAY OVER THIS

And without controversy great is the mystery of
godliness: God was manifested in the flesh, justified in
the Spirit, seen by angels, preached among the Gentiles,
believed on in the world, received up in glory.

1 TIMOTHY 3:16

PONDER THIS Don't ever cast out matters of faith because you can't understand them. How are you going to understand Almighty God, with you being finite and He being infinite? It may sound contradictory to you and outside the realm of logic, but I want to remind you that there are many things you must believe that are contradictory and outside the realm of logic. Here are a couple of examples.

Infinity. Which of you understands infinity—that things go on and on and on? Have you ever thought about that? Even though your mind cannot begin to conceive of infinity; you believe it.

Eternity. Everything we know has a beginning and an end. But we know that time cannot cease to exist. You can't totally grasp that eternity never had a beginning and never has an ending, yet you believe it.

You also don't understand that God is everywhere at the same time. It is contrary to human logic. But God is a presence whose center is everywhere and whose circumference is nowhere. We don't have to understand it. Likewise, the idea of the Trinity does not rise or fall on logic, but by divine revelation. It is a sacred mystery.

- How do you react when it comes to matters of faith you don't fully understand?
- How do God's vastness and mysteries grow your awe of Him?

PRACTICE THIS Write out some of the questions of faith you wrestle with. Ask God to help you trust Him even in the things you won't ever fully understand in this life.

PRAY OVER THIS

In Him you also trusted, after you heard the word of truth,
the gospel of your salvation; in whom also, having believed,
you were sealed with the Holy Spirit of promise, who is
the guarantee of our inheritance until the redemption of
the purchased possession, to the praise of His glory.

EPHESIANS 1:13-14

PONDER THIS I want you to see the saving ministry of the Trinity. First, you're selected by God the Father. If God had not first chosen you, you never would have chosen Him. Aren't you glad that God took the initiative? God looked down through the corridors of time and chose you. God knew from all eternity that you would receive Him and trust Him. Then, you're saved by the Son. Apart from the precious blood of the Lord Jesus Christ, no one is saved. And once you trust the Lord Jesus, it's the dear Holy Spirit of God who seals you unto the day of redemption.

In Scripture, the word *seal* is like a seal we would put on a document, a stamp. The Bible says the king's seal no man can break. You're sealed with the Holy Spirit. A seal in Bible times meant a finished transaction: signed, sealed, and delivered. It meant a transfer of ownership. You have been selected by the Father, saved by the Son, and sealed by the Spirit. Is that not wonderful? This is the saving ministry of the Holy Trinity.

- When did you begin to follow Jesus?
- How has your life been changed by the work of the Holy Spirit?

PRACTICE THIS Reflect on your own testimony about how God has been at work in your life through the work of the Father, Son, and Holy Spirit.

23

PRAY OVER THIS

And Mary said: "My soul magnifies the Lord, and my spirit has
rejoiced in God my Savior. For He has regarded the lowly state
of His maidservant; for behold, henceforth all generations
will call me blessed. For He who is mighty has done great
things for me, and holy is His name. And His mercy is on
those who fear Him from generation to generation."

LUKE 1:46-50

PONDER THIS Jesus was a Lamb without a spot, without blemish. He was the
virgin-born Son of God. The Infinite became an infant, and God lay in a manger.

Why was He born of a virgin? So that He could be sinless. Why did He need
to be sinless? So that He could make a blood atonement. The Bible says it is the
blood that makes atonement for your sin. There needed to be a sinless sacrifice
that no child of Adam could satisfy because in Adam all die. The bloodline
comes from the father. While Mary was the earthly mother, God the Father
was the heavenly Father, and the blood that flowed through the veins of Mary's
Lamb was the very blood of God.

He was a special Lamb and a slain Lamb. He was born of a virgin that
we might be born again. He was made the Son of Man that you and I might
become sons and daughters of God. Thank God for that.

- How does it make you feel when you consider all that God has
  done so that you might be reconciled with Him?
- How does the humility of God in the nativity narrative challenge
  you?

PRACTICE THIS Talk to a friend in the faith about how God exemplified humility
as He became an infant and spotless lamb. Challenge one another in how you
can grow in humility like Him.

PRAY OVER THIS

Then the angel said to her, "Do not be afraid, Mary, for you have found favor with God. And behold, you will conceive in your womb and bring forth a Son, and shall call His name Jesus. He will be great, and will be called the Son of the Highest; and the Lord God will give Him the throne of His father David. And He will reign over the house of Jacob forever, and of His kingdom there will be no end."

LUKE 1:30-33

PONDER THIS Have you been to Jesus for cleansing power? Are you washed in the blood of the Lamb? I tried my hand at poetry, I thought I would try to rewrite, "Mary Had a Little Lamb." Here's what I wrote:

Mary had a little Lamb. His fleece was white as snow.
Son of God from Heaven above, for sinners here below.
Mary's Son, Eternal God, He, the Great I AM
With wool so white on Christmas night became a little Lamb.
Mary had a little Lamb. His fleece was white as snow.
That spotless Lamb was crucified to pay the debt I owe.
Oh, spotless Lamb, with wool so white, thy crimson blood, I know,
Can take away my crimson sin and wash me white as snow.

I thank God for Mary's little Lamb that died upon that cross. But not only was this Lamb a special Lamb, a slain Lamb, and a saving Lamb, He was to be a shared Lamb. That's why when we come to the Lord's Table, we have a celebration. We feed on the Lamb.

- How has your relationship with Jesus changed the way you celebrate Christmas?
- How are you looking to share the hope of Jesus this Christmas season?

PRACTICE THIS Pick one activity to do on your own or with your loved ones to feed on the Lamb as you prepare for Christmas Day.

PRAY OVER THIS

Now when He had taken the scroll, the four living creatures and the twenty-four elders fell down before the Lamb, each having a harp, and golden bowls full of incense, which are the prayers of the saints. And they sang a new song, saying: "You are worthy to take the scroll, and to open its seals; for You were slain, and have redeemed us to God by Your blood out of every tribe and tongue and people and nation..."

REVELATION 5:8-9

PONDER THIS Jesus is a strong, searching Lamb. He is omnipotent. He is omniscient. He knows what you're thinking about at this very moment. He sees every move you make. He is the sovereign Lamb. He and He alone is the secret of history.

If you were to ask Him, "What right do you have to take that scroll"? He would say, "I have the right of creation. I made it all, and I have the right of Calvary. I died; I shed my blood for it, and I have the right on conquest. I was raised from the dead. I have the right to take this book and to open it, for I AM the great I AM who was born a Lamb."

You've seen the Lamb in prophecy, you've seen the Lamb in history, you've seen the Lamb in victory, but now see the Lamb in majesty. Mary had a little Lamb; His fleece was white as snow. Worthy is the Lamb. He is exclusively worthy, exceedingly worthy, and eternally worthy.

- How have you recognized Jesus' worth this Christmas?
- How do you feel when you recognize the baby lying in the manger as the victory, strength, power, and peace of our God?

PRACTICE THIS Take a moment today to celebrate Jesus for who He is, from before the manger, to His life on Earth, to His death and resurrection and the victory to come.

26

PRAY OVER THIS

My brethren, count it all joy when you fall into various trials, knowing that the testing of your faith produces patience. But let patience have its perfect work, that you may be perfect and complete, lacking nothing.

JAMES 1:2-4

PONDER THIS What is God's plan for you? God wants to enlarge you, not indulge you. God is not so interested in making you happy and healthy as He is in making you holy. So, God will use the trouble in your life. The Lord Jesus wants to develop us. Psalm 4:1 says: "You have relieved me in *my* distress." Now think about that. Think about the times when you have grown the most. When there was trouble, that's when you were stretched, and that's when your faith was enlarged. We all enjoy not having trouble, but I want to tell you—and I can give this testimony—that I have grown the most in my own life in times of deepest despair. I know that when Joyce and I had a little baby boy step over into Heaven, we grew a quantum leap during that time. I know when I had a daughter go through deep heartache and distress, God stretched my heart and my life. I would never want it to happen again, but it did happen, and I'm here to tell you that I'm a better person because of it.

- When has God grown you during a time of trouble in your life?
- How do you approach God when you experience trouble?

PRACTICE THIS Take some time to think about the different ways God has grown your faith in the past year and what events or circumstances contributed to that.

PRAY OVER THIS

Jesus said to her, "I am the resurrection and the life. He who believes in Me, though he may die, he shall live. And whoever lives and believes in Me shall never die. Do you believe this?"

JOHN 11:25-26

PONDER THIS Jesus is the only reason we live. As a matter of fact, He came so that we might live. He said in John 10:10, "I have come that they may have life, and that they may have it more abundantly." He's the only reason I live.

Most people today don't have life, they have existence. They are fighting to live while they're living to fight. They're growing and breathing, and one day is turning into another. They have existence, but they don't have life. They've got it all backward.

Jesus has come that you might have life. Satan has come to rob you of life—he comes to steal, kill, and destroy. (See John 10:10.) And he has stolen, killed, and destroyed life from many people. They don't understand life, and they look at it very pessimistically. That may be true if you don't know the Lord Jesus, but if you are in Christ, you have the key to true life.

- How have you experienced life because of Jesus?
- Who are some people you know who are only existing and not truly living because they do not experience the hope and life of Jesus?

PRACTICE THIS Pray for someone you know who does not yet have the life and hope of Jesus.

28

PRAY OVER THIS

Then they took away the stone from the place where the dead man was lying. And Jesus lifted up His eyes and said, "Father, I thank You that You have heard Me. And I know that You always hear Me, but because of the people who are standing by I said this, that they may believe that You sent Me." Now when He had said these things, He cried with a loud voice, "Lazarus, come forth!" And he who had died came out bound hand and foot with graveclothes, and his face was wrapped with a cloth. Jesus said to them, "Loose him, and let him go."

JOHN 11:41-44

PONDER THIS Jesus raised Lazarus from the dead to give us an illustration of the greater spiritual truth of eternal life. When He said, "I am the resurrection and the life. He who believes in Me, though he may die, he shall live" (John 11:25), He shared the greatest truth we need to learn.

Jesus raised Lazarus from the dead, but He didn't raise everybody from the dead. So, what is the message in the miracle? Jesus is God's answer to man's death. Miracles of glory speak of greater miracles of grace. We should believe in miracles but trust in Jesus. Do you understand what I'm saying? These miracles are not to have us put our faith in miracles. Our faith is to be in the Lord Jesus Christ. If you want a full and wonderful life, and the abundant life that we've been talking about, you must experience life in Jesus.

- How has your relationship with Jesus changed your perspective on death?
- Who is one person you know that you have seen experience life in Jesus?

PRACTICE THIS Ask a mature Christian you know to share a testimony about experiencing life in Jesus. Consider some lessons you can use in your own life.

29

PRAY OVER THIS

And they commanded the people, saying, "When you see the ark
of the covenant of the Lord your God, and the priests, the Levites,
bearing it, then you shall set out from your place and go after it.
Yet there shall be a space between you and it, about two thousand
cubits by measure. Do not come near it, that you may know the way
by which you must go, for you have not passed this way before."

JOSHUA 3:3-4

PONDER THIS Why are some Christians victorious and others not? All Christians possess Jesus. The difference in Christians is not in possession; it is in position. When the Lord becomes the leader, when the Resident becomes the president, when the Christ who abides comes to preside, when the Lord begins to lead, He leads to victory. Every Christian is a possessor of God's ark of the covenant, but not every Christian follows the Lord Jesus Christ into victory.

Learn to follow after the ark. Consider your New Year's resolutions this year. Think about committing to God. You may say, "I am not going to take a step without my eyes on the ark, wherever the ark goes that's where I'm going." When you live your life like that, I promise you'll have good success, and you'll have true victory. Victory is seeing which way God is going and then joining Him. That's it. Are you experiencing victory?

- Would you say you are living in victory in Jesus? Why or why not?
- What are some areas where you have seen God at work in the world around you?

PRACTICE THIS Consider what things you are planning for the year to come. What would it be like to make a resolution to look for where God is going and join Him?

PRAY OVER THIS

Therefore do not worry, saying, "What shall we eat?" or "What shall we drink?" or "What shall we wear?" For after all these things the Gentiles seek. For your heavenly Father knows that you need all these things. But seek first the kingdom of God and His righteousness, and all these things shall be added to you. Therefore do not worry about tomorrow, for tomorrow will worry about its own things. Sufficient for the day is its own trouble.

MATTHEW 6:31-34

PONDER THIS Some people were out in a boat on a stormy night. The passengers were frightened, so they sent somebody to talk to the captain. He asked the captain about the boat's condition. The captain said, "I'm going to give it to you straight. This is a leaky old ship, and we may go down. But the boilers on this ship are very weak. We may go up. Whether we go down or up, we're going on."

That's where we are as we look at the year to come. This old world is not what it ought to be. We don't know what's going to happen. But we don't have to know where we are going. God may keep you in the dark so that you'll keep your eyes on Him. Aren't you glad you don't know the future? What if you knew the sorrows or challenges that might come? It might choke you down. But in Christ, we can have confidence, no matter what the day, month, or year brings.

- How do you feel about the year to come? What are you excited or anxious about?
- How has God changed the way you handle the unknowns in your life?

PRACTICE THIS Be honest with God about the unknowns of the coming year that scare you. Consider what it would look like to fix your eyes on Him in the future.

PRAY OVER THIS

Forever, O LORD, Your word is settled in heaven. Your faithfulness endures to all generations; You established the earth, and it abides.
PSALM 119:89-90

PONDER THIS While you are preparing for this coming year, keep your eyes on the Lord Jesus Christ. He will not only guide you through the unknown places but also grant you unfading promises. Do you know what a covenant is? A covenant is a promise that is unfading and unfailing. The Lord Jesus Christ had the last meal with His disciples and said, "This cup is the new covenant in my blood" (Luke 22:20). He is our ark of the covenant. All the promises of God are yes and amen in Him. He will guide us through unknown places. He will grant us the unfailing promises of God. Don't let 2,000 years keep you from a promise. The promises didn't die with Moses or Joshua. The promises are for all saints; they are for all seasons; they are for all situations. Don't think that somehow God blessed these people, but God won't keep His covenant with us. If you'll say, "My New Year's resolution is to follow the ark, and wherever it goes, I'll go after it," He will guide you in the uncharted places, grant you unfading promises, and guard you with unfailing power.

- What are some New Year's resolutions you have considered making? What would need to change for you to commit to "follow the ark"?
- When have you been tempted to forget the promises of God?

PRACTICE THIS Write a list of your New Year's resolutions and write down some things in your life that might change if you commit to following the ark.

Printed in the USA
CPSIA information can be obtained
at www.ICGtesting.com
CBHW071131221223
2852CB00008B/242